2007

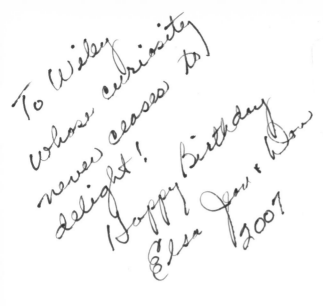

To Wiley
whose curiosity
never ceases to
delight!
Happy Birthday
Elsa Jean & Dave
2007

D1230079

Porcupine
Picayune
& Post

Porcupine
Picayune
& Post

*How Newspapers
Get Their Names*

JIM BERNHARD

University of Missouri Press
Columbia and London

Copyright © 2007 by
The Curators of the University of Missouri
University of Missouri Press, Columbia, Missouri 65201
Printed and bound in the United States of America
All rights reserved
5 4 3 2 1   11 10 09 08 07

Library of Congress Cataloging-in-Publication Data

Bernhard, Jim.
   Porcupine, Picayune, & Post : how newspapers get their
names / Jim Bernhard.
      p.   cm.
   Summary: "Porcupine, Picayune, & Post examines the history
and etymology of newspapers' names. Bernhard focuses on
printed general-interest English-language dailies and weeklies,
from the Choteau (Montana) Acantha to the Moab (Utah) Zephyr,
with everything in between"—Provided by publisher.
   Includes bibliographical references and index.
   ISBN 978-0-8262-1748-6 (alk. paper)
   1. Titles of newspapers—United States.   2. Titles of newspapers—Great Britain.   I. Title.
   PN4888.T58B47 2007
   071.3—dc22   2007012895

♾™ This paper meets the requirements of the
American National Standard for Permanence of Paper
for Printed Library Materials, Z39.48, 1984.

Jacket Designer: Susan Ferber
Page Designer: Stephanie Foley
Typesetter: The Composing Room of Michigan, Inc.
Printer and binder: The Maple-Vail Book Manufacturing Group
Typefaces: Bodoni Family and Times New Roman

For Ginger

Contents

It all began with the *Jimplecute*. A few years ago while wandering around the northeast Texas town of Jefferson—I do a lot of wandering when I travel—I noticed someone reading what looked like a newspaper with the word *Jimplecute* in large letters across the top of the page. I am shy around strangers, so I didn't have the nerve to just walk up to the person and ask directly, "What's a 'Jimplecute'?" A question like that might get your face slapped, or worse.

Later I came across a whole stack of these papers, and then I saw a glass-front office labeled "The Jefferson Jimplecute." I was beginning to put the pieces together and reach the conclusion that this peculiar word, which sounded as if it might be a winsome facial feature, or maybe a tiny winged insect, or else an especially unpleasant surgical instrument, must in fact be the local newspaper, as improbable as that might seem.

Residents of the town whom I asked could not immediately provide any definitive explanation of this name, and my curiosity was piqued. I did some preliminary research, and as I got into the subject, I came across other unusual names, causing me to think about the whole fascinating range of newspaper titles and wonder how they became attached to the various newspapers that bear them. Why is a *Gazette* called that? How did the name *Picayune* come about? How do you explain peculiar names on newspapers such as the *Courant,* the *Pantagraph,* or the *Repository*? For that matter, how did the plain old *Times* or *News* come to be known that way?

I am not the first person to be fascinated by journalistic onomastics (that last word means "the study of names" and will not appear again in this book). A former newspaperman in Australia named Eric Shackle has a Web site devoted to what he calls "quirky" newspaper names, and I have borrowed from it copiously. The Wordsmith.com webmaster Anu Garg has devoted brief attention to the subject. The American poet Walt Whitman took note of odd newspaper names in his book of essays *November Boughs,* when he wrote: "Among the far-west newspapers have been, or are, *The Fairplay* (Colorado) *Flume, The Solid Muldoon,* of Ouray, *The Tombstone Epitaph,* of Nevada [*sic*—it's actually in Arizona], *The Jimplecute,* of Texas, and *The Bazoo,* of Missouri."

This book, however, goes further than any previous work with which I am familiar in exploring the history and etymology of how dozens of newspapers got their names. There are tens of thousands, perhaps hundreds of thousands, of publications throughout the world that might be called "newspapers." The British Newspaper Libel and Registration Act of 1881 defines a "newspaper" as "any paper containing public news, intelligence or occurrences, or any remarks or observations therein printed for sale, and published . . . periodically or in parts or numbers at intervals not exceeding twenty-six days between the publication of any two papers."

Even with a definition as specific as this, more limitations in the scope of my research had to be established, so that it could be accomplished in the one lifetime, or what may be left of it, that I have to devote to it.

First, I determined to concentrate only on what I deemed to be general-interest printed newspapers in the English language that appear on a regular schedule, usually daily or weekly. I thus excluded such periodical publications as magazines, as well as online newspapers that have no printed edition. I also excluded special-interest newspapers that are aimed only at specific segments of the population, such as ethnic groups, labor organizations, religious denominations, fraternal lodges, high school and university students, breeders of Shih Tzus, and so on. The alert reader who wishes to be a pain in the neck may point out that I do not follow these exclusionary rules with scrupulosity and that occasionally some of the interdicted publications are mentioned.

I should explain what this book is not. It is not a history of journalism, by any stretch of the academic imagination, although some historical tidbits do crop up now and again. It is not a comprehensive list of every English-language general-interest newspaper in the world, nor is it a scholarly study with footnoted documentation—nary an *ibid.* nor an *op. cit.* will be found in these pages. Some newspaper titles have eluded my attempts to track down their origins; others I have purposely omit-

ted because they struck me as uninteresting; and some have undoubtedly escaped my attention altogether owing to research methodology that
might be described as pococurante.

Having made these disclaimers, I modestly confess that I have tried
with some assiduousness to provide a reasonably complete list of the
most commonly found newspaper titles, as well as the most whimsical
and arcane. Readers who wish to call my attention to omissions or—per-
ish the thought!—errors may do so by e-mailing me at fjb@sbcglobal
.net, and the suggestions will be given the consideration they deserve for
subsequent editions of this book, if there are any.

The art of naming newspapers, especially the actual printed kind, is
dying because the number of newspapers in North America and Europe
is declining, owing to the growth of television and the Internet as sources
of information and to the sharp reduction in the number of fish-and-chip
shops in need of wrappers for their hot, greasy food. Someday there may
be no printed news, and the idea of a title on a printed page over the day's
information will be outmoded. Daily newspaper readership in the United States has decreased from almost 70 percent of the populace in 1972
to just over 30 percent in 2006, according to the National Opinion Research Center, as reported by the New York *Times.* The number of U.S.
daily papers also has steadily decreased from 1,772 in 1950, to 1,520 in
1997, and only 1,456 in 2003.

Worldwide, in 2004 there were 6,580 daily newspapers, actually representing an increase of about 2 percent over the previous year—but the
gains were primarily in China, Japan, and India. The United States and
Great Britain both showed declines, according to the World Association
of Newspapers.

It is difficult for modern readers to imagine the profusion of newspapers that used to be customary in every major city. It was not unusual to
find a large city with a dozen or more dailies, and even moderate-sized
towns normally had several. For example, early in the twentieth century
New York City had the *Times,* the *Post,* the *News,* the *World,* the *Telegram,* the *Sun,* the *Journal,* the *American,* the *Mirror,* the *Herald,* and
the *Tribune;* today it has only four. And as recently as the 1920s, Pittsburgh, Pennsylvania, boasted of the *Dispatch,* the *Leader,* the *Post,* the
Sun, the *Press,* the *Gazette-Times,* and the *Chronicle-Telegraph.* Today,
except for the largest of metropolises, most cities are lucky to have one
surviving daily paper, or two at the most. With a population of about

85,000, Columbia, Missouri, is the smallest U.S. city with two competing daily newspapers (the *Tribune* and the *Missourian*).

A note on the typographical presentation of newspaper titles in this book might relieve any distress caused by readers who have recently dipped into the *Chicago Manual of Style* or who are infused with the punctilious spirit of Lynne Truss's *Eats, Shoots & Leaves*. Newspapers themselves, it should be noted, can be cranky about how their titles are treated in print. Some of them include the word *The* and the name of their city in the title on the nameplate: *The New York Times*. Others include the city but not the word *The: Los Angeles Times*. Still others do not include the city of publication at all: *The Times,* which you're supposed to know is published in London. And some omit both the name of the city and the word *The* in their nameplate: *Daily News,* which might be in New York or Los Angeles, so you'd better know where you are before you start reading.

The *Chicago Manual of Style* pays no attention to these niceties and instructs writers not to italicize the word *The* (in English-language papers, but to italicize the equivalent article in foreign titles), and to add the city and italicize it whether it appears in the newspaper's title or not. Well, if the *Manual* can be cavalier, so can I, and since this book is about newspaper names per se and not about their places of publication (and certainly not about the word *The*), I have chosen to italicize only the actual substantive word under discussion, even if the newspaper itself does include *The* and the place of publication in its title: for example, the New York *Times* and not *The New York Times*.

There is an exception to that rule, which is when a newspaper has a double-barreled name—quite common in the eighteenth century—and it would look peculiar to hop back and forth between italics and Roman type: for example, the Massachusetts *Gazette and Boston News-Letter.* I have also chosen to italicize the words *Daily, Weekly, Morning,* and *Evening* and a few other modifiers when they form part of the paper's name, because it looked odd not to. There may be other exceptions that have insinuated their way into the text. If these discrepancies bother you, please keep in mind that the purpose of this method of italicization is clarity of understanding, not foolish consistency, which, as the Sage of Concord has told us, is the hobgoblin of little minds.

Finally, please permit me to thank those who have helped make this little volume possible. A sort of bibliography of works (and Web sites) consulted is appended, but like one's friends, some of them were more helpful than others, and I have made no attempt to evaluate them. I would like to acknowledge that I have relied for etymologies and definitions on *Webster's New International Dictionary of the English Language,* second edition (1949), *Merriam-Webster's Collegiate Dictionary,* tenth edition (1993), and *The Compact Edition of the Oxford English Dictionary* (1971); for historical data, Frank Luther Mott's *American Journalism: A History of Newspapers in the United States through 250 Years, 1690 to 1940* (1947) and Anthony Smith's *The Newspaper: An International History* (1979) have been useful; for chronological listings, I have consulted the British Library Newspapers Catalogue online; and for anecdotal material Eric Shackle's e-book *Life Begins at 80 . . . On the Internet* has been a font of odds and ends. The rest of the information in this book has come from snippets culled from various references and histories, from correspondence with newspaper publishers and editors, and, most especially, from the Web sites of the newspapers themselves. (A special blessing on those that provide a history of their publications under the heading "About Us.") My great thanks to all of them for their help.

More thanks than I can convey are due to my wife, Virginia Bernhard, herself an author and historian, who has kindly read and commented on this manuscript, making many useful suggestions and also refraining from criticizing my self-indulgent and erratic methods of research, which depart with casual insouciance from the rigorous academic standards to which she is accustomed. Thanks are also due to Donna Martin, Dorothy Hackney, Ann Holmes, D. J. Hobdy, Kathryn Rodwell, and Michael Freeman, each of whom kindly read all or some of the manuscript and offered useful comments. Beverly Jarrett, Sara Davis, and Julianna Schroeder, of the University of Missouri Press, have been exceedingly helpful. All the above should be glad to know that, try as I might, I can think of no way to implicate them, or indeed anyone but myself and possibly my computer, in causing any factual errors or solecisms that may have wormed their way into this text.

Now, with the hope that readers will find some moments of delight and not too many of insufferable dullness in the pages that follow, let the names begin!

Porcupine
Picayune
& Post

1

What's in a Name?

If you are one of the 1,750 Montanans who live in the town of Choteau, you can get the local news from a newspaper called the *Acantha,* which is a word that means either a thorn on the side of a plant or a spine on a fish. In Galesburg, Illinois, or in Moab, Utah, you can read the *Zephyr,* which is a soft, gentle breeze from the west. In Jefferson, Texas, there is a newspaper called the *Jimplecute,* the meaning of which no one seems to know.

If you counted them all, you would find many thousands of English-language daily and weekly newspapers throughout the world, every one of them identified by a name, usually at the top of the front page, in what is called the nameplate, the flag, the title piece, or sometimes, incorrectly, the masthead. (In case you're interested, the masthead is the box that appears usually on the editorial page and lists the newspaper's owner and key staff.) New Yorkers, Los Angelenos, and Londoners may all bury their noses in a *Times,* while people elsewhere turn to a *Herald,* a *Gazette,* a *Journal,* a *Post,* a *Chronicle,* a *Tribune,* or a seemingly omnipresent *News.* Readers in Big Bear, California, glean information each week from a paper called the *Grizzly;* residents of Venice, Florida, read the *Gondolier;* while President George W. Bush, should he decide one day to read newspapers, could join other residents of Crawford, Texas, in perusing the pages of the *Iconoclast.*

The rationale for putting titles on newspapers stems from a universal human impulse to name things, primarily to distinguish one from another, but also to impart to them the qualities for which they are, or are wished to be, noted. The prolific linguist David Crystal, in his estimable *Cambridge Encyclopedia of the English Language,* explains naming practices this way: "There seems to be a universal and deep-rooted drive to give individual names to things. People, places, pets, and houses are among the most obvious categories, but anything with which we have a special relationship is likely to be named. . . . It is important to appreciate the variety of reasons which lead us to name things. Pride, affection, and nostalgia combine with such hard-nosed factors as practicability, recognizability, memorability, and saleability."

The naming of items for public identification typically follows certain unwritten rules, which vary from one industry to another. It is common, for example, to find restaurants and bars displaying the first names of their owners or chefs: Joe's Bar and Grill, Chez Suzette, or just plain Emeril's. It is rare, on the other hand, to find Bill and Ted's Excellent Bank and Trust, or Mary Jane's Life Insurance Company, financial institutions generally preferring to project a more substantial image of security—Fidelity Bank, Guaranty Trust, Prudential Insurance—or, at least, to invoke the pedigreed family names of their memorable and presumably once fiscally solid founders such as Morgan, Chase, or Barclay.

The tendency in most corporate names is to condense. Less is evidently much, much more when it comes to identification in the marketplace. The International Business Machines Corporation is known only as IBM, and Koninklijke Luchtvaart Maatschappij finds it attracts more airline passengers by calling itself KLM. Standard Oil Company of New Jersey shrank to Esso, the spelled-out enunciation of its first two initials, and thence (inexplicably) morphed to Exxon. Northwestern National Life Insurance Company first became Reliastar, then ING, as though it were a participle looking for a verb. Minnesota Mining and Manufacturing Company understandably prefers 3M. The Entertainment cable network gets by with just one letter and a punctuation mark—E! The ultimate in product minimalism must be the chain of hotels (as well as a certain head of state) known simply as W.

Broadcast and cable companies usually go for three-letter words or initials—ABC, BBC, CBC, CNN, FOX, HBO—presumably for convenience in printed schedules. Hotels and theaters tend to conjure up thoughts of aristocratic luxury with names like Princess, Palace, Royal, Grand, Empire, Imperial, Majestic, George V, and Prince of Wales. Luxury liners are even more grandiose, invoking both royalty, such as Queen Elizabeth, Queen Mary, and some unnamed Princess, as well as romantic idealizations, in such words as Rhapsody, Splendor, Radiance, Serenity, Elation, and (does it get it any better than this?) Ecstasy.

Perfumes dally with sex and danger—My Sin, Nude, Obsession, Opium, Poison, and, with what is probably merely wishful thinking, Orgasm. It makes you wonder how something so prosaic as No. 5 competes successfully with more daringly christened fragrances. The Roman designer Valentino has introduced a perfume called V, which, come to think of it, is twice as minimalist as W.

Even such high-minded institutions as colleges and universities play the name game. The New York *Times* reported that enrollment increased significantly when Pennsylvania's Beaver College changed its name to Arcadia University. (Do you think Harvard might do better as, say, Elysian U.?)

There are some names—those for racehorses, sailboats, rap performers, and household pets among them—whose rubrics defy all explanation.

In the case of newspapers, a variety of historical, political, philosophical, personal—and sometimes purely whimsical—reasons determined their names. Most newspaper founders have followed traditional patterns, employing names that have been in use since the earliest days of newspapers, sometimes merely by default. But other names are carefully chosen to symbolize a political point of view, a philosophy, or a perceived mission, or else they are created by word-association with the paper's location or its role in the community.

The vast majority of newspapers today have names that were first used for that purpose between the years 1600 and 1800. More than 60 percent of English-language newspapers are called by one of only fifteen commonly used titles. There are, for example, probably a thousand or more daily or weekly newspapers worldwide that use the name *News,* and almost that many are called the *Times.* The other most frequent names for English-language newspapers are *Herald, Journal, Tribune, Press, Star, Sun, Gazette, Record, Courier, Independent, Leader, Post,* and *Democrat.* Next are *Review, Enterprise, Chronicle, Observer, Citizen, Register, Reporter, Advocate, Eagle, Standard, Dispatch, Telegraph* (or *Telegram*), *Ledger, Messenger, Express,* and *Bulletin.* In Britain and in Canada, *Advertiser, Mail, Echo, Free Press, Guardian,* and *Mirror* are also among the most often encountered.

But if most newspapers tend to use tried-and-true titles, there are glorious exceptions—those wonderfully idiosyncratic, comical, or outlandish names like the Banbury *Cake* in England, the Grand River *Sachem* in Ontario, the Gawler *Bunyip* in South Australia, the Snow Hill

Laconic in North Carolina, and the *Alibi* in Albuquerque, New Mexico. About half of the three hundred or so newspaper names surveyed are unique—proudly splashed across the nameplate of only one publication anywhere on earth. Some names are amusing oddities, and others have meanings that may be surprising or, like the *Jimplecute,* virtually impossible to pin down.

A title on a newspaper's nameplate—whether it's the prosaic *News* or the enigmatic *Jimplecute*—fulfills two marketing goals: like a brand name, it distinguishes one entity from others in the field, permitting competitive activity, and it instills a desire for the product in the potential customer. Without a title at the top of the page, there would be no proprietary interest or sense of continuity in the conveyance of news and, hence, no loyalty from satisfied customers. These repeat customers are the source of a newspaper's circulation, which determines its advertising revenue.

Newspapers, especially those in markets with more than one news source, take infinite pains to ensure that their names are prominently associated with the editorial content. The name of the paper is proclaimed at the top of every page in what is called the "folio," and it is mentioned frequently in news stories to remind the reader of the source of a particular item. Bylines commonly identify reporters not only by name, but also by adding a self-evident explanation like "of the *Times* Staff." Qualifying phrases, such as "it was learned by the *News,*" are gratuitously peppered throughout articles. How else, one wonders, would the paper be able to report anything, if it hadn't "learned" it? Readers are constantly reminded, in various ways, "You saw it here first!" It is vital to the management that their customers remember that they have read a given item in the *Times,* the *Express,* or the *Mirror,* and not in the *Guardian,* the *Telegraph,* or the *Sun.* Exclusivity is of paramount importance to newspapers. Journalists everywhere strive for that elusive "scoop," a bit of information that no other media possess. In the same quest for exclusivity, every newspaper hopes to inculcate in its readership a permanent attachment to its name.

That name, like the accuracy of its reporting and the slant of its editorial policy, is an essential part of a newspaper's identity. It is elevated like a totem, inviting reverence from the public, as if, akin to the archetypal feline in T. S. Eliot's *Old Possum's Book of Practical Cats,* the newspaper's management is constantly engaged in deep thoughts about the singular name that adorns its pages.

The vast majority of newspaper names fall into one of several categories. First are the names that refer directly to the paper's contents, that is, to the happenings themselves, such as *Courant, Facts, Item,* and the ubiquitous *News.* Nothing could be more straightforward.

Equally direct in nomenclature are references to the reportage—synonyms for the written account—such as *Bulletin, Chronicle, Journal, Ledger, Record, Register,* and *Transcript,* or those that refer to the means, either mechanical or human, by which the information is conveyed: *Courier, Dispatch, Express, Herald, Intelligencer, Mail, Mercury, Messenger, Post, Press, Reporter, Telegram,* and *Telegraph.*

Some newspapers derive their names from the period of time in which the happenings occur: *Age, Day, Daily, Era, Monthly, Times, Today,* and *Weekly.* Other names denote the place in which the happenings occur, taking either a broad view—*Globe, World, State*—or a narrow one—*Ruralite, Townsman, Villager. USA Today,* the largest-circulation daily in the United States, combines time *and* place. The names may even be geographically specific: *Briton, Chattanoogan, Labradorian, Oklahoman, Oregonian, Saratogian, Scotsman, Tennessean, Trentonian, Virginian,* and so on.

Among the most frequent names for newspapers are those that try to instill the notion that they are working with relentless fervor on behalf of the readers, by promising to lead them to a better life, protect them from all manner of harm, or uncover truths that someone is trying to keep from them. Names of this sort include *Advocate, Aegis, Argus, Banner, Blade, Champion, Citizen, Enquirer* (or *Inquirer*), *Examiner, Free Press, Guardian, Leader, Monitor, Observer, Palladium, Pathfinder, Pioneer, Plain Dealer, Progress, Sentinel, Standard, Tribune,* and *Vindicator.* Some go even further by offering (often misleadingly) the expression of a specific political point of view: such as *Constitution, Democrat, Independent, Republic, Republican, Union,* and *Whig.* Such a title, it must be noted, is no guarantee that the views actually expressed will conform to what is promised. In fact, they might be diametrically opposed.

Others see themselves as combatting the darkness of ignorance, with either natural or man-made illumination: *Beacon, Comet, Light, Headlight, Searchlight, Spotlight, Meteor, Mirror, Pharos, Reflector, Star,* and *Sun.*

A few newspapers betray their origins as marketing tools with mercantile names like *Advertiser, Commercial,* and *Enterprise.* Others attempt, with varying logic, to appropriate to themselves the qualities of animals or natural phenomena, as in *Avalanche, Bee, Breeze, Eagle,* and *Zephyr,* or the attention-getting characteristics of natural sounds or musical instruments: *Bugle, Call, Clarion,* and *Echo.*

Finally, there are those newspaper names that are in a class by themselves, whose peculiarity defies easy categorization and provokes wonder about their origins—names like *Acantha, Alibi, Ark, Bunyip, Cake, Chad, Flume, Gondolier, Iconoclast, Jimplecute, Laconic, Optic, Oran, Picayune, Pine Cone, Rocket, Rustler, Sachem, Shuttle, Tomahawk,* and *Vidette.* Names such as these invite—nay, cry out with irresistible demands—for deeper investigation.

2

In the Beginning

Journal

The world's first newspaper name was the *Journal,* and Julius Caesar was one of its publishers. All right, it wasn't exactly a newspaper—it was more of a carved tablet—and Caesar wasn't a true forerunner of William Randolph Hearst, Joseph Pulitzer, and Lord Beaverbrook as a journalism mogul. As early as 131 BC in republican Rome, about the same time the Chinese were inventing paper, the *Acta Diurna,* or "daily events," an account of official business inscribed on stone or metal, was posted in public places such as the Forum, so that the citizens could gather around and read it, or have it read to them. While this device was not a real newspaper that you could use to swat flies or wrap fish, its contents included not only official government edicts and proclamations, but also juicier items like accounts of gladiatorial contests, astrological omens, marriages, births, divorces, deaths, fires, appointments to public office, trials, and executions—the very stuff that still lures readers to newsstands. In fact, in a sensational story that might be vividly splashed on the pages of today's supermarket tabloids, one issue of the *Acta Diurna* reported the sighting of an actual phoenix!

As emperor, Julius Caesar got involved in the newspaper biz in 59 BC when he ordered that handwritten copies of the *Acta Diurna* be sent to the Roman provinces. The satirist Juvenal mentions a Roman housewife pausing in her domestic tasks to read the *Acta Diurna,* much as a homemaker today might scan the day's headlines over a second cup of coffee.

More than a millennium later, by the fourteenth century, the word *diurnal* drifted into French and then into English. It appeared first as *Di-*

urnall, but sometimes it dropped its *d* and became *Iurnalle,* and it was a name for an ecclesiastical service book with prayers for each day of the year. Then, as the capricious Latin *i* was wont to do, it changed to a *j,* resulting in *Jurnal,* or as the French would have it, *Journal,* from their word *jour* ("day"). By 1540 the word was used as a record of daily transactions.

In 1615 a German bookseller named Egenolph Emmel began issuing what can be thought of as the first true newspaper, a weekly publication that he called the *Frankfurter Journal,* which had nothing to do with sausages but was published in the city of Frankfurt. The name *Journal* caught on for a profusion of newspapers that began to pop up in the seventeenth century: a number of publications called *Diurnalls,* which listed Parliamentary acts, in London in 1641; the *Nouveau journal universel,* a French-language paper first published in the Netherlands in 1688; the *Daily Journal* in London from 1723; the New England *Weekly Journal* in Boston in 1727; and the New York *Weekly Journal* in 1733. The first daily newspaper in France was the *Journal de Paris* in 1777.

In France, in the early eighteenth century, the *Journal des Scavants* was one of three periodicals licensed by the government, each with a different purpose. The *Gazette de France* printed official notices, the *Mercure de France* contained social and literary news, and the *Journal des Scavants* ("Journal of Scholars") was primarily for scientific information. As Anthony Smith points out in his history of world newspapers, the format of the *Journal*—which dealt with specific categories of information, such as artistic, theatrical, financial, weather, and miscellany—became the standard, triumphing over *Gazette* and *Mercury* as the customary name of French newspapers.

Although *Journal* had its origin in a Latin word meaning "daily," it never meant that it was necessarily published every day. So much for truth in advertising! According to Frank Luther Mott, in his fact-crammed 1947 *American Journalism,* the English *Diurnalls* of the seventeenth century were weeklies that gave day-by-day accounts of occurrences; *diurnal,* then, did not refer to daily publication but to the sequential method of recounting events that happened some days ago. When the weekly *Journals* appeared in the early eighteenth century, the name had lost all reference to "daily."

Journal has remained a popular title for newspapers (and also for collections of scholarly writings) and has become a synonym for any newspaper no matter what its title. *Journalism* is the highfalutin word for the task of news-gathering and dissemination, and people who work in the profession call themselves *journalists* when they want to seem dignified.

Journal is the fourth most frequent name today for newspapers, among them the *Journal*s of Aberdeen, Scotland *(Press & Journal);* Edmonton, Alberta; Montreal *(Le Journal);* Albuquerque, New Mexico; Akron, Ohio *(Beacon Journal);* Atlanta, Georgia *(Journal-Constitution);* Daytona Beach and Pensacola, Florida *(News-Journal);* Lincoln, Nebraska *(Journal Star);* Louisville, Kentucky *(Courier-Journal);* Madison, Wisconsin *(State Journal);* Milwaukee, Wisconsin *(Journal Sentinel);* Oklahoma City *(Journal Record);* Providence, Rhode Island; Springfield, Massachusetts; Syracuse, New York *(Herald-Journal);* Topeka, Kansas *(Capital-Journal);* Wilmington, Delaware *(News Journal);* White Plains, New York *(Journal News);* Winston-Salem, North Carolina; and the paper whose business is business, the *Wall Street Journal.*

As more newspapers came into being, new names for them were coined. Obviously, the possibility of a widely circulated sheet conveying recent information would depend on the invention of some method of putting words on paper that was faster than handwriting. That occurred between 1436 and 1450, when a clever German metalworker named Johannes Gutenberg got the idea for the printing press by looking at a winepress, possibly while sampling its product. *In vino inventio!*

It is difficult to speak with accuracy about names that were given to the very earliest newspapers because it is difficult to define a newspaper. Printers published numerous precursors of the modern newspaper in various formats under many names. The names were used at first as generic descriptions of a certain type of news publication, but they gradually came to be associated with specific publications that consistently used the same name as a heading. The name attached to a paper sprang from its purpose: the kind of information it conveyed, the audience to whom it was addressed, and the role it saw itself playing with respect to its intended readership.

The historian Anthony Smith distinguishes these early erratic news publications from true "newspapers"—the crucial distinction being a continuing relationship between reader, printer, and originator of the information. Another scholar, M. A. Shaaber, is more exacting, demanding that a true newspaper must be a miscellany of news items, published periodically, with each issue connected by a uniformity of ownership, title, style of makeup, and policy. A more liberal definition will better serve the purpose of this survey of names, and *newspaper* will be used broadly, for any kind of printed sheet conveying information to the general public about recent happenings under a title repeated in multiple issues.

In case you're interested, the first recorded use of the term *news paper*—two words—was not until 1670, in a letter to Charles Perrot, editor of the London *Gazette,* from a customer who wrote, "I wanted the news paper for Monday last past." (It is not recorded whether he got it.) By 1688 "newspaper" saw print as one word.

Principally in Holland, Germany, Italy, France, and England during the sixteenth and seventeenth centuries, the notion of a newspaper that was issued regularly under the same name, thus maintaining continuity, came about in gradual stages. As early as 1488 in Paris, printers issued sporadic news accounts on single sheets called *occasionels.* In Poland in 1513 a publication called *New Zeitung auss Litten und von den Moscowitter* ("News from Lithuania and concerning the Muscovites") appeared; *zeitung* has survived to this day as the German word for "newspaper."

In 1540 in Vienna, a printer named Hans Singreiner received government permission to publish *Novitäten,* which might be translated as "new things," a collection of official proclamations. Between 1588 and 1593 a publisher named Michael von Aitzing in Frankfurt issued *Relatio Historica,* summaries of recent events in six-month intervals. And by 1605, in the Low Countries (Netherlands plus Belgium), Abraham Verhoeven of Antwerp had begun publication of the *Nieuwe Tijdingen* ("New Tidings").

The *relation* (or *relacioun*), a "report" of some happening of widespread interest, sometimes not written until a year or more after the event, became the favored name for this early form of news dissemination. One of the first of these was *Relation aller Fürnemmen und gedenckwürdigen Historien* (which may be translated as "Report of all Notable and Memorable News"). Commonly known as the *Relation of Strasbourg,* it was published in that city by Johann Carolus, perhaps as early as 1605. It was followed by *Avisa Relation oder Zeitung* ("Report of Opinions or Newspaper"), issued in 1609 by Heinrich Julius, Duke of

Brunswick-Wolfenbuttel. The name *Relation* has not survived as a modern newspaper title (nor, for that matter, has Brunswick-Wolfenbuttel as a dukedom).

Courant

Next in the development of newspaper formats, primarily in Holland, came a continuous series of *relations* called by the Italian name *coranto,* sometimes *corante,* or *courant* in French and *krant* in Dutch—which meant "current news." The word, which also meant "messenger," originated from the Latin *currere,* "to run," which is also the root of the modern English word *current.* Corantos were not true newspapers in today's sense of the word, since the publication, though sequential, was irregular, and the title on the top of the page might change from one issue to the next, so that there was not a real sense of continuity. The corantos arranged the news under headings indicating the place and date of its origin, like datelines in modern newspapers.

Before 1621 a number of corantos were translated—from French and Italian—and published in England. Among them was a series published in French in 1620 by Jacob Jacobsz, the first of which was called *Courant d'Italie et d'Almaign* ("News from Italy and Germany"). On December 23, 1620, an English-language newspaper printed in Amsterdam called *Corrant out of Italy, Germany &c.* appeared and continued regularly until September 18, 1621.

At the outset of the Glorious Revolution in 1688, on the day after King James II fled the country, two newspapers appeared, with the titles London *Courant* and English *Courant.* The first daily newspaper in England was the *Daily Courant* in London, first published in 1702, followed by the Edinburgh *Courant* in 1705.

In 1721 James Franklin, the older brother of fifteen-year-old Benjamin, founded Boston's third newspaper, the New England *Courant,* to which precocious young Ben, not content to be a mere printer's helper, contributed a number of satires under the name Silence Dogood, before fleeing big brother for the greener pastures of Philadelphia.

Today, the name *Courant* survives in only a few British and American newspapers, notably the Hartford *Courant,* founded in Connecticut in 1764.

Courier

Closely related to *courant* etymologically is *courier,* from two French words, *coureur* ("runner") and *courier* ("professional messenger"). The words had separate meanings in French, but were combined in English and eventually made to conform to the spelling of *courier.* From the fourteenth century the word was used to mean a "running messenger," a messenger sent in haste, gasping for breath all the way. In 1630 in France an organization of royal dispatch riders known as *les grands courriers* carried news to major centers in the country.

The German town of Hildesheim had a publication in 1705 known as the *Relations-Courier* ("Report Deliverer"), which has survived to this day but is now known as the Hildesheimer *Allgemeine Zeitung* ("Hildesheim General Newspaper"). There was a Dublin *Courier* in 1758, a Cork *Courier* in 1795, and *Courier*s in both Bombay and Madras during the 1790s.

The *Chelsea Courier* was established in Norwich, Connecticut, in 1796, and the *Courier* was the name given to a newspaper established in Charleston, South Carolina, in 1803. The *Kurjer Wilenski* ("Vilnius *Courier*") was in Lithuania from 1815. The Boston *Courier* came shortly thereafter, in 1824.

Today, among notable *Couriers* are the *Post and Courier* in Charleston, South Carolina, the South's oldest daily newspaper, tracing its origin to the *Courier* of 1803; the Louisville (Kentucky) *Courier-Journal* (founded as the *Courier* in 1844); and the *Courier & Press* in Evansville, Indiana. The word found its way into Italian as *corriere,* and is well known today in *Corriere della Sera* ("Evening Courier"), one of Italy's leading newspapers.

Mercury

Another seventeenth-century development was an account of events in book form known as a *mercury,* also called in German an *intelligenzblatt* ("information sheet"). The name *Mercury* had a lot going for it, since Mercury was the Roman god of commerce and business, derived from the Greek Hermes, who was a messenger, or herald, to the gods. (The attentive reader will note that *Messenger* and *Herald* are also frequent newspaper names, but they will be dealt with later.) Hence, a

Mercury was a carrier of tidings, a bearer of news, a symbol of eloquence, and possibly also an early precursor of the *Wall Street Journal* or *Financial Times.* On a more somber note, readers of a *Mercury* might not have wished to know that among the Roman god's duties was escorting the dead to the underworld.

The *Mercurius Gallobelgicus,* or "News of the Low Countries," was among the earliest of a number of periodical summaries that began to appear in Europe in the late sixteenth century. Starting in 1594, it was issued twice a year in Latin by a German named Michael ab Isselt and contained mostly current war news. (As in our own time, there was always a war somewhere.)

The English poet John Donne, famous for reminding us for whom the bell tolls, might have had an unpleasant experience with the *Mercurius Gallobelgicus* similar to those of Carol Burnett and Cameron Diaz with the *National Enquirer,* for he wrote in a poem aimed at the newspaper: "Change thy name; thou art like Mercury in stealing, but liest like a Greek."

In 1611, the French began a publication called the *Mercure français. Mercurius Britannicus* in 1625 became the first English news periodical with a regular title. The English Civil War gave rise to many political newssheets, each with its own slant, and many of them chose the name *Mercurius.* A newsbook issued in London in 1643 carried the title *Mercurius Civicus—London's Intelligencer, or Truth Impartially Related from thence to the whole Kingdome, to prevent mis-information.* There were also *Mercurius Aulicus* (a pro-Monarchy propaganda piece), *Mercurius Pragmaticus* (an anti-Cromwell publication), *Mercurius Politicus* (pro-Commonwealth), *Mercurius Publicus* (Parliamentary), and *Mercurius Academicus* and *Mercurius Rusticus* (both Royalist). As if that were not enough mercurial activity, there were also short-lived papers known as *Mercurius Dogmaticus, Mercurius Morbicus, Mercurius Honestus, Mercurius Jocosus, Mercurius Phreneticus, Mercurius Phanaticus, Mercurius Insanus Insanissimus, Mercurius Infernus, Mercurius Democritus,* and *Mercurius Fumigosus, or the Smoaking Nocturnal*— the subtitle of which purported that it contained "many strange Wonders Out of the World in the Moon, the Antipodes, Magy-land, Greenland, Faryland Tenebris, Slavonia and other adjacent parts," all published for the "mis-understanding of all the Mad-Merry-People of Great Bedlam." A publication called the *Marine Mercury* specialized in news of sea beasts, of which, presumably, there were a sufficient number sighted to fill its pages. By the turn of the eighteenth century, *Mercurius* or its English form *Mercury* or sometimes *Mercurie* was well established as a common newspaper name.

In 1695 the Lincoln, Rutland and Stamford *Mercury,* the oldest surviving provincial newspaper in England, was first published. The Leeds *Mercury* came along in 1717. The *American Weekly Mercury* became the first American newspaper outside of Boston in 1719. The Newport *Mercury* in Rhode Island was founded in 1758 by Benjamin Franklin's nephew, James Franklin (Junior), and it survives today as the Newport *Mercury and Weekly News.* Other notable surviving *Mercury*s are in Manhattan, Kansas; Leicester, England; and San Jose, California *(Mercury News).*

Gazette

Another venerable name for a newspaper is *Gazette,* which has a long and circuitous history. Its usage began in Venice as early as 1556. The Venetian government's policy was to post a document known as *Notizie scritte,* or "written news," which people could read, or have read to them, upon payment of an admission fee of one *gazeta,* a Venetian coin of small value—about three-fourths of a penny. Just as certain publications in more recent times acquired nicknames such as "dime novels" or "penny dreadfuls," the *Notizie* soon became known, from its cost, as the *Gazeta.* Before long, the French, as they will do, adopted the word as their own, changing it to *Gazette.*

Some scholars ungraciously take a different view, maintaining that *Gazette* is derived from the Italian *gazzetta,* or "little magpie," alluding to the newspaper as a chattering nuisance (or possibly comparing the paper's output to bird droppings).

Newssheets known as *gazettes* must have been printed in England by the early seventeenth century, for in Ben Jonson's 1605 play *Volpone,* Sir Politic Would-Be is humiliated and laments that he'll be a public laughingstock:

> O, I shall be the fable of all feasts;
> The freight of the Gazetti; ship-boies tale;
> And, which is worst, even talke for Ordinaries.

The first French newspaper was the *Gazette de France,* founded in 1631 by Théophraste Renaudot with the backing of no less than Cardinal Richelieu. Some of the articles were even edited personally by King Louis XIII, who was thus able to use the royal "we" and the editorial "we" simultaneously. Renaudot was hounded by satirists and rivals, who issued competing publications, including one called the *Antigazette.* Renaudot's use of the term *Gazette* popularized it throughout the Continent as the title of publications specializing in diplomatic news.

In England, the Oxford *Gazette,* later renamed the London *Gazette,* was established in 1665 by a Royalist publisher named Henry Muddiman; it is still published in the twenty-first century and can be considered the oldest continuous newspaper in the world. The *Gazette* is the official newspaper of the United Kingdom, in which the texts of laws and government regulations are required to be published. It is not a conventional newspaper offering general news coverage, and it does not have a large circulation. A similar purpose is served in other parts of the United Kingdom and Ireland by the Edinburgh *Gazette,* which came along in 1699, the Dublin *Gazette* (1706, later known, mostly by those who speak Gaelic, as *Iris Oifigiúil*), and the Belfast *Gazette* (1921).

In 1784 the King's Printer in Bermuda began publishing the Bermuda *Gazette,* and Australia's first paper was the Sydney *Gazette* in 1803.

In 1756, the oldest surviving American newspaper, the New Hampshire *Gazette,* was founded by Daniel Fowle. It is edited today by a collateral descendant named Steven Fowle. Its claim to be the oldest surviving newspaper is slightly clouded by the fact that from 1960 until 1989 it was merged with the Portsmouth *Herald.* The Hartford *Courant* (founded in 1764) then jumped into the breach with its own claim to being the eldest, but Fowle maintains the *Gazette* was alive and kicking the whole while that it was merged with the *Herald.* It is certainly kicking today—most notably at Republicans and at its fellow New Hampshire paper, the *Union Leader.* The *Gazette* Web site maintains a department called "Republican Chickenhawk Database," listing people who it says enthusiastically endorse a policy of preemptive war but who have assiduously avoided any military service themselves.

Earlier American papers that have since bitten the dust were the Boston *Gazette,* founded in 1719; the New York *Gazette,* founded in 1725; the Maryland *Gazette* in Annapolis in 1727; and the Pennsylvania *Gazette,* founded in 1728 by Benjamin Franklin. *Gazette* proved among the most popular of newspaper names, helped along by the notoriety of Alexander Hamilton's *Gazette of the United States* and Thomas Jefferson's *National Gazette,* both founded as political organs.

With this profusion of *Gazette*s, it is no surprise that a character named Sir Gregory Gazette, a newspaper-obsessed politician, appears in the Cornish actor-playwright Samuel Foote's 1749 farce, *The Knights.*

*Gazette*s continue to abound in the twenty-first century in such places as Armagh, Northern Island; Chichester, England; Colorado Springs, Colorado; Katoomba, New South Wales; Montreal, Quebec; Saskatoon, Saskatchewan; Little Rock, Arkansas *(Democrat-Gazette);* Pittsburgh, Pennsylvania *(Post-Gazette);* and Texarkana, Texas and Arkansas.

A Chinese publication, commonly known in English as the Peking *Gazette,* appeared regularly beginning in the T'ang dynasty (AD 618– 905), but it did not become known under the name *Gazette* until the eighteenth century. It contained imperial replies to official questions, court edicts, and government announcements. Issued daily, but not printed until the fifteenth century, it was actually known as a *dibao* until the early 1700s, when, emulating the Western naming practice, the Beijing (Peking) *Gazette* as such was christened by Emperor Yung Cheng.

News

"What's the news? What's the news?" demands the wily old Roman senator Menenius in *Coriolanus.* The same question is asked by Hamlet, Desdemona, Mistress Overdone, and other characters in plays written by Shakespeare between 1590 and 1612. They might have found the answer to their question in one of the many newspaper prototypes with the word *News* in their titles, which had appeared at least as early as 1570.

The word stems from the Old English *niwe* or *niowe,* meaning "not existing before, or not previously known." Originally the word *newes,* in the plural, meant "new things" or "novelties," but by the 1420s it was used in England to refer to an account of recent occurrences—or the occurrences themselves—as reported to one for the first time.

The printing of the news conferred upon the report a kind of legitimacy. A factor (one who wrote newsletters by hand) in Ben Jonson's 1621 masque, *News from the New World,* says, "I would have no news printed; for when they are written, though they be false, they remain news still." To this, the masque's printer replies, "It is the printing of 'em makes 'em news to a great many who will indeed believe nothing but what's in print." Human credulousness has remained steadfast in the last five hundred years but has now been transferred to the Internet.

Although plural in form, *news* has usually been construed in the singular since as early as 1566, according to the *Oxford English Dictionary.* There have been some notable departures from this custom. In the Jonson masque just quoted, *news* is treated as a plural, and a news gatherer in Jonson's 1625 play *The Staple of News* asks, "Where are the news that were examin'd last?" Horace Greeley, the famed founder and editor of the New York *Tribune,* always insisted that the word "news" was to be used in the plural. He once wired one of his reporters, "Are there any news?" Not to be outdone, the reporter wired back, "Not a new."

One of the earliest instances of the word *News* as a heading for an English publication was *News Concernynge the General Councell Holden at Trydent* (Trent), published in London, translated from the German, in 1549, a mere two or three years after the actual council, which was a key event in the Roman Catholic Counter-Reformation. Other early examples of the *News* were the *Newes from Northumberland* and *Joyfull Newes for true Subiectes,* both printed in 1570. Two newsbooks published in 1601 by Thomas Pavier bore similar titles: *Newes from Ostend,* followed by a sequel, *Further Newes from Ostend,* which were accounts of the siege of that Belgian city by the Spanish. In 1605 came the breath-defying *Newes out of the Lowe cuntreies with a report of all things happened from the begynninge of this Last Summer till this present wynter betwene the States and the Archduke in Brabant and Friseland this yere 1605.* Such a title probably did not come trippingly from the tongues of the newsmongers.

The first real English newspaper to use the name *News* began as a translation by Nathaniel Butter, a printer, of a Dutch coranto called *Corante, or newes from Italy, Germany, Hungarie, Spaine and France,* dated September 24, 1621. Together with two London stationers, Nicholas Bourne and Thomas Archer, Butter published a stream of corantos, including a numbered and dated series of *Weekley Newes* beginning in 1622. Some forty years later, in 1663, there was a single issue of a publication with the unadorned title of the *Newes.*

Meanwhile, in Paris in 1631, the *Nouvelles Ordinaires de Divers En-*

droits, which might be translated as "Daily News from Various Places," was a short-lived venture by the booksellers Louis Vendosme and Jean Martin, who ran afoul of a rival who had the unbeatable backing of Cardinal Richelieu.

In 1696 *Lloyd's News,* issuing from Edward Lloyd's coffeehouse, which had become a center of marine insurance, was an early source of shipping information. Later British instances of this name include the *Weekly News* (1842), *Reynolds News* (1850), and the racy and still flourishing *News of the World* (1843).

The first successful American paper was the Boston *News-Letter,* founded in 1704, and in 1846 the *Daily News* in London was established, edited by none other than Charles Dickens. The paper survived, later known as the *News-Chronicle,* until the late twentieth century.

The *News* remains the single most popular title for newspapers all over the English-speaking world. In Canada, the *News* is delivered in dozens of cities including Halifax, Niagara Falls, and Victoria. In the United Kingdom, you will find a *News (of the World)* in London, and also in Belfast, Cambridge, Carlisle, Edinburgh, and Manchester, among many others. In the United States there is a *Daily News* as well as a *Newsday* in New York, and others in Los Angeles, Dallas, Denver, Detroit, Birmingham, Philadelphia, Dayton, Buffalo, and on and on and on.

Oh, yes—the northeast Texas town of Uncertain (population 150) has a newspaper that is issued semiannually. It is called, with disarming candor, the *Uncertain News.*

Others

In the sixteenth and seventeenth centuries, the early days of proto-newspapers, a number of titles were attached to them that have not generally survived as names of modern newspapers. Some of these descriptive words included: *Discourse, Description,* and *Rehearsal,* all used for news of the monarch's activities; *Articles, Declaration, Collections and Relations,* and *True Report,* for official news issued by the Crown; *Narration, Argument, Petition, Treatise, Information, Defense, Admonition,* and *Historie,* attached to pieces of religious propaganda; and *Summarie, Tidings, Recital, Manifest, Abstract,* and *Canticle,* which were headings for war news and foreign translations. In the same era, the tradition of news ballads sprang up. They were accounts of usually lurid events, such as crimes, unnatural occurrences, and ghostly apparitions, written in verse, and often intended to be sung to popular melodies. They had such sensational titles as *Tydinges of a Huge and Ougly Childe borne at Arneheim in Gilderland* and *A true relacon of the birth of Three Monsters in the Citty of Namen in Flaunders.*

One very early "newspaper," an account published in 1485 by Hungarian king Matthias to spread the word of his conquest of Vienna, sported a name that did not become popular for succeeding publications, and it's easy to understand why (even though certain public figures who feel mistreated by the press might still find it appropriate). It was called *Dracola Waida,* or the "Devil Prince."

3

Rule, Britannia!

British fractiousness begat scores of newspaper names in the seventeenth and eighteenth centuries. The Dutch, the Germans, the Italians, and the French devised the earliest titles—the *Corantos, Gazettes, Journals,* and *Mercurys*—and these names quickly became entrenched across the Channel. But as newspapers came and went in England—hundreds of them between 1640 and 1660—new names for them sprang from the polemics of two centuries of constant British political and religious turmoil: the beheading of a king, a civil war and several foreign ones, restoration of the monarchy, a bloodless revolution, and a very bloody one ending in the loss of the American colonies. Some of these newspaper names were created to express opinions now obscured in the mists of time, and they are no longer much in use—*Hermit, Ghost, Jesting Astrologer, Lover,* and *Wandering Whore,* for example, do not grace the tops of many front pages these days—but others from this period remain in wide circulation. Even when the papers themselves were short-lived, their titles have survived in a string of successors: *Intelligencer, Observer, Review, Examiner, Inquirer,* and *Guardian.*

Intelligencer

An "intelligencer" in the seventeenth century was a secret agent or spy. The word was formed from *intelligence,* meaning "information," and by adding an "er," which was probably influenced by the French word for "spy," *intelligencier.* From the 1630s the word was used to mean "a bringer of news, an informant, or sometimes a newsmonger." During this period of political intrigue between Crown and Parliament, the cloak-and-dagger connotations of *intelligencer* made it an ideal word to describe a politically active newspaper's "insider" information. *Intelligencer* was perhaps deemed a little more polite than the brazen word *Spy,* although one anti-Royalist publication in 1644 called itself exactly that—the *Spie*—and there were others that later incorporated that word into their titles.

In 1641 the *Mercurius Britannicus* used *English Intelligencer* as a subtitle, and in 1643 in London there was a paper called *Intelligencer Mercurius Civicus.* Throughout the Civil War, from 1642 until 1649, there were several papers that used the name *Intelligencer,* including the *Kingdomes Weekly Intelligencer,* which bore a subtitle that must have sold a few copies: *Speciall passages and certain information from severall places collected for the use of all that desire to be truely informed.* Who could resist such a come-on?

The *Compleate Intelligencer* and the *Daily Intelligencer* came out in 1643 and the *Exchange Intelligencer* in 1644. A weekly called the *Moderate Intelligencer,* first issued in 1649 and published by John Dillingham, a former tailor turned journalist, became a thorn in the side of Oliver Cromwell, the virtual dictator of England during the Commonwealth period. Dillingham, for all his "moderation," was engulfed in controversy, one unhappy reader referring to him as a "Prick louse vermin Taylor." A rival, Gilbert Mabbot, thought he would stir up a little confusion by publishing a paper under the same name, but the House of Lords ruled that Dillingham was exclusively entitled to use the name *Moderate Intelligencer,* thus establishing the importance of proprietary rights to a newspaper's title. The word *Intelligencer* in other combinations, however, was still up for grabs, including the *Impartial Intelligencer* in 1653 and the *Faithful Intelligencer* in Edinburgh in 1660. John Thurloe, the secretary of state under Cromwell in the government of the Commonwealth, supervised a publication called the *Publick Intelligencer,* beginning in 1655.

Intelligencer continued to be used into the eighteenth and nineteenth centuries, including the North Country *Journal or Impartial Intelligencer* (1734), Leeds *Intelligencer* (1754), and Newcastle *Intelligencer* (1755). Some early American *Intelligencer*s were the *Gazette and Norfolk Intelligencer* in 1774; the Connecticut *Gazette and Universal Intelligencer* in 1778; the *Political Intelligencer and New Jersey Advertiser* in 1783; the *National Intelligencer and Washington Advertiser* around 1800; and *Intelligencer*s in Green Bay, Wisconsin, in 1833 and La Grange, Texas, in 1844.

Today, the name survives in only a few newspapers, most notably the *Post-Intelligencer* in Seattle, Washington. The name also appears in the titles of papers in Doylestown and Lancaster, Pennsylvania *(Intelligencer-Journal);* Stonington, Connecticut; Wheeling, West Virginia; and Belleville, Ontario.

Observer

In 1681, Roger L'Estrange, who held the censorious job of surveyor of the press under King Charles II, began publication of a newspaper to attack Whigs, a party of "dissenting Protestants" who were opposed to the accession to the throne by the Roman Catholic duke of York. The paper seemed to have been successful in its goal, inasmuch as the duke did become King James II. L'Estrange called his paper the *Observator,* a word whose root is the Latin *observare,* meaning "to watch, attend to, guard, or keep." By the seventeenth century, the word had also taken on the meaning of "to say, or remark upon." The implication of the title, then, is that it is both looking on and commenting about political activities. In the first issue, April 13, 1681, Sir Roger minced no words in explaining what the paper's name implied:

"Q. You call yourself the *Observator.* What is it now that you intend for the Subject of your Observations?

"A. . . . My business is to encounter the Faction, and to Vindicate the Government; to detect their Forgeries; to lay open the Rankness of their Calumnies, and Malice; to Refute their Seditious Doctrines; to expose their Hypocrisy, and the bloody Design that is carried on, under the Name and Semblance, of Religion."

Sir Roger could afford to be doctrinaire. His royal grant from King Charles gave him "all the sole privileges of writing, printing, and publishing all narratives, advertisements, mercuries, intelligencers, diurnals, and other books of public intelligence."

More than a hundred years later, in 1791, an entrepreneur named W. S. Bourne chose *Observer,* a variant form of *Observator,* for a newspaper that he established with motives more pecuniary than political. It was a

Sunday gossip rag, and Bourne's avowed purpose in founding it was to earn a rapid fortune. In this aim, alas, he was disappointed, and he had to sell the paper, but it did survive through several subsequent owners and widely varying policies: a government propaganda organ, a luridly graphic crime and scandal sheet, and then the respected journal of serious social and political commentary that it provides for British readers each Sunday to this day.

The name *Observer* has been adopted by numerous newspapers in English towns, among them Bishop's Stortford, Bognor Regis, East Grinstead, Hastings, Slough, Watford, Wigan, and Windsor, as well as in Canada, Australia, and the United States, notably the Charlotte *Observer,* the Fayetteville *Observer,* and the Raleigh *News & Observer,* all in North Carolina. In Italy, the Vatican likes to watch and comment in *L'Osservatore Romano.*

Review

Politics was usually the driving force underlying the founding of early newspapers. Such was the case with the *Review of the Affairs of France, and of All Europe,* started in 1704 by Daniel Defoe. Defoe was an ardent Whig who loved to stir up a good political fight, and he continued to publish the *Review* three times a week until 1713. Later he wrote the works for which he is best known today, *Robinson Crusoe* and *Moll Flanders.*

The word *review* stems from the Latin *re* ("again") + *videre* ("to see"), by way of the French word *revue,* and its earliest usage in the sixteenth century referred to the act of looking over something with the idea of improving it. It took on numerous meanings, and by 1700 one of them was "a retrospective survey of past actions."

After Defoe named his paper the *Review,* it gained general usage as a name for newspapers, especially those devoted to commentary on current events or literature. Among its later emulators were the Reading *Journal and Weekly Review* (1744), the Preston *Review and County Advertiser* in Lancashire (1793), the *Sunday Review* in London (1804), and the Nottingham *Review and Weekly Advertiser* (1808).

The name is used today most commonly for literary and scientific publications and by a few general-interest newspapers, including Cana-

da's Richmond and Niagara Falls *Review*s, and in the United States the
Las Vegas *Review-Journal* and Pittsburgh *Tribune-Review,* along with
numerous smaller daily and weekly papers.

Examiner

Like Defoe's *Review,* the early *Examiner* also had an impressive literary pedigree. The word itself is from the Latin *examen,* which originally meant "the tongue of a balance" and the related verb *examiner,*
which by extension meant "to weigh, or to test." The English word *examine* (spelled variously) by the fourteenth century meant "to test by an
appropriate method, inspect carefully in order to determine the character of, investigate, scrutinize, interrogate closely as in a judicial pro-
ceeding." By the sixteenth century an *examiner* was a synonym for an
"investigator."

Among its earliest uses as the title of a newspaper was the Tory publication the *Examiner* in 1710, which was edited by Jonathan Swift, the
Irish satirist who also wrote *Gulliver's Travels.* At the same time, there
was an opposition paper that called itself the *Whig Examiner,* to which
the playwright and essayist Joseph Addison was a contributor.

Continuing this literary tradition, a later *Examiner* was founded in
1808 by the poet Leigh ("Abou Ben Adhem") Hunt, who continued to
edit the politically aggressive paper from prison after he was convicted
of libeling the prince regent. In America, there was an *Examiner* in Richmond in 1798; it was a journal that positioned itself as an ally of Thomas
Jefferson and lasted until 1804. A later Richmond *Examiner,* founded in
1849, was one of the most severe critics of Jefferson Davis, president of
the Confederacy during the American Civil War.

The San Francisco *Examiner* was published from 1865 until 2000, as
part of the Hearst media empire since 1880. It, too, had a literary back-
ground, with Ambrose Bierce, Mark Twain, and Jack London among its
contributors. Hearst also operated the Los Angeles *Herald-Examiner*
until 1989, when the paper closed. Today the *Examiner* name survives
in San Francisco and also in Washington, D.C., and Baltimore, as a free
daily tabloid.

Other *Examiner*s can be found in the United States, Canada, Britain,
and Australia, including the Bartlesville (Oklahoma) *Examiner-Enter-*

prise, the Independence (Missouri) *Examiner,* the Ogden (Utah) *Standard-Examiner,* Huddersfield and Isle of Man *Examiner*s in England, plus Canadian *Examiner*s in Barrie, Ontario, and Edmonton, Alberta; an *Irish Examiner* in Dublin; and Australia's Launceston (Tasmania) *Examiner.*

Inquirer/Enquirer

The *Free-Enquirer* was a virulently anti-Christian publication that appeared in nine issues over a three-month period in 1761. It was published by a Liverpudlian named Peter Annet, who made it clear that he was strongly opposed to all revealed religion. So strident were the irreligious views expressed in the *Free-Enquirer* that Annet was convicted of blasphemy in 1762 and sentenced to twelve months' hard labor. The name *Enquirer* was apparently not much in favor for some while after Annet's unfortunate experience.

The word itself might well give pause to the ultraorthodox, since it stems from the Latin words *in* ("in") and *quarere* ("to seek"), and means "to seek to know by asking questions, to investigate, to examine critically."

In 1804 in the New World, the Richmond *Enquirer* was established as a successor to the *Examiner,* and like its predecessor was also a supporter of Thomas Jefferson.

Insisting on the Latinate, rather than the Frenchified, spelling of the word, an *Inquirer* appeared in Dublin in 1815, in Nantucket in 1823, and in Philadelphia in 1829. The Philadelphia *Inquirer,* still published in the twenty-first century, is the third-oldest surviving newspaper in the United States, after the New Hampshire *Gazette* and the Hartford *Courant.*

Edgar Williams, in "A History of the *Inquirer*" published on the Web site philly.com, describes how the name was adopted by the founders of the Philadelphia paper, John Norvell and John Walker, on June 1, 1829: "Norvell picked up a proof of Page One, nodding toward the flag. 'There can be no better name than "The Inquirer,"' he is reputed to have said. 'In a free state, there should always be an inquirer asking on behalf of the people: Why was this done? Why is that necessary work not done? Why is that man put forward? Why is that law proposed? Why? Why? Why?'"

Reverting to the eighteenth-century spelling, the Cincinnati *Enquirer* was founded in 1841 and is published to this day. A newer American paper, which also favors the *E* spelling but specializes in the *G* word (for "gossip"), pushes the meaning of its name to the limit: the inquisitive weekly *National Enquirer,* founded in 1926.

Guardian

In the fourteenth century a *guardian* was a type of government official, particularly as used for the offices of Guardian of the Peace, analogous to today's Justice of the Peace, and Guardian of the Poor, an official in charge of administering the poor laws in a particular district. The word acquired other meanings and connotations, for one who protects and defends, as in a guardian angel, or a legal guardian appointed to have custody of someone incapable of managing his or her own affairs.

The *Guardian* was the name that political gadfly Richard Steele chose for the opinionated newspaper that he founded in 1713, after the demise of the *Tatler* (founded 1709) and the *Spectator* (founded 1711), in all three of which his good friend Joseph Addison was a coconspirator. Other *Guardian*s that followed include the *Guardian, or Historical and Literary Recorder* in London in 1819, and the *Poor Man's Guardian* in 1831—a populist paper named in an obvious allusion to the Manchester *Guardian,* which had been founded in 1821 by John Edward Taylor with a specific agenda to promote liberal interests. The Manchester *Guardian*'s initial prospectus, justifying its name, declared that it would "zealously enforce the principles of civil and religious Liberty" and "warmly advocate the cause of Reform."

The *Guardian* had the same editor, C. P. Scott, for fifty-seven years, from 1872 until 1929. Always noted for the militant independence that its name implied, the *Guardian* set forth its most important principles in an article celebrating its hundredth birthday in 1921: "Comment is free, but facts are sacred. The voice of opponents no less than that of friends has a right to be heard."

For a time, the *Guardian* fell upon evil days and suffered from an eccentric news agenda, poor printing, and profuse typographical errors—having once printed its own name as the *Gaurdian,* provoking the satirical *Private Eye* magazine to christen it with the nickname the

Grauniad. Having moved to London in 1976, abandoning its Manchester designation, the *Guardian* today is one of England's leading national newspapers and almost invariably spells its own name correctly.

The *Poor Man's Guardian,* incidentally, hung around until 1835, vying for attention with the *Destructive, or Poor Man's Conservative.*

In other parts of the English-speaking world, only a few newspapers carry the name *Guardian,* or sometimes its variant, the *Guard,* which, having fewer letters to be concerned about, is much easier to spell.

Others

Among other provocative names for newspapers in England during the disputatious seventeenth and eighteenth centuries were *Hermit, Rhapsody, Whisperer, Lover, Ghost, True-Informer, Tatling Harlot, Wandering Whore, Jesting Astrologer, Dove, Vulture, Screech-Owl, Craftsman, Auditor, Miscellany, Freethinker, Grumbler, Adventurer, Honest Gentleman, Post-Angel, Lay-Monk, Crab-Tree, Flapper* (meaning "reminder"), *Connoisseur, Humanist, Medley, Old Common Sense, Lounger, Patrician* (issued as a response to the *Plebeian*), *Prompter, Trifler, Rambler,* and *Idler* (the last two the work of Samuel Johnson and inspired by the earlier *Tatler* and *Spectator*). Oh, yes, one should not forget the 1679 publication that gave readers fair warning of its impish intent: the *Snotty-Nose Gazette: Or, Coughing Intelligence.* These names survive today mostly in musty memory—and the much less musty archives of the Harry Ransom Humanities Research Center at the University of Texas at Austin or the British Library in London.

4

You've Got Mail

"Neither snow nor rain nor heat nor gloom of night stays these couriers from the swift completion of their appointed rounds." That's how the Greek historian Herodotus praised the Persian postal system in the fifth century BC—not the United States Postal Service of today. Many people, however, do think that's the USPS official motto—but it isn't, so don't expect your mail to be delivered in a hurricane. It's merely a quotation that the architect had engraved on the frieze of a New York Post Office building in 1913. The saying might apply with some truth to the delivery of your daily newspaper, and it was, in fact, the speed and reliability of the British postal system that inspired the names of numerous newspapers in the seventeenth and eighteenth centuries.

This system initially depended on riders on horseback and was soon emulated in the United States. As technology developed, ships, trains, and telegraphy were also utilized, and ultimately this delivery system became the Royal Mail in Great Britain and the Postal Service in the United States, where it achieved such feats of derring-do with its legendary Pony Express that even Charlton Heston became one of its riders, in a 1953 film that glorified the mail-delivering exploits of "Buffalo Bill" Cody. Among the newspaper names that allude to these methods of delivering messages are *Post, Packet, Mail, Dispatch, Herald, Messenger, Telegraph, Telegram, Express,* and *Clipper.*

The proliferation of newspaper names was noted by the poet George Crabbe in 1783 in "The Newspaper," a sardonic commentary in verse on what Crabbe believed was the sheer banality of newspapers. He provided this rhymed litany:

> I sing of NEWS, and all those vapid sheets
> The rattling hawker vends through gaping streets;
> Whate'er their name, whate'er the time they fly,
> Damp from the press, to charm the reader's eye:
> For soon as Morning dawns with roseate hue,
> The HERALD of the morn arises too;
> POST after POST succeeds, and, all day long,
> GAZETTES and LEDGERS swarm, a noisy throng.
> When evening comes, she comes with all her train;
> Of LEDGERS, CHRONICLES, and POSTS again.
> Like bats, appearing when the sun goes down,
> From holes obscure and corners of the town.

Such ubiquity, from rosy dawn to darkest night, is exactly what the newspaper publishers hoped to achieve for their news-starved readers, and they gleefully appropriated a pouchful of titles from the postal services on which the public was increasingly reliant.

Post

Post comes from the Latin *ponere,* "to place," and refers to a station or fixed point of duty, especially an official one. From the beginning of the sixteenth century, *post* described the system of men with horses stationed at suitable points along the "post"-roads, their duty being to ride with all speed to the next stage of the road, carrying the king's packet (or dispatches), and eventually the letters of other persons. From 1674, *post* was in use to mean the system that evolved into the national postal service.

As a result, in the late seventeenth and early eighteenth centuries, *post* was incorporated into the names of printed papers conveying the news, much of which, in fact, came to them via messages delivered by those very post riders. These papers included the Worcester *Post-Man* in 1690; London *Post-Man* and *Post-Boy* in 1699; the London *Post,* published by Benjamin Harris from 1699 to 1705; the London *Post-Angel* (1701); the Norwich *Post* (1701); the Bristol *Post-Boy* (1702); the Dublin *Post* (1702); *Whalley's Flying Post* in Dublin (1704); the *Flying Post* in Edinburgh (1704); and the London *Evening Post* (1711). London's *Morn-

ing Post, published from 1772 until 1937, counted William Wordsworth, Samuel Taylor Coleridge, Robert Southey, and Charles Lamb among its writers.

The names of these early *Posts* reflected the continuation of the tradition of handwritten newsletters that had flourished since the fifteenth century. The *Post-Man,* the *Flying Post,* and others had blank pages for purchasers to write their personal news in longhand and forward to other readers in the countryside by the actual postal service.

The New York *Evening Post* was founded in 1801 by Alexander Hamilton and was edited for many years by William Cullen Bryant, who in his spare time waxed poetic, most famously over a waterfowl and about the contemplation of death. The New York *Post* is the oldest U.S. newspaper in continuous daily publication. Larger in its early days than most other newspapers (it measured about twenty-two inches by thirty inches), it was sometimes irreverently called "Bryant's Mighty Horse Blanket." The name *Post* gave rise to a punning anecdote in the late nineteenth century, when the *Post* was highly critical of the New York *Sun*'s Democratic editorial policies under editor Charles A. Dana. The *Post* referred to the *Sun* as a "yellow dog" paper. The *Sun* in an editorial serenely responded: "The *Post* calls the *Sun* a 'yellow dog.' The attitude of the *Sun* will continue to be that of any dog toward any post."

In the twenty-first century, *Posts* are found in Great Britain in Birmingham, Bristol, Dundee, Leeds, Liverpool, Nottingham, Reading, and York, among other cities; in Canada in Toronto *(National Post);* Regina and Saskatoon, Saskatchewan; and Sydney, Nova Scotia; in Wellington, New Zealand; in the United States, in Birmingham, Alabama *(Post-Herald);* Cincinnati, Ohio; Denver, Colorado; Palm Beach, Florida; Pittsburgh, Pennsylvania *(Post-Gazette);* Seattle, Washington *(Post-Intelligencer);* St. Louis, Missouri *(Post-Dispatch);* and Washington, D.C. Other *Posts* are in Bangkok, Berlin, Hong Kong, Jakarta, Jerusalem, and Lusaka.

A much-played march by John Philip Sousa titled "The Washington Post" was commissioned by that newspaper in 1889 for an essay contest awards ceremony. Publisher Frank Hatton, who had just acquired the *Post,* started the contest as a promotional stunt, and it attracted fifteen hundred entries from schoolchildren. One day Hatton ran into Sousa, a fellow member of the Gridiron Club and also the leader of the United States Marine Band, and asked if he would compose a special piece to liven up the awards presentation. Sousa agreed, and on the following June 15 a crowd of twenty-five thousand, including abolitionist hero Frederick Douglass, who was one of the judges, tapped their toes as the Marine Band premiered "The Washington Post." The piece became hugely popular as an accompaniment to a new dance craze, the "two-step," and it catapulted the name of the newspaper into the world's consciousness. Whether Sousa was paid by the newspaper for composing the march is not known, but he later sold the publishing rights for thirty-five dollars.

Packet

Related to the name *Post* is *Packet,* a word for a "collection of dispatches or letters." Its first recorded use in that sense for a news publication was in 1646 by the *Packet of Letters,* which had only one issue, and in 1648 a longer-lived *Packet of Letters from Scotland.* In 1678 the *Weekly Pacquet of Advice from Rome* was published, and in 1714 a paper known as the *Loyal Packet* appeared in Norwich. In 1763 came the New York *Pacquet.* (As often happened, some Anglo-French spellers thought a *qu* more kingly than the quotidian *k.*)

In the mid-eighteenth century, *packet* came into use as an abbreviated form of *packet boat,* a vessel used to transport postal dispatches. Some newspapers were named with this meaning of the word in mind, including the tongue-twisting Essex *Journal and Merrimack Packet or the Massachusetts and New Hampshire General Advertiser* (that's all one paper) in 1773. There were also the Dublin *Evening Packet* in 1770, the Norwich *Packet* in 1773, and, in 1775, the Pennsylvania *Packet,* which became the first successful daily in the New World—aided, no doubt, by the breaking news from the Second Continental Congress resulting in the Declaration of Independence.

Today the name *Packet* survives in only a few newspapers. In the United States, you'll find the Princeton (New Jersey) *Packet,* and the *Island Packet* in Hilton Head, South Carolina, whose founders in 1970 specifically named it after the packet boats that are the communications link between the mainland and the barrier islands along the Intracoastal Waterway.

In England there is a *Packet* group of newspapers in Falmouth, Truro, and other towns. The Falmouth *Packet* was founded in 1801 as the *Cornwall Gazette and Falmouth Packet.* A story is told that press mogul Lord Beaverbrook's son, who was an avid sailor, heard that the Falmouth *Packet* was for sale and bought it, sight unseen, under the impression that it was a boat.

Mail

By the thirteenth century the word *mail,* spelled variously *male, maylle,* and *maale,* came into English from the Dutch, meaning "traveling bag or wallet." By the seventeenth century it was a synonym for *packet,* meaning a "bag of letters or dispatches for conveyance by post." That meaning was transferred to the person or vehicle that carried the postal material, and thence became used for the "system by which letters are transported," or, in other words, as a synonym for *post.*

In this sense it was adopted as a newspaper title: the Blackburn *Mail* and the London *Evening Mail,* both in 1800, soon followed by the Manchester *Mail* in 1805, the Waterford (Ireland) *Mail* in 1827, the Dublin *Mail* in 1828, and the Liverpool *Mail* in 1836.

Today the *Daily Mail* is one of London's leading newspapers, and in Canada, the Toronto *Globe and Mail* is similarly prominent. In Australia, the weekly *Golden Mail* is published in Kalgoorlie, playing on the mining town's famous "Golden Mile," touted as the richest one-mile stretch of gold ore in the world. In the United States the *Daily Mail* in Charleston, West Virginia, is among the largest newspapers of that name, and Columbia City, Indiana, has what must be regarded as the redundantly named *Post & Mail.*

Dispatch

Yet another postal term is found in the name *Dispatch.* The letters and official documents sent by the postal service were known as "dispatches." The word stems from the Italian *dispaccio* or Spanish *despacho:* "a message sent with speed, especially an important official message." Its Latin root is *dis* ("to undo") + *pactare* ("fasten or fix"); hence "to remove from a fixed position, i.e. to send with haste." According to the *Oxford English Dictionary,* it was first used in this sense in 1582, but it is not found as a newspaper name until the beginning of the nineteenth century.

The *Weekly Dispatch* appeared in London in 1801, followed by *Bell's Weekly Dispatch* in 1812, the *Twopenny Dispatch* in 1836, the Edinburgh *Dispatch* in 1886, and many others. Depending on whether the speller was feeling Italianate or Hispanic, the word sometimes appeared as *Despatch,* as in the Birmingham, England, paper founded in 1902 and later merged into the *Evening Mail and Despatch,* another paper with a superfluity of postal allusions. Today the name is seen less frequently, but can be found (with another bit of redundancy) in the *Post-Dispatch* in St. Louis, Missouri; the *Times-Dispatch* in Richmond, Virginia; the *Dispatch* in Columbus, Ohio; and in numerous smaller papers.

Herald

The Middle English word *heraud* or *herault* is probably from the Old German *hariwald,* from *heri* ("army") and *walto* ("govern") and originally meant "commander of an army." It may be also related to the Old High German *haren,* meaning "to call." In any event, from the fourteenth century in England a *herald* was an officer with the duty of making royal or state proclamations or carrying official messages. It was eventually used to mean any kind of messenger, envoy, or harbinger of things to come.

In Ben Jonson's 1621 masque *News from the New World Discovered in the Moon,* two characters known as "Heralds" attract the audience's attention with their opening cries of "News! News! News! Bold and brave news! New as the night they are born in—or the fantasy that begot 'em!" Long before a printed newspaper used the name, heralds were regarded as sources of news.

Early examples of *Herald*'s use as a newspaper title are the *Morning Herald and Daily Advertiser,* London, 1780; *Volunteers Journal, or, Irish Herald,* Dublin, 1783; the *Evening Herald,* Dublin, 1786; and the *Morning Herald,* Dublin, 1789; the Pennsylvania *Herald,* 1789; the Edinburgh *Herald,* 1790; the York (England) *Herald,* 1791; and the Bath *Herald and General Advertiser,* 1792.

The New York *Herald* was founded in 1835 by James Gordon Bennett, who was so anxious to promote the newspaper's name that he issued an edict that it should always be printed in italics. One typesetter showed unflinching, or maybe just unthinking, obedience to the order when an article reported that a Christmas concert included "Hark, the *Herald* Angels Sing."

Today's *Herald*s famously proclaim the news in many venues, including, but certainly not limited to, Boston, Massachusetts; Durham, North Carolina *(Herald-Sun);* Birmingham, Alabama *(Post-Herald);* Lexington, Kentucky *(Herald-Leader);* Sarasota *(Herald-Tribune)* and Miami, Florida; Omaha, Nebraska *(World-Herald);* Arlington Heights, Illinois; Biloxi-Gulfport, Mississippi *(Sun Herald);* Portland, Maine *(Press Herald);* Portsmouth, New Hampshire; Calgary and Grand Prairie *(Herald Tribune),* Alberta; Halifax, Nova Scotia; Glasgow, Scotland; Plymouth, England; Sydney and Melbourne *(Herald Sun),* Australia; Auckland, New Zealand; and Buenos Aires, where the *Herald* has been an English-language daily since 1877.

Herald is the third most frequent newspaper name, after *News* and *Times.*

Messenger

More or less synonymous with *herald,* from the thirteenth century, was a *messenger,* from the Latin *mittere,* "to send." During the English Civil War's spate of newspapers, the *Moderate Messenger* in 1647 appeared for what historian Joseph Frank calls "a single inoffensive issue." The same title was used for papers that came out in 1649 and 1653. In the eighteenth century, one of the lurid Sunday newspapers, emphasizing details of brutal crimes, was known as *Bell's Weekly Messenger.* The name survives in a number of mostly small daily and weekly newspapers in the United States, Canada, and Great Britain.

Telegraph and Telegram

The word *telegraph* comes from the Greek *tele* ("far away") + *grapho* ("write") and means, literally, "written communication from far away." It generally refers to an apparatus used for transmitting messages from a distance, usually by some kind of signs. Its first usage is cited in 1794 by the *Oxford English Dictionary,* applied to a device invented by Claude Chappe in France, in 1791, consisting of a post with movable arms, with coded signals made by various positions of the arms. Other later devices used flashing lights, movable discs or shutters, and sounds. Such devices today would probably be called semaphores.

London had a *Telegraph* and Newfield, Connecticut, an *American Telegraph,* both in 1795, and Dublin, Ireland, had the *Hibernian Telegraph and Morning Star* in 1799. The same year saw the Portsmouth *Telegraph* in England, followed in 1800 by the Bridgeport (Connecticut) *Telegraph,* in 1808 by the Plymouth and Dock *Telegraph,* and in 1809 by the Leith and Edinburgh *Telegraph.* London's *Telegraph* of 1795 is not the same paper as today's widely read *Daily Telegraph,* which began in 1855 as the first penny paper. In the United States, the *American Telegraph* was founded in Brownsville, Pennsylvania, in 1814, and the Rochester (New York) *Telegraph* in 1818.

The first story based on an electrically telegraphed report that was printed in a newspaper was not, however, in one called the *Telegraph,* but in the *Times* of London. It was on August 6, 1844, and was the news of the birth of a son to Queen Victoria. This method of telegraphy, using a single wire to send short and long coded signals, was successfully developed by an American portrait painter named Samuel Finley Breese Morse, who began to dabble in electricity in 1832 and by 1844 was able to demonstrate to the U.S. Congress the practicality of his device by sending the famous message "What hath God wrought" from Washington to Baltimore.

After the invention of the electric telegraph, the word *telegram* was coined in 1852, to refer to a telegraphic dispatch, and this form of the word was favored by papers in the United States, where the New York *Telegram* (later famously merged into the *World-Telegram & the Sun*) was founded in 1867, the Worcester (Massachusetts) *Telegram* (now the *Telegram & Gazette)* in 1884, the Long Beach (California) *Press-Telegram* in 1897, and the Fort Worth (Texas) *Star-Telegram* in 1906. There were some English *Telegram*s as well, in Darlington, Sunderland, and Deal.

Express

The word *express* has been around since at least 1385 and has enough meanings to fill six columns of the *Oxford English Dictionary.* Its original etymology is from the Latin *ex* ("out") + *premere* ("to press"), and one of its earliest meanings was "directly or distinctly stated, as opposed to implied." By the seventeenth century the word was also applied to messages sent with speed. The poet John Milton in 1642 referred to King Charles's *expresses,* meaning his "dispatches." It seems to be in this sense that the word was first used as the title for a newspaper. Among the earliest examples to be found are the *Englishman, or Sunday Express* in London in 1803; the *British Volunteer and Manchester Weekly Express,* 1805; the Dublin *Evening Express,* 1811; and the Windsor and Eton *Express,* 1812.

The *Daily Express* of London was founded in 1900 and for many years was the personal fief of the Canadian emigrant Max Aitken, later named Lord Beaverbrook. Tanzania has an *Express* in Dar es Salaam. In the United States, the most prominent *Express* is probably the *Express-News* in San Antonio, Texas.

Clipper

By the 1840s, clipper sailing ships were used to carry the mail across the Atlantic. They were called *clipper*s, by analogy with the nautical term *cutter,* which was a boat that knifed its way rapidly through the water. They could cross the Atlantic in less than two weeks, bringing news items for the newspapers, a few of which adopted the name *Clipper,* as others had done earlier with the mail-carrying packet boats.

There was a *Clipper* in 1858 in Baltimore, Maryland, and another in Brownsville, Pennsylvania. By 1874 there was a London *Clipper* and in 1901, the New York *Clipper.*

There are still half a dozen *Clipper*s in existence, but the provenance of their names may have little to do with the clipper ships of yore. The Web site of the Davis County *Clipper* in Bountiful, Utah, explains: "About 1891, [the print shop owner] started *The Little Clipper,* a small paper that—true to its name—contained clippings of interesting articles from a variety of other published sources."

There are also *Clipper*s in Duxbury, Massachusetts, not founded until 1950, long after the era of clipper ships; and in Bethany, Missouri *(Republican-Clipper),* and Lexington, Nebraska *(Clipper-Herald),* cities that are far enough away from the shore to raise questions about how seafaring their names may be.

5

Gray Ladies No More

For at least half a century the New York *Times* has been known affectionately, or perhaps, by some, distastefully, as "the Old Gray Lady." (The Arkansas *Gazette* at one time also laid claim to that sobriquet, but it did not have so firm a grip upon it.) The rationale for the nickname was the tendency of the newspaper to print columns of small type punctuated by very few illustrations, a condition that no longer exists thanks to the splashy color photographs that have now turned the Old Gray Lady into a Painted Bird of Paradise. Nonetheless, the *Times* of New York, along with its London counterpart, also known as the *Times,* both like to think of themselves as "newspapers of record," or, as the New Yorkers put it, one that provides "all the news that's fit to print." In New York, the *Times* has even become enshrined as a physical part of the city—its busiest and most famous intersection—Times Square. The very name "the *Times*" connotes a sober-sided gravitas that is reinforced by the fact that neither the New York nor the London *Times* has a comics section. Other newspaper names—*Tidings, Register, Chronicle, Record, Transcript, Index, Facts, Truth, Item, Bulletin, Ledger, Repository*—tend to sound equally solemn, even though it must be acknowledged that their actual contents are sometimes as frivolous and inconsequential as the *National Lampoon.*

Times

The *Times* has a long lineage in English newspaper history. The singular form, the Old English *tima,* meaning "a limited stretch of continued existence," was in the language by the ninth century. Not until the fifteenth century is there a record of the use of the plural, *times,* denoting "a period in the world's history, an age, or an era." In the sense of "the general state of affairs of a given period of history," the first usage cited by the *Oxford English Dictionary* was in 1713 by Richard Steele in the *Spectator.*

In Germany, in the early sixteenth century, the word *Zeitung* was used to describe sheets containing recent news. *Zeit* in German means "time," and *Zeitung,* which since the 1860s has been the generic German word for newspaper, cognate with the English word *tiding,* can be interpreted as "happenings, i.e. news items, of the time." In the early sixteenth century, German publishers began issuing news reports that covered a year, six months, or one month, called *Jahres-Zeitung, Sammel-Zeitung,* or *Monats-Zeitung.* In 1513 a German publication in Poland was called the *New Zeitung auss Litten* ("Recent News from Lithuania"), and the word *Zeitung* was used frequently in the sixteenth century for a newssheet throughout German-speaking areas. The word survives today not only in Germany, but also in the United States in a few German-language newspapers such as the New Yorker *Staats-Zeitung,* as well as in the title of the English-language *Herald-Zeitung* in German-influenced New Braunfels, Texas.

Although *Zeitung,* the German equivalent of the word *times,* was seen frequently from the early sixteenth century, it was not until 1788, with the naming of the *Times* in London, that the usage is found in an English newspaper. The *Times* for years has positioned itself as the British newspaper of record, a semiofficial publication of court appointments, important marriages, and society births and deaths.

Although its staid appearance might have identified it as another "old gray lady," since 1830 this *Times* has been dubbed "The Thunderer." This nickname originated in the intrigue surrounding the *Times*'s criticism of procedures in an inquest into a supposed suicide by a noted peer—the appropriately named Lord Graves—followed a few days later by the *Times*'s reversal of its criticism in a printed statement that contained this phrase: "then we thundered out that article . . . which caused so great a sensation." A rival paper, the *Morning Herald,* had great fun in mocking the *Times* as the "Great Earwigger of the Nation . . . otherwise the Awful Monosyllable, otherwise The Thunderer, but more commonly called 'The Blunderer.'" "The Thunderer" stuck, and it has been the paper's nickname ever since.

During the nineteenth century, *Times* became a very popular title, second only to the *News.* The Bombay *Times,* founded in 1838, became the *Times of India.* The New York *Times* was established in 1851, and in 1854 a Chicago *Times* (later merged into the *Sun-Times*) began. From 1861, the Otago *Daily Times* was published in Dunedin, Australia. Today, the *Times* can be found all over the globe—either standing alone or, frequently, combined with other names. You can read the *Times* not only in New York and in London (where there are three of them, including the *Sunday Times* and the *Financial Times*), but also in Dublin, Bombay, New Delhi, Karachi, Singapore, Lagos, Hong Kong, Johannesburg and Cape Town, Amman, the United Arab Emirates, Moscow, St. Petersburg (both Russia and Florida), Manila, Taipei, Los Angeles, and Seattle, as well as in Washington, D.C.; Contra Costa County, California; Roanoke, Virginia; and hundreds of other cities and towns.

Departing from the more serious aura of the name, Blossom, Texas, has an operetta-inspired *Blossom Times,* and at Tennessee's Riverbend Maximum Security Institution, prisoners publish the aptly named *Maximum Times.* Greenwich, Connecticut, puns on the English home of the Royal Observatory, by dropping the "s" and calling its paper the Greenwich *Time.* In an even trickier play on words, which might at first look like a typographical error, the South Fork, Colorado, newspaper is known as the South Fork *Tines.* A newspaper in Bradford, Vermont, unashamedly calls itself *Behind the Times*—which is inevitable, since it's published only once a month.

Tidings

Related to the word *times, Tidings,* from the Anglo-Saxon *tîdan* ("to happen"), was used as a newspaper title in 1871 in Penzance, England; in 1886 in St. George's, Grenada; and in 1946 in London. Today it pretty much enjoys retirement at the old words home—except when it pops up at Christmas in the phrase "good tidings of great joy"—and in the *Daily Tidings,* which has been an up-to-the-minute newspaper in Ashland, Oregon, since 1876.

Register

The English word *register,* from the Latin *regerere,* "to set down," was used as early as 1377 to mean a written record of details considered sufficiently important to be formally recorded. It applied to legal documents, such as parliamentary bills, deeds, and wills; church records of baptisms, marriages, and burials; and military and commercial records.

A kind of protonewspaper on religious topics called *A compendious register* was published in England in 1559, but *Register* does not appear to have been used for a real newspaper until the Liverpool *Advertiser and Mercantile Register* in 1756, followed by the *Public Register, or Freemen's Journal* in Dublin in 1763, the *Daily Universal Register* in London in 1785 (which changed its name to the *Times* in 1788), the New-York *Journal and Weekly Register* in 1787, and the Raleigh (North Carolina) *Register* in 1799.

In the early nineteenth century came the Salem (Massachusetts) *Impartial Register* and the South Australian *Gazette and Colonial Register.* The name lingers today in major newspapers in Des Moines, Iowa; Mobile, Alabama; New Haven, Connecticut; Orange County, California; Springfield, Illinois *(State Journal-Register);* Wheeling, West Virginia *(News-Register);* and dozens of other communities.

Chronicle

Related to the idea of a register was the Middle English word *cronykle,* originally from the Greek *chronikos,* "concerning time." A *chronicle,* as it was spelled after the sixteenth century, was "a detailed and continuous register of events in order of when they occurred." Its first use in this sense was noted in 1303. A collection of manuscripts dating back to the tenth century and providing a chronological record of historical events in the British Isles came to be known as the Anglo-Saxon Chronicle.

In 1493 a Nuremberg physician named Hartman Schedel published a history of the world titled in Latin *Liber Chronicarum.* Lavishly illustrated with more than eighteen hundred prints made from woodcuts, the initial edition of this work circulated twenty-five hundred copies and was known in English as the *Nuremberg Chronicle.* In 1580 the English translator Raphael Holinshed published a history of England, Scotland, and Ireland that was known as *Holinshed's Chronicles* and was much used as source material by Shakespeare and other Elizabethan playwrights. *Chronicles* had also been used in the English translation of the Bible as the name of two historical books in the Old Testament.

Chronicle was thus a conveniently ready-made name to apply to a newspaper, especially one that had aspirations to be an authoritative record of events. In *News from the New World Discovered in the Moon,* a masque written by Ben Jonson for presentation in 1621, a character known as the Chronicler speaks of the need for news items to fill up his great book—his "Chronicle," by which he meant a chronological listing of recent happenings. In a 1625 Jonson satire on news reporting, *The Staple of News,* there is a reference to a news publication as a *Chronicle.*

More than a hundred years after Jonson's use of the word, in January 1757, the London *Chronicle, or Universal Evening Post,* appeared with an introductory article by Dr. Samuel Johnson. As a contributor to the paper, Dr. Johnson made a point of reading it regularly, according to his biographer, James Boswell. It contained domestic and international news, essays, poetry, and the inevitable advertisements for books, patent medicines, auction sales, and other goods and services.

Dozens of *Chronicle*s followed. In 1759 came the Edinburgh *Chronicle,* in 1760 the Bath *Chronicle,* in 1762 the Manchester *Chronicle* and the *American Chronicle* in New York, in 1764 the Newcastle *Chronicle,* in 1767 the Liverpool *Chronicle* and the Pennsylvania *Chronicle,* in 1770 the *Morning Chronicle* of London, and in 1776 the Cumberland *Chronicle, or Whitehaven Intelligencer,* in northern England. The name had definitely caught on.

*Chronicle*s are found nowadays throughout the British Isles, in Bangor, Bath, Essex, and Newcastle, among other places; in Quebec (the *Chronicle-Telegraph,* founded in 1764 and claimant to the title of Canada's oldest newspaper) and in other Canadian cities; and in the United States, in Anchorage, Alaska; Houston, Texas; and San Francisco, California, among many others.

Record and *Recorder*

The noun *record* was a legal term in the fourteenth century and meant "facts committed to writing as evidence in a matter of legal importance." The origin of the word was the Latin *re* ("again") + *cordis* ("heart or mind") and originally referred to a recollection or memory of something. Like a *Register* or a *Chronicle,* it was an obvious straightforward descriptive name for what was intended to be an accurate account of happenings, with semiofficial status, as in the phrase "newspaper of record."

The *Village Record* in Westchester, Pennsylvania, appeared in 1818. The *Record* was the name given to a newspaper published in London in 1828, to the Dublin *Record* in 1835, and to the Guernsey *Record* in 1839.

Today's *Record*s include a Glasgow tabloid, whose splashy format strays a bit from the original meaning of the word; also the Bergen County *Record* in Hackensack, New Jersey; papers in Middletown, New York *(Times-Herald Record);* Greensboro, North Carolina *(News & Record);* and many other towns in the United States and Canada.

The *Record*'s cousin, the *Recorder,* is also well represented among newspaper names. As early as 1681 there was a publication in London known as the *Monthly Recorder, of All True Occurrences Both Foreign & Domestick.* In 1785 came the *American Recorder* in Charlestown, Massachusetts; and then the *American Herald and Federal Recorder* in Boston and Worcester in 1788; *Carey's United States Recorder* in Philadelphia in 1798 (published by James Carey, considered the first professional news reporter in America and brother of Matthew Carey, a more famous early American publisher); the London *Recorder* in 1806; the Baltimore *Recorder* in 1810; right up to today's Americus (Georgia) *Times Recorder* and several others with the word in their titles.

Transcript

A *transcript* in legal parlance is similar to a *record.* From the Latin *trans* ("across") + *scribere* ("to write") it was used by the thirteenth century to mean a handwritten copy of a legal document. By the seventeenth century it meant any kind of printed copy or reproduction of something in writing. Its usage as a newspaper title came along in the 1830s and 1840s with the New York *Transcript,* one of the first of the "penny papers"; the Albany (New York) *Transcript;* the Baltimore *Commercial Transcript;* the Montreal *Transcript and General Advertiser;* and the Boston *Daily Evening Transcript,* the readers of which are the subject of a poem by T. S. Eliot ("The *Boston Evening Transcript*").

Today you'll find a daily *Transcript* in Norman, Oklahoma, but most of the others are either weeklies or special-interest papers.

Index

From the Latin *indicare* ("to point out"), an *index,* since the sixteenth century, has been primarily "a pointer, a guide, or an indicator." It can also mean a "guiding principle," and its most common usage today, also from the sixteenth century, is an "alphabetical listing of topics."

Its use as a name for a newspaper apparently sprang from its meaning as a listing, as with *Lloyd's Daily Index* in London in 1838, which was a summary of ships arriving in and sailing from port. The *Index* was used in 1862 as the name of a British weekly journal of politics relating to the mutual interest of the Confederate States of America and Great Britain, in which the various topics to be covered were set forth in an orderly list.

The Moberly (Missouri) *Monitor-Index and Evening Democrat* was established in 1869 as a listing of properties for sale and was originally called the Moberly *Herald and Real Estate Index.* The Petersburg (Virginia) *Index* was established in 1865 and later became known as the *Index-Appeal,* and the Sonoma (California) *Index-Tribune* has been around since 1879.

The Tacoma (Washington) *Daily Index* began in 1890 as the *Daily Court and Commercial Index* and lived up to that name by publishing primarily legal notices, calls for bids, court records, public documents, contractor listings, and, of course, advertisements, so that it was, in fact, a useful indexing of the commercial life of the city.

Other papers using the word *Index* in their titles are in Marianna, Arkansas *(Courier-Index);* Greenwood, South Carolina *(Index-Journal);* Mineral Wells, Texas; and West Liberty, Iowa.

Facts

"Just the facts, ma'am," was the no-nonsense interrogation technique of Sergeant Joe Friday on the radio and television crime show *Dragnet.* For no-nonsense news reporting, the name *Facts* serves at least two U.S. newspapers, one in Redlands, California, and one in Clute, Texas. There was also a short-lived *Facts* in 1914 in London, subtitled the *People's Investigator.*

At their simplest, *facts* are simply "deeds" or "occurrences," a word the English got from the Latin *facere* ("to make or to do"). But over the years the *fact* has acquired a heroic mantle investing it with the implication that it is the unequivocal, absolute, and immutable truth. It is therefore a bold and self-confident publisher who offers his readers unvarnished *Facts*.

That is precisely what E. F. Howe had in mind in 1890 when he founded the *Facts* in Redlands, California. Howe was a vigorous proponent of the prohibition of alcoholic beverages, a cause that inspired him in his journalism, and many of his "facts" were no doubt directed toward the evils of demon rum.

Prohibition also played a role in the creation of the Brazosport *Facts* in Texas, although rather remotely. Brazosport is not actually a town, but the informal name for an aggregation of seaports clustered along the Brazos River on the Texas Gulf Coast southwest of Galveston. The Brazosport *Facts* began life in 1913 as the Freeport *Facts,* a pleasingly alliterative title coined by a printer whose name was also alliterative, Roy Ruffin. Most of the other Brazosport towns had their own papers, one of which was the Velasco *World,* owned by a man named Oscar Nation, whose stepmother was Carry A. Nation—the woman who tried in the early 1900s to enforce her own brand of Prohibition with a hatchet, which she used to chop up many a bar. The *World,* along with the Brazoria County *Review,* the West Columbia *Light,* and the Angleton *Times* were all bundled together in 1952 in a paper first called the *Daily Facts-Review* but soon changed to just the *Facts,* ma'am.

Truth

If mere facts are not sufficient, the *Truth* itself is available in Elkhart, Indiana, for just fifty cents a copy. That sounds like a real bargain, especially when you recall that Mark Twain said the most valuable thing in the world was truth (which is why he was economical with it). The word, from the Anglo-Saxon *trēow* ("fidelity or faith"), means in "conformity with reality."

Item

Item is a Latin adverb meaning "just so, likewise, moreover," which arrived in English in the fourteenth century and became a noun without even changing its hat. In its English garb, it was written down at the beginning of a line on any kind of list to introduce a new article or entry.

From that usage it came to mean a physical thing or unit. From about 1819, it meant a detail of information, or a separate piece of news, especially when it was printed in a newspaper.

As the name of an entire paper it was used by the Philadelphia *Evening Item,* founded in 1847 by Thomas Fitzgerald, who fancied himself a playwright but proved far more successful as a newspaperman. The Huntsville (Texas) *Item* was founded in 1850 and is still going strong in the execution capital of the world. The New Orleans *Daily City Item,* founded in 1877, later merged with the *States* to become the *States-Item* but is now defunct. The town of Picayune, Mississippi—which was actually named for a newspaper, by Mississippi native Eliza Jane Nicholson, publisher of the New Orleans *Picayune*—has had a newspaper called the *Item* since 1904. Other *Item*s can be found in Lynn, Massachusetts; Sumter, South Carolina; and three towns in Pennsylvania: Sunbury, Shamokin *(News-Item),* and Carnegie *(Signal Item-Star).*

Bulletin

A medieval *bulla* was a seal attached to a Latin document such as a papal edict, and hence began to refer to the document itself—in English, *bull* (no pun is intended). *Bulletin* is from the Italian *bulletino,* a diminutive of *bulla,* coined to describe a brief or condensed statement of the contents of a bull; and hence, a *bulletin* is a condensation of news of any kind, especially official government, military, or medical information. In the sense of a short note or memorandum, or as an official certificate, *bulletin* was first used in English in 1645. As a short account of public news, its first recorded use was in 1791 by Edmund Burke.

As a newspaper title, the Boston *Bulletin* appeared in the 1820s and the New Orleans *Commercial Bulletin* in the 1830s. The Philadelphia *Evening Bulletin* (first called the *Telegraphic Bulletin*) came along in 1847, and by the 1850s there was a *Morning Bulletin* in Glasgow, and an *Evening Bulletin* in San Francisco and Washington, D.C. In 1863 the Providence (Rhode Island) *Bulletin* was founded, and in 1880 came the Edmonton (Alberta) *Bulletin.* Today's *Bulletin*s include the *Star-Bulletin* in Honolulu, Hawaii, and the *Post-Bulletin* in Rochester, Minnesota.

The word *bulletin* is also frequently used by news-gathering agencies to alert clients to a news item of great importance that has been learned only in the last few minutes. A "bulletin" is exceeded in urgency by a "flash."

Ledger

Most people today know that a ledger is a book of accounting records, full of those pesky things called double entries, but in the sixteenth century *ledger* referred to a book that was kept in one place, presumably a book of important permanent information, like a religious breviary or an official register of vital statistics. This meaning stemmed from the original Dutch *legger,* which came into Middle English as *liggen* ("lie") and *leggen* ("lay"). A *ledger,* then, was a book that "lay" in one place.

As it took on the associated meaning of "a repository of information of importance," newspaper publishers latched onto it, and in 1760 the *Public Ledger,* the oldest British periodical with continuous daily publication, appeared in London.

The Pennsylvania *Ledger and Weekly Advertiser* was in existence in Philadelphia in 1777, followed in subsequent years by the *Public Ledger* in Philadelphia, the *Independent Ledger* in Boston, Massachusetts; and *Daily Ledger*s in Kansas, Tennessee, Minnesota, and Indiana, among other places. In 1836 the Philadelphia *Ledger* merged with the *Daily Transcript* to form the *Public Ledger and Daily Transcript.*

Certainly no *Ledger* today thinks of itself as "lying"—in any sense of the word—and you will find papers of that name, theoretically reporting only the truth, in Newark, New Jersey *(Star-Ledger);* Jackson, Mississippi *(Clarion-Ledger);* Norfolk, Virginia *(Ledger-Star);* Lakeland, Florida; Columbus, Georgia *(Ledger-Enquirer);* and numerous other places.

Repository

A *repository,* from the Latin *repositorium,* is a storage place for something of great value, or, in other words a "treasure house." What better name could any publication ask for? Several chose it, including *Salmons Mercury, or, Entertaining Repository,* in Bath, England, in 1777; the Dundee (Scotland) *Repository* in 1793; the *Farmer's Repository* in 1808, in Charleston, West Virginia; the *Western Repository* in 1809 in Canandaigua, New York; and the Canton (Ohio) *Repository* in 1815. Evilminded jokers, as you might have guessed, sometimes refer to the Ohio paper as the *Suppository.*

6

"Print the News and Raise Hell"

A feisty fellow named Sheldon McKnight was the first editor of the Detroit *Free Press,* founded in 1831 and originally known as the *Democratic Free Press and Michigan Intelligencer.* McKnight explained the paper's name in a ringing editorial: "The Democratic citizens of this territory, having found the two newspapers already established here completely under the control of the city aristocracy, we have been compelled to set up an independent press." A later, even feistier, editor, Wilbur F. Storey, wrote in 1853: "It is a newspaper's duty to print the news and raise hell." John S. Knight, who acquired the paper in 1940, was less pugnacious, but no less blunt in asserting: "we are ourselves free and our paper shall be free . . . free to truth, good manners and good sense."

This characterization of a newspaper—as a kind of crusading knight in stainless-steel armor, a fearless whistle-blower unencumbered by obligations to the powerful, a righteous truth-teller raking through the muck of official corruption and greed to champion the interests of the populace—influenced the naming of many newspapers in the 1700s.

Before the eighteenth century, most newspapers were published by the authority of the government, which also happened to be their greatest source of information. In 1644 John Milton argued in *Areopagitica* for liberty of unlicensed printing, but it was not until 1695 that licensing and censorship laws were abolished in England. At last, in the heady atmosphere of the eighteenth-century Enlightenment—the Age of Reason—when the notion of unfettered thought championed by John Locke was becoming widespread, publishers demanded freedom from censorship. In the defense of printer John Peter Zenger, who was acquitted of publishing libelous and seditious material in New York in 1735, Zenger's

lawyer, Andrew Hamilton, speaks of "a right—the liberty—both of ex-
posing and opposing arbitrary power . . . by speaking and writing truth."
This notion was codified in 1791 in the First Amendment of the United
States Constitution, which bars Congress from making any laws "abridg-
ing the freedom of speech, or of the *press*"—a word that was understood
to mean the aggregate of newspapers and the news they printed.

This crusading spirit is found not only in the individual newspaper
names of *Press* and *Free Press,* but also in such other symbols of expression free of government control as *Plain Dealer, Champion, Advocate, Leader, Statesman, Chief, Chieftain, Pioneer, Vanguard, Advance,
Tribune, Citizen, Patriot, Minuteman, Blade, Scimitar, Vindicator, Standard,* and *Banner.*

Press and *Free Press*

In Germany by around the year 1500, the word *Presse,* the machinery by which printing was done, came to mean "the process of periodical publication." A couple of centuries later, the *press* became a collec-
tive term for the periodicals themselves. It is surmised that this usage
developed through such phrases, as "a free press" and "the liberty of the
press," which referred initially to the desire to put the printing machine
under the control of its owner, free from any government interference,
but then became a reference to the products of the printing machine, that
is, the newspapers it produced. Ultimately, the phrase "free press" meant
the ideas expressed in the publications.

In 1797 in Dublin a newspaper called the *Press* was founded. Its first
issue explained its name: "By some fatality of late, the Press of the ha-
rassed country has been either negligent or apostate; it has been a centinel asleep on its post. It is now proposed to establish a newspaper, to
be solely and unalterably devoted to the people of Ireland and their interests, under the appellation of *The Press.*"

In 1803 came the *British Press* in London, in 1836 *La Presse* in Paris,
and in 1848 *Die Presse* in Vienna. The Glasgow *Free Press* (1823), the
Antigua *Free Press* and the Tipperary *Free Press* (1826), the London
Free Press (1827), the Detroit *Free Press* (1831), and the Winnipeg *Free
Press* (1872), were among the many that followed, with the word *Free*
added to underscore their independence from government control—not,

as the owners would have been quick to point out, to indicate the absence of a purchase price.

Both *Press*es and *Free Press*es abound today, including the *Times Free Press* in Chattanooga, Tennessee; the *Press* in Bristol, England; Aberdeen, Scotland; Christchurch, New Zealand; Asbury Park, New Jersey; and Grand Rapids, Michigan; *La Presse* in Quebec; and *La Prensa* in numerous Spanish-speaking communities.

The word *free* comes via Old Norse and German from the Sanskrit *priya,* which means "dear or beloved," and it gains its meaning of "absence of bondage" by its usage in referring to family members, as opposed to slaves. *Free* finds itself in a number of newspaper titles, including the *Free Lance,* the *Freelancer,* the *Free Times,* the *Freeholder,* the *Freeman,* and the *Freethinker.*

Plain Dealer

Telling the public the truth is the self-announced goal of the half-dozen newspapers in the United States that use the name *Plain Dealer.* The most noted of them is in Cleveland, Ohio, a paper named in 1842, when two brothers, A. N. and J. W. Gray, acquired the Cleveland *Advertiser* and rechristened it the *Plain Dealer.* Of the new name they wrote:

> We offer no apologies for changing the name of this paper but the Scripture command—"Put not new wine into old bottles, lest they break." We think the good taste of our readers will sanction the modest selection we have made. Had we called it the *Torpedo,* timid ladies never would have touched it. Had we called it the *Truth Teller,* no one would believe a word in it! Had we called it the *Thunder Dealer* or *Lightning Spitter,* it would have blown Uncle Sam's mailbags sky high. But our democracy and modesty suggest the only name that fits the occasion, the PLAIN DEALER.

Webster's New International Dictionary defines *plain dealing* as "straightforward conduct and speech; open, frank and candid dealing" and a *plain dealer* as one who practices those virtues. It is the opposite of a *double-dealer.* A Calvinist theological tract in 1571 mentions the "righteous and plaindealers" of Psalm 34. Winston Churchill once said the *Plain Dealer* was "the best name for a newspaper of any in the world."

There is, however, another connotation of *plain dealer,* which might make it less desirable for a newspaper's name. This stems from playwright William Wycherley's use of the word in the title of his 1666 play *The Plain Dealer.* The title character is named Manly, who describes himself as "An honest man . . . who speaks what he thinks"—but, as Wycherley pointedly reveals, not always with happy consequences. His straightforward conduct makes him an easy dupe for treacherous friends who betray him. Consequently, one now-obsolete meaning of *plain dealer* was "simpleton."

Nonetheless, one assumes the newspaper publishers were thinking of the more favorable definition when they chose the name. Among the first were the *Plain Dealer* in London in the early 1700s and another in Dublin in 1729. In 1775 there was a newspaper called the *Plain Dealer* published in a tavern (what a jolly newsroom that must have been!) in Bridgetown, New Jersey, for the purpose of supporting the cause of American independence. It appeared every Tuesday morning and is thought of as New Jersey's first regular newspaper.

In the early 1700s the title "Plain Dealer" was used for a series of articles in the Maryland *Gazette* that gave advice to men about how to deal with women. The articles were reprinted by Benjamin Franklin in his Pennsylvania *Gazette.*

In very much the same vein as the *Plain Dealer*s, newspapers in Newport, Tennessee, and Vermillion, South Dakota, tell it like it is under the title *Plain Talk,* which had been earlier used by a London paper in 1913, with the all-inclusive subtitle "About Everything That Matters."

Champion

Nowadays we tend to think a *champion* is a winner of a competition—such as a title-holding prizefighter, or an incredibly quick crossword-puzzle solver, or a person who can put away more corn dogs than anyone else without becoming nauseated. The original meaning of the word, however, was not necessarily "a winner," but "a combatant, one who engages in conflict, a fighter"—from the Latin word *campus,* meaning "field" and, specifically, "field of battle." A champion came to mean not only a fighter, but a fighter for another person or cause; in other words, an advocate.

It was in this sense that the word was used by the earliest newspapers that called themselves *Champion,* including one in London in 1739; another *Champion* in London in 1814, which changed in 1822 to the *Investigator;* the *Champion of the East* in Lincolnshire in 1830; and yet another London *Champion* in 1834.

In its long struggle for independence, Ireland spawned a number of papers devoted to advocating this cause. *Champion* was therefore a popular title; the Sligo *Champion* traces its origins to 1836, and others followed in Kerry, Galway, and Clare.

The manifesto in the first issue of the Clare *Champion,* a 1903 reincarnation of an earlier nationalist Irish paper forced to close in a libel action, expressed in fiery terms the notion of a newspaper as a fierce advocate. Editor Tom Galvin wrote,

> The *Champion* will stand as the inveterate foe of landlordism, shoneenism, grabbers and Castle hacks. The wants of the people will be firmly espoused in our columns until their grievances are redressed. We shall agitate for an Irish Ireland and an Irish Parliament to govern and make laws for the Irish people. Should the present Land Bill not meet the requirements of the tenant farmers, we shall loyally support their cause until justice is done them and until the last vestige of landlordism disappears from the country.

(The *shoneenism* that is so heartily condemned in this pronouncement is an Irish term for people who put on airs, pretending to social status they do not, in fact, possess. Such persons have been known to exist in places other than Ireland.)

Australia has some community papers in the Sydney area called the *Champion,* and there's another in the United States in Morton Grove, Illinois—none of which, it will come as no surprise, seem as ferociously militant as their Hibernian counterparts.

Advocate

From the Latin *ad* ("to") + *vocare* ("to call") an *advocate* is "one who pleads the cause of another." As a newspaper title, one advantage of the word is that it doesn't pin down the paper to any particular point of view—in fact, it can indicate completely opposite points of view, as evidenced by papers in Baton Rouge, Louisiana, and Victoria, Texas, founded about the same time. The Baton Rouge *Advocate* traces its publishing history back to the *Democratic Advocate,* a newspaper started in 1842 with an agenda of defeating the Whig Party candidates. The Victoria *Advocate* was founded in 1846, within months of the admission of Texas into the United States, and was a pro-Whig paper supporting the candidacy of Zachary Taylor for president.

Among the earliest usages of *Advocate* as a title was the *National Advocate* in New York in 1812. The name became popular in the nineteenth century, often associated with a political, religious, or ethnic cause— Conservatives, Christianity, Temperance, the Irish, the Indians—on which the advocacy was lavished. The Los Angeles *Advocate,* founded in 1967 and devoted to gay issues, was such a newspaper, although in 1996 it changed its format to that of a magazine. Today's *Advocate*s are more generalized and are found mostly in Canada and the United States, notably in Stamford, Connecticut; Greenville, Alabama; Danville, Kentucky *(Advocate-Messenger);* and many other cities.

Leader

Some newspapers keep themselves above the fray of ideological allegiance and cast themselves not as advocates of any cause—but simply as generic *Leaders. Lead,* from the Anglo-Saxon *lædan,* means "to guide by going ahead," and it doesn't really specify if you're moving forward, backward, or sideways. In the mid-nineteenth century, *Leader*s popped up in London (1850); Cleveland, Ohio (1852); Tipperary (1855); Melbourne (1856); St. Johns, New Brunswick (1858); New York (1858); Philadelphia (1858); and Des Moines, Iowa (1870).

Today's *Leader*s can be found in abundance throughout the United States—oh, would that it were literally so!—in such places as Davenport, Iowa; Lexington, Kentucky *(Herald-Leader);* Manchester, New Hampshire *(Union Leader);* Staunton, Virginia *(News Leader);* Wilkes-Barre, Pennsylvania *(Times Leader);* and Springfield, Missouri *(News-Leader).* There are also *Leader*s in Banbridge, Northern Ireland; Chester, England; Mold, Wales; Regina, Saskatchewan; and in Ireland in Limerick, Longford, and Leinster, where perhaps they like the alliteration.

In British journalistic parlance, a "leader," short for "leading article," is also a long opinion piece, equivalent to what Americans would call an "editorial."

Statesman

Even better than a *Leader,* it can be argued, is a *Statesman,* which from the fifteenth century meant not only a leader of people, but one who is especially skilled in conducting government business. No doubt with this noble creature in mind, publishers in Austin, Texas *(American-Statesman);* Boise, Idaho; and Salem, Oregon *(Statesman Journal)* have so named their papers. The weekly in Versailles, Missouri, wants to be sure there is no mistake about its status as the one for the people to follow and calls itself the *Leader-Statesman.* In Spokane, Washington, with a paronomasian nod to the city's name, there is a no *Statesman* but instead a *Spokesman-Review.*

Chief and Chieftain

Mostly in communities with names based on American Indian languages, *Chief* and *Chieftain* are sometimes used as the denoters of leadership. Both words stem from the Latin *caput* ("head"), *chief* having descended through the French *chef,* and *chieftain* from the Latin derivative *capitanus* and French *chevetaine,* specifically meaning "the head of a troop of soldiers." By the sixteenth century, the words were used to describe the principal authority of a clan, a tribe, or other loosely organized group of people lacking more specific governmental titles.

In the United States you can find *Chieftain*s in Clatskanie and Wallowa County, Oregon; Poway, California; Pueblo, Colorado; and Socorro, New Mexico *(El Defensor Chieftain).* The Squamish, British Columbia, paper uses the shorter *Chief* as its title. There is a newspaper in Nebraska that includes the name of a U.S. general whose rashness led to a fatal last stand against a superior force of Sioux Indians led by Chief Sitting Bull—and the paper's full name memorializes (perhaps inadvertently) both sides in this battle: it's called the *Custer County Chief.*

Pioneer

Another type of leader is the *pioneer* (from the French *pionnier*), who was not a commander of troops, but a foot soldier who led by being sent ahead of the main body of the army to help repair roads, dig trenches, and generally pave the way for the rest of the guys. The digging activity of a pioneer was emphasized in sixteenth-century usage, such as Hamlet's reference to his father's ghost, whose voice comes from underground: "Canst work i' th'earth so fast? A worthy pioneer!" By the early seventeenth century, the word meant an "originator, forerunner, initiator, investigator, colonist or explorer." In the nineteenth century, *pioneer* was specifically used to refer to a settler of the American West.

Today's newspaper *Pioneer*s tend to be in the western or midwestern sections of the United States, most notably the Saint Paul (Minnesota) *Pioneer Press,* which a printer named James M. Goodhue founded in 1849 as the Minnesota *Pioneer.* Goodhue originally planned to call his paper the *Epistle of Saint Paul,* but was dissuaded by friends who thought that might presumptuously claim a bit too much canonical authority for a mere newspaper. Wales and Canada also have their *Pioneer*s, in Colwyn Bay and Summerside, Prince Edward Island, respectively.

Vanguard

Nipping at the heels of the French army's *pionniers* were the *avant-garde,* troops who marched in front of the main body of the army—a position not calculated to ensure a long and happy life. Despite the obvious dangers, some people still like to be out in front; hence, *avant-garde* and its English equivalent, *vanguard,* now refer to anyone that you regard as more hip, reckless, or *outré* than you are—people who drive hybrid cars, understand Sudoku, vote for Democrats in Texas, and boldly go where no man, and precious few women, have gone before.

Most of the newspapers that called themselves *Vanguard*s have been vigorous proponents of religious or social causes. These include journals for the Church of England Purity Society in 1887, the Sheffield Temperance Electoral Association in 1888, the Liverpool Christian Temperance Society in 1903, the Bradford Socialist and Trade Union Party in 1908, the Communist Party in India in 1923, the Protestant Church in

Scotland in 1944, Zionist advocates in London in 1948, the Grenada Nationalist Party in 1959, and the Marxist Spartacist Society in New York in 1971.

In the midst of all this activist *Vanguard* propaganda, the weekly Yarmouth (Nova Scotia) *Vanguard* would appear to have as its principal cause the more modest and entirely laudable goal of staying ahead of its competition in the Atlantic and Canadian Community Newspaper Associations.

Advance

When the *pionniers* and the *avant-garde* say it's okay, the rest of the troops *advance,* a word from Latin *abantiare* (*ab*="away," *ante*="before") via the French *avancer,* which means "to move toward the front." You may or may not be inclined to think of this movement as progress. The British Library's earliest recorded newspaper named the *Advance* was in Ipswich in 1885, followed shortly by the Staten Island (New York) *Advance* in 1886; it continued as a popular title, in Manchester, England (1888), New York (1893), Melbourne (1914), and London (1936).

Today, progress is made in many directions by such papers as the *News & Advance* in Lynchburg, Virginia; the *Advance Leader* in Oakmont and Plum, Pennsylvania; and the unadorned *Advance* in Atmore, Alabama; Bloomer, Wisconsin; Novato, California; Elizabeth City, North Carolina; Parkston, South Dakota; Barrie and Grand Bend, Ontario; Creston Valley, British Columbia; and Wynyard, Saskatchewan.

As a newspaper title, *Advance* connotes visionary thought and progressive action, but in more mundane newspaperese, an "advance" is simply an article about a future event.

Tribune

The Roman *tribune* was an officer in the Roman Republic appointed as early as 494 BC to protect the rights of plebeians when infringed upon by the patricians. The word *tribunus* originally meant "head of a tribe." The English word *tribowne* was first used in 1375, and by the sixteenth century a *tribune* was any judge or protector of the people. Often, however, a *tribune* meant a demagogue (a definition frowned upon by newspapers that use the name).

Ireland, frequently the first to coin new newspaper names, had a Dublin *Tribune* by 1729. There were a number of *Tribunes* started in Paris in 1848, during the revolution by the restive bourgeoisie, all modified with antiroyalist nomenclature: *Tribune populaire, Tribune des réformes, Tribune des prolétaires, Tribune des peuples.*

In 1841 Horace Greeley founded the New York *Tribune,* not exactly with the proletariat in mind—even though Karl Marx (yes, that one) was once the London correspondent. The first issue proclaimed, "The *Tribune,* as its name imports, will labor to advance the interests of the people, and to promote their moral, social and political wellbeing." It did so by espousing Whig candidates and by urging those who wished to make good in life to "Go west, before you are fitted for no life but that of the factory." The famous phrase "Go west, young man," often attributed to Greeley and the *Tribune,* actually appeared first in another newspaper, the Terre Haute (Indiana) *Express,* in an 1851 editorial by John B. L. Soule that was titled "Go West, Young Man, and Grow Up with the Country." Greeley, who got the credit for saying it, didn't use it in print until 1865.

Many years later, the *Tribune* merged with the New York *Herald,* to become the *Herald Tribune,* one of New York's leading papers till it folded in 1966, and it now survives only in the name of the *International Herald Tribune,* published in Paris, oddly enough, by the New York *Times.*

The Chicago *Tribune* was founded in 1847 and was acquired in 1855 by a group that included American press baron Joseph Medill. The *Tribune* was the chief backer of Abraham Lincoln for president.

Tribune is the sixth most popular U.S. name for newspapers—but it is found hardly at all in Great Britain. Look for it in Addis Ababa, Ethiopia; Chandigargh, India; Bahrain; Albuquerque, New Mexico; Minneapolis–St. Paul, Minnesota *(Star Tribune);* Cheyenne, Wyoming *(Tribune-Eagle);* Oakland, California; Pittsburgh, Pennsylvania *(Tribune-Review);* Salt Lake City, Utah; San Diego, California *(Union-Tribune);* Tampa, Florida; Tacoma, Washington *(News-Tribune);* Tulsa, Oklahoma; South Bend, Indiana; Columbia, Missouri; and Scranton, Pennsylvania. In Greeley, Colorado, the town's founder, who had worked as a reporter for Horace Greeley in New York, honored him by establishing the Greeley *Tribune.*

Citizen, Patriot, and Minuteman

A *citizen,* which comes to English from the Latin *civis* by way of the French *citoyen,* originally meant "the resident of a Roman city"—who enjoyed the rights that would have been protected by the tribunes. It later took on the meaning of "a member of a state," with an implied loyalty to that state and with reciprocal rights such as life, liberty, and property. A *citizen* is unlike a *subject,* who owes allegiance to a king or other master. By 1789 during the French Revolution, *Citoyen* took the place of *Monsieur* as a title, implying social equality.

Ireland had one of the first newspapers to incorporate the concept of citizenship in the *Censor or Citizen's Journal* in 1749 in Dublin. The *American Citizen* came in 1800, a continuation of the *Argus* in New York. Strongly devoted to politics, it was the organ of the Clinton faction of the Democratic Party in New York—no, not Bill or Hillary, but an earlier family of Democratic Clintons, George and his nephew De-Witt, both of whom had the distinction of running for president against James Madison and losing.

The Ottawa *Citizen* was published in Canada in 1800, and even though the British are known as subjects and not citizens, they had newspapers by that name in Glasgow in 1844 and in London in 1849. In 1858 many American communities had *Citizen* newspapers, including Ithaca, New York; Beaver Dam, Wisconsin; Paris, Kentucky; Flint, Michigan; Smithport, Pennsylvania; Lowell, Massachusetts; Des Moines, Iowa; and Knoxville, Tennessee.

Today you will find *Citizen*s in Tucson, Arizona; Key West, Florida; Wilkes-Barre, Pennsylvania; Pasadena, Texas; Gloucester and Milton Keynes, England; and in numerous other U.S. and Canadian cities.

A sort of hyped-up version of a *Citizen* would be a *Patriot,* a word that had its origin in the Greek *patrios* ("established by one's forefathers") and today means a person who is zealously devoted to his country's interests. In eighteenth-century England, the word *patriot* was used ironically to describe seditious antigovernment dissenters, specifically a Whig faction opposed to Sir Robert Walpole. There was a London newspaper called the *Patriot* in 1714.

As nationalism became a vital political force, newspapers adopted the *Patriot* name through the late eighteenth and early nineteenth centuries. A French writer named Jacques-Pierre Brissot was visiting America in 1789, and when he heard the news of the beginnings of the French Revolution, he returned to Paris and founded the *Patriote français,* which had below its title a motto that translates as "a free newspaper is the forward sentinel of the people."

Similarly strong political views inspired the London *Patriot* in 1792 and the Green Mountain *Patriot* in Vermont by 1798. Dublin, never shy to introduce new newspaper nomenclature, had a *Patriot* by 1810, and others soon sprang up in Carlisle, Stamford, Sheffield, Hertford, and Leeds, England; Edinburgh and Glasgow, Scotland; Galway, Ireland; Concord, New Hampshire; Boston, Massachusetts; Baltimore, Maryland; Madison, Wisconsin; and even in Calcutta, where the *Hindoo Patriot* in the 1850s began a long publishing history that continued into the 1920s.

Today *Patriot*s may be found in Barnstable, Massachusetts; Cuba, New York *(Patriot and Free Press);* Harrisburg, Pennsylvania *(Patriot-News);* Jackson, Michigan *(Citizen Patriot);* Quincy, Massachusetts *(Patriot Ledger);* and Waconia, Minnesota.

A *Minuteman* might be defined as a patriot with a gun, and the name was applied to a class of armed citizens during the American Revolution who pledged to take to the field at a minute's notice. Now a synonym for an especially militant patriot, the word is usually found attached only to American missiles, vigilante border patrols, and newspapers in the historic revolutionary cities of Lexington, Massachusetts, and Fairfield and Westport, Connecticut.

Blade and *Scimitar*

"All newspapers," wrote H. L. Mencken in 1919, "are ceaselessly querulous and bellicose. They never defend anyone or anything if they can help it; if the job is forced upon them, they tackle it by denouncing someone or something else."

What could be more bellicose than a newspaper named the *Blade?* Well, possibly one called the *Scimitar.* The *Blade* has been the newspaper in Toledo, Ohio, since 1835. How did it get its name? As explained on the paper's Web site:

> Toledo, Ohio has a sister city in Toledo, Spain. So it made sense
> that the newspaper be named after a well-known product of that

city—the steel-bladed sword. Also, at the time the newspaper was founded, the Ohio-Michigan War was being waged for control of Lucas County, Ohio. It was believed that *The Blade* would "always leap from its scabbard whenever the rights of individuals, or the community, shall be infringed."

Another meaning of the word *blade,* dating at least to the sixteenth century, is a "wild, reckless, sharp-witted young man." A weekly newspaper devoted to same-sex issues published in Washington, D.C., and New York is now known as the *Blade.* Alas, it no longer uses its original title, a reference to an eighteenth-century phrase for a libertine—the *Gay Blade.*

The *Scimitar* was a newspaper in Memphis, Tennessee, founded in 1880 by George P. M. Turner, a Civil War officer under Nathan Bedford Forrest. The word *scimitar*'s origin was Persian and means "a sword with a curved blade," and perhaps Turner carried such a weapon in the war. In 1904 the *Scimitar* merged with the *News* and continued as the *News-Scimitar* for the next two decades, when it merged with the Memphis *Press* and continued publishing until 1983 as the *Press-Scimitar.*

Vindicator

A pretty scary term for a newspaper is the *Vindicator,* which sounds as if it might be the name of an Arnold Schwarzenegger movie. The word comes from the Latin *vindicare,* meaning "to lay claim to, to defend, or to avenge." Nowadays it usually means to prove something or someone to be right against objections to the contrary.

In 1828 an Irish physician named Daniel Tracey founded the *Vindicator* in Montreal, named after a paper in Ballyshannon, Ireland. It opposed British control of Canada, and its motto was "Justice to all classes; monopolies and exclusive privileges to none."

The Staunton (Virginia) *Vindicator* was founded in 1845 as the Augusta *Democrat* by two men named Stevenson and Geiger, who must have had a change of heart four years later when the paper's name was changed to the *Republican Vindicator.* In 1858 it became the Staunton *Vindicator and General Advertiser,* but in 1861 the exigencies of the Civil War forced it to suspend publication. There was an Indian newspaper

named the *Vindicator* in 1872 in New Boggy, Oklahoma, which advo-
cated the interests of the Choctaw and Chickasaw nations. In 1857 there
was briefly a New York *Vindicator,* and since 1869 the *Vindicator*—
breezily nicknamed the *Vindy*—has been the principal newspaper in
Youngstown, Ohio.

Standard and *Banner*

Banner is from Latin *bandum,* "sign," thence into French as *bannière,*
"a piece of cloth, attached on its edge to a pole or staff and used by a
king, a feudal lord, or a knight as a standard and as the rallying point for
his men in battle." In the sense of a nation's flag, *banner* is now chiefly
historical (as in the "Star-Spangled Banner"), but poetically it is often
applied to anything displayed as an expression of principles. *Standard* is
from the Old French word *estandard,* originally, but now obsolete, for
"something elevated as a signal or a beacon." Now it means an emblem
symbolizing an organized body of people, as the eagle was the standard
of the Roman legion; hence "the personal flag of a ruler or state, or,
loosely, a banner." Thus, as the dictionaries tell us in these roundabout
definitions, a banner is a standard and a standard is a banner, and they
both mean "flag." They are both common newspaper titles—but the
word *flag* itself for some reason is rarely, if ever, seen in a nameplate.

Newspapers named *Standard* sprouted all over the British Isles in the
early nineteenth century, from the London *Standard* (later the mass-
circulation *Evening Standard*) in 1827, to the Essex *Standard* in 1831, the
Carlow (Ireland) *Standard* in 1832, and other *Standard*s in Gloucester,
Cheltenham, Liverpool, Wiltshire, Chatham, Rochester, Devon, Surrey,
Newcastle, York, Lincoln, Cork, Coventry, Londonderry, Dublin, Mon-
tego Bay, New Brunswick, and many others.

*Banner*s evidently started flying a little later, Ulster's in 1842, Aberdeen's in 1844, London's *British Banner* in 1848, the Jackson County
Banner in Wisconsin and the Ogle County *Banner* in Illinois both in
1858, and the *Scottish Banner* in Glasgow, 1859. The Nashville *Banner*
proudly waved in Tennessee from 1865 until 1998, when it was lowered
for the last time.

The *Standard Banner* of Jefferson County, Tennessee, founded in
1928, today waves both flag names. Not to be confused with the fight-

ing spirit of any *Banner*s is the *Banter* of Bainbridge, Ohio, whose title indicates that its interests run more to persiflage than perseverance.

It should be noted that a "banner" in newspaperese is also a headline running across the full width of the page, usually reserved for a story of really earthshaking significance such as ARMED BANDIT ROBS LIQUOR STORE!

7

Party Time

As newspapers freed themselves from the government control of the seventeenth century and embraced their newfound freedom of expression in the eighteenth, many new publications were created as outlets for specific political parties or ideological positions. Major politicians sponsored papers pledged to their support, such as Thomas Jefferson's *National Gazette* and George Canning's *Anti-Jacobin*. Many papers expressed political preferences not only in their editorial policies, but also in their titles. As they evolved, however, the allegiance promised in their names sometimes failed to match the actual views of papers called the *Democrat, Republican, Republic, Whig, Tory, Union, Constitution, Commonwealth, Independent,* and *Impartial Reporter.*

Democrat, Republican, and *Republic*

The name of a specific political party in its title only occasionally provides a clue about which candidate a newspaper will support in an election. As Frank Luther Mott observes of two nineteenth-century newspapers: "An oddity of nomenclature existed in the fact that the two leading St. Louis papers contradicted their titles in their editorial policies: the Missouri *Democrat* was a Republican journal, while the Missouri *Republican* was Democratic." Mott explains that the *Republican,* founded as the Missouri *Gazette* in 1808, changed its name long before the birth of the Republican Party and retained its founding "Democratic" principles—those of the party then known as "Democratic-Republicans." The *Democrat* was founded in 1852 in the Free-Soil cause, and during the

U.S. Civil War it was critical of Lincoln, allying itself with the group called "radical" Republicans. It later became famous as the St. Louis *Globe-Democrat.*

The Donegal *Democrat* in Ballyshannon, Ireland, uses the name in a nonpartisan sense. Someone who is a "little-*d* democrat"—from the Greek *dēmos* ("people") + *kratos* ("authority")—is an adherent of any system in which sovereign power resides with the people who are to be governed. The Ballyshannon paper was founded in 1919 by John Downey, who stated in the first issue that it was to be a "non-political paper in a world of politics . . . and it shall be ever our object to uphold anything that will further the national and local interests." The paper had a militant nationalist policy, which led to several raids by police and British soldiers (so much for nonpolitical!).

Republican first emerged as a newspaper name in the eighteenth century in the fervor accompanying the founding of a new nation in America and a new government in France, both of which were republics. In its nonpartisan sense, *republic,* from the Latin *res* ("thing") + *publicus* ("the people"), is a form of democracy in which sovereign power rests with an electorate who choose representatives who are, in theory, accountable to the people. Among the first newspapers to adopt this name was the Massachusetts *Centinel and Republican Journal* in 1784. The Boston *Gazette and Republican Weekly Journal* followed by 1794, as well as the *American Watchman and Delaware Republican* in 1809, the East-Jersey *Republican* in 1816, the Springfield (Massachusetts) *Republican* in 1824, and the *National Republican* in 1832.

The Brits took up the cause when Richard Carlile began publishing a radical reform paper called the *Republican* in 1819, in response to the Peterloo Massacre, a violent suppression of a public gathering in Manchester resulting in eleven deaths.

*Republican*s came into full flower in the United States in the 1850s, when the name became attached to a new political party with an Illinois rail-splitter named Abe Lincoln as its standard-bearer. Newspapers named the *Republican* jumped with alacrity onto this new bandwagon, springing up in scores of American cities by 1858. Despite this profusion, *Republican* has not survived on nameplates as widely as *Democrat.* Today there are more than 150 newspapers with *Democrat* in their titles, making it the fifteenth most popular U.S. name. By comparison, there are fewer than half as many *Republicans.*

The nominal preponderance of *Democrats* over *Republicans* is no cause for delight by the Democratic Party, for many papers that call themselves *Democrat* have editorial policies that actually support Republicans. Among the so-called *Democrats* that backed presidential nominee George W. Bush in 2004 are the Albany (Oregon) *Democrat-Herald;* the Little Rock (Arkansas) *Democrat-Gazette; Foster's Daily Democrat* in Dover, New Hampshire; the Natchez (Mississippi) *Democrat;* and the Orangeburg (South Carolina) *Times & Democrat.* To be fair, it should be noted that Democrat John Kerry was indeed backed by the Rochester (New York) *Democrat & Chronicle* and the Santa Rosa (California) *Press-Democrat*—as well as by the Springfield (Massachusetts) *Republican!* Go figure.

Jim Cox, editor of the Clark County *Democrat* in Grove Hill, Alabama, dealt with the discrepancy of newspapers' names versus their politics in a column in 2004. Clark explains that the name of his paper refers to a democrat with a small *d.* But he acknowledges that when Isaac Grant founded the *Democrat* in 1856, the Democratic Party was dominant in the South and that for years the *Democrat* was a staunch supporter of Democratic Party candidates.

Dating from the post–Civil War era, there is a newspaper in Osage County, Missouri, known as the *Unterrified Democrat.* The paper was founded in 1866 by Colonel Lebbeus Zevely, a native of North Carolina, who refused to sign the "Ironclad Oath" of loyalty to the Union required in Republican-controlled Missouri's postwar constitution; as a result he was dubbed an "unterrified Democrat" and used the nickname for his newspaper. Under its present ownership, the political affiliation of the *Unterrified Democrat* is listed in the Official Manual of the State of Missouri as Republican—though whether of the terrified or unterrified variety is difficult to say.

The Arizona *Republic* in Phoenix began life in 1890 as the Arizona *Republican* and was intended as the political mouthpiece of the territory's conservative Republican governor. It was bought by a cattle and land baron in 1912, and upon his death in 1929, the *Republican* was acquired by two of its top staff members. Shortly thereafter, aiming for a less partisan image, they changed the name to the *Republic.* Even so, the *Republic* has remained staunchly Republican and endorsed George W. Bush for the presidency in both 2000 and 2004.

Democrats might be tempted to think the worst about the *Republican-*

Rustler in Basin, Wyoming—especially in the western United States, where *rustling* can mean the theft of horses and cattle, a serious crime. But in early American slang, the word also meant "to move with great energy, especially in business." In any event, the *Republican-Rustler* is the result of a 1928 merger between the *Rustler* (of whatever kind it was), founded in 1889, and the *Republican,* founded in 1905 to counteract the *Rustler's* Democratic views—which it did by eventually absorbing its rival.

The publisher of the *Daily Democrat* in Durant, Oklahoma, says his paper does not give editorial support to any candidates in national elections: "Nobody cares who we endorse for President," he says, with rare insight and refreshing candor.

The circuitous political paths followed by newspapers bearing party names can be dizzyingly illustrated, although not fully grasped, by the history of the Easton (Maryland) *Star-Democrat.* It descends from the *Republican Star and Eastern Shore Political Luminary,* founded in 1799 as a supporter of Thomas Jefferson. In those days "Republicans" were members of the Democratic-Republican Party, who after 1828 became known as Democrats. Their adversaries were the Whigs, a precursor of the modern Republican Party, and in 1828 the *Eastern Shore Whig and People's Advocate* was founded in Easton—but it did not support the Whig Party. Its name honored an entirely different kind of "Whigs"— patriots who had supported the American Revolution against the British. The *Whig and People's Advocate* backed Andrew Jackson and the Democratic Party. Also in 1828 the *Republican Star* bolted to the Whig side and refused to back Jackson. The *Whig and People's Advocate* acquired the *Republican Star* in 1832, bringing it back into the Democratic camp and eventually scrapping the word *Republican.* In 1885 the Easton *Independent* began publishing, but the following year it changed its name to the Easton *Democrat.* In 1896 the *Star* and the *Democrat* merged to become today's *Star-Democrat*—which endorsed Republican Bush in 2004. Got it?

Whig and *Tory*

The name *Whig* was used by papers in both America and England but with different meanings. The word is derived from the Scottish *whigga-*

maire, which referred contemptuously to any horseman (*whig* meaning "drive" + *maire* meaning "mare") who rode to Edinburgh in 1648 to protest against the king. *Whig* later meant a member of the Scottish Presbyterian Covenanters opposed to the accession of James II, a Roman Catholic. Thereafter, a Whig referred to a member of one of the two main parties, which evolved into the Liberal Party. In the colonies a Whig was a pro-revolutionary American partisan. From 1834 the word was attached to a political party favoring strong central government, a forerunner of today's Republican Party.

Among dozens of nineteenth-century newspapers called *Whig*s were the *Independent Whig* in London (1720); the *Washington Whig* in Bridgetown, New Jersey (1815); the *Northern Whig* in Hudson, New York (1817); the *Constitutional Whig* in Richmond, Virginia (1828); and the *Northern Whig* in Belfast, Ireland (1829). *Whig*s still lurk (for which of their many political purposes who knows?) in Elkton, Maryland, and Quincy, Illinois *(Herald-Whig),* as well as in Kingston, Ontario *(Whig-Standard).*

In England, the Whigs' adversaries were the Tories, a name derived from the Irish *tôruidhe* ("pursued man") and applied to seventeenth-century Irish outlaws and then to supporters of the Roman Catholic James II. Royalists in the American Revolution were also called Tories. British Tories remained a force into the nineteenth century and eventually evolved into the Conservative Party. A few newspapers adopted the name, including the *Tory* in London in 1827 and the *Tory* in Liverpool in 1898.

Union

Allied historically to newspapers calling themselves *Republican* are those with the name *Union,* which in most cases has nothing to do with teamsters or steelworkers. The years leading up to the American Civil War saw the founding of the Republican Party, one of whose principal political goals was the preservation of the federal union of American states. Accordingly, a number of newspapers founded during this time, mostly in the Northern states, showed their patriotism by calling themselves the *Union.*

The word *union* (and its cousin *onion*) both come from the Latin *unio* and originally referred to "a large pearl, or a pungent bulb vegetable," but later came to mean "oneness" of any kind. Only a slight etymological detail made the American alliance of states a federal union rather than a federal onion.

Founded in 1854—the same year as the Republican Party—Sonora, California's *Union-Democrat* was an anomaly in its name. California had just become a state in 1850, so pro-Union sentiment was strong. But the paper's founder, Albert N. Francisco, a failed gold miner, came from New Orleans, where he had been a printer at the *Picayune*—and where Democrats prevailed. The *Union-Democrat* today is the oldest California paper published continuously under the same name.

Once the war started in 1860, the word *Union* was on everyone's lips in the North. A stirring popular song of the period urged: "Always stand on the Union side / And battle for the right." In this atmosphere, a number of papers were founded to give editorial support to the North. The Springfield (Massachusetts) *Union* was founded in 1864, largely to appeal to the hordes of Union soldiers who were stationed there. Its major competition was the *Republican,* which got its name in 1824, when Republicans were really Democrats.

One Southern newspaper, the Milledgeville (Georgia) *Federal Union,* founded in 1830, whose naming predated the Civil War, found itself in a pickle when hostilities began and its name put it on the wrong side. The owner quickly and prudently changed the name to the *Confederate Union*—and then just as prudently switched back to *Federal Union* when the fighting was over and the North had won. In 1872 it merged with the *Southern Recorder* and is now the *Union-Recorder.*

The *Union* of Manchester, New Hampshire, began in the late 1850s as a weekly, and by 1863 was a daily, called the Manchester *Daily Union.*—printed with a period after its name, if you please. Always noted for its bellicosity, the *Union* in 1865 had an editor who railed equally against the Northern Radical Republicans, who favored suffrage for the former slaves, and the Democratic former slaveholders, who opposed it. Editorial raillery continued into more recent times. Now known as the *Union Leader,* the paper was notorious for vitriol under the leadership of the late William Loeb, who famously heaped insults on the wife of Maine senator Edmund Muskie during his 1972 presidential race. Muskie's emotionally unrestrained response dashed his election hopes.

The Florida *Times-Union* in Jacksonville has had a schizophrenic ca-

reer, veering between Northern Union support and the Southern sym-
pathies of the state surrounding it. It was founded in 1864 as the *Union*
by J. K. Stickney, an olive grower and former Detroit newspaperman,
who favored the North in the Civil War. After the war, although still pro-
Union, Stickney hired as editor a former obstetrician named Holmes
Steele, an unreconstructed Southern Democrat who had commanded a
Confederate infantry troop. When Stickney insisted that the paper support a bill that disenfranchised Confederates, Steele quit. Stickney then
sold the paper to a staunch Republican and former Union officer, Boston
lawyer Edward Cheney. Cheney had to sell the paper for financial reasons but stayed on as editor and supported Republicans in the election
of 1876, when Democrats swept the state of Florida. The *Union* was then
sold again, to H. B. McCallum, an ardent Democrat and Baptist preach-
er, who hopped back and forth between soapbox and pulpit. By this time,
the *Union* had stiff competition from the Jacksonville *Times,* and the two
papers merged in 1883. By 2004, the *Times-Union* was back in the Republican camp, with an endorsement of President George W. Bush.

Other papers with *Union* in their titles are now published in San
Diego, California (the *Union-Tribune*); Walla Walla, Washington *(Union-
Bulletin);* Junction City, Kansas; Princeton, Minnesota *(Union-Eagle);*
and several other towns.

Constitution

The Atlanta *Constitution,* founded in 1868, was predicated on the notion of restoring the pre–Civil War Union. Carey Wentworth Styles,
James Anderson, and W. A. Hemphill bought the Atlanta *Opinion* and
changed its name to reflect their advocacy of a return to constitutional
prewar government. In 1879 the *Constitution* ran the first Uncle Remus
story by Joel Chandler Harris. Merged in 2001 with the Atlanta *Journal,*
the *Constitution* has won several Pulitzer Prizes and employed many noted writers, including sports editor Grantland Rice, editor Ralph McGill,
and humorist Lewis Grizzard.

Constitution had previously been used in the names of numerous
newspapers in Ireland, as early as 1799 in Dublin for a paper opposed to
union with Britain, and in London, during the early nineteenth century
when parliamentary reform was much in the news. The word *constitu-*

tion, from the Latin *constituere* ("to form the essential part of"), refers to the body of laws or customs, either written or unwritten, by which a people is governed.

Commonwealth

James Kimble Vardaman was a Mississippi lawyer, politician, and newspaperman, known as a progressive educational reformer, opponent of child labor, and advocate for ordinary working folks—as long as they were white. With equal fervor he opposed both the wealthy landed gentry and all black people. While he was speaker of the Mississippi legislature, he sought the Democratic nomination for governor in 1895 and 1899 but was sharply rebuffed by party leaders. This annoying experience reinforced his strongly populist views—and also undoubtedly influenced the naming of the newspaper he founded in Greenwood in 1896—the *Commonwealth,* which is still published today.

The word is a combination of *common* (from the Latin *communis,* "belonging to the community") + *wealth* (from the Old English *weola,* "well-being or prosperity"). It means "the people constituting a state or other organized political community" and refers especially to a democratic form of government deriving its power from all the people. Power from the people, at least from those with pale skin, is precisely what finally propelled Vardaman into the governor's office in 1903, when he was elected under a new law calling for popular primaries instead of nomination by party bosses.

Vardaman had ample historical precedent for use of *Commonwealth* as a newspaper title, there having been many others previously, frequently allied with various workers' causes—in London in 1848; Glasgow in 1853; Philadelphia, Pennsylvania, and Frankfort, Kentucky, in 1858; Birmingham, England, in 1880; Freetown, Sierra Leone, in 1888; Melbourne, Australia, in 1892; and Boston, Massachusetts, in 1895.

Independent

For papers that like to emphasize their nonencumbrance with any specific political baggage, the name *Independent* has been popular, both as adjective and noun, starting with the *Independent Advertiser,* published in Boston in 1748 as the organ of a political club founded by American revolutionary leader Samuel Adams.

American clergyman Henry Ward Beecher edited a weekly Congregationalist antislavery journal called the *Independent* in New York from 1861 to 1863. Beecher perhaps demonstrated a wee bit too much independence in his relationship with Elizabeth Tilton, the wife of Theodore Tilton, who had succeeded him as editor of the paper. Between 1870 and 1875, Mrs. Tilton confessed, then denied, then recanted her denial, that she and Beecher had had an adulterous affair. Beecher, whose older sister Harriet Stowe wrote *Uncle Tom's Cabin,* continued his illustrious preaching career, unfazed by his publicized deviation from a major Commandment, until his death in 1887. The *Independent* was published until 1928.

Historically, several hundred newspapers have incorporated *Independent* into their titles, up to the present day. In 1986 a new British national daily called the *Independent* was founded with its mission "to take the broader view." There are newspapers bearing the title *Independent* in dozens of American towns and cities, as well as in Dublin and several other Irish locales, and in several Australian cities, including Brisbane.

Political independence, however, does not mean a newspaper can't take sides when push comes to shove (and in politics it usually does). In 2004 the Anderson (South Carolina) *Independent-Mail* endorsed Democrat Kerry, while the Ashland (Kentucky) *Daily Independent* came out for Republican Bush.

Impartial Reporter

In a land noted for its bitter and sometimes bloody rivalry between Protestants and Catholics, the *Impartial Reporter* purports to maintain, improbable as it may be, an even keel in Enniskillen, County Fermanagh, Northern Ireland. It is believed to be the oldest newspaper in existence managed by only one family in direct succession. Okay, see if you can top the longevity of a paper that was first edited by William Trimble in 1825 and is managed today by his great-great-granddaughter. A newspaper dynasty without bruising family fights is a rarity indeed!

Trimble, a fervent Scotch-Irish Presbyterian who arose at 5 a.m. every day to read six chapters of the Bible, might seem a tad doctrinaire to maintain neutrality, but he nonetheless lived up to the paper's name in his first editorial, when he wrote, "Regardless alike of the frowns of party, and the smiles of power, we shall state our own convictions on all subjects which come under our review. We shall defend the Protestant when we consider him in the right, and the Roman Catholic may expect similar treatment." Trimble promised the paper would be "the organ of no party," and its masthead sounded like the oath administered in a court of law, declaring that it would print "the truth, the whole truth, and nothing but the truth."

Of course, Trimble's impartial reporting could extend only so far, and the paper became an ardent crusader in behalf of tenant farmers who Trimble believed were oppressed by absentee landlords. The *Impartial Reporter,* for all its impartiality, was despised by the established government and church, and it became known as the "Farmer's Friend." Trimble's parting words to his son, who took over the paper in 1886, were: "Get into the coachbox of the *Reporter* and drive straight. Never give up the reins, fear God, and never forget the poor."

8

Sound the Alarm

While some newspapers nominally cast themselves as representatives of the people, with a mission to safeguard their interests from miscreants or politicians of the wrong party, others go a step further than that, seeing themselves as ferocious watchdogs, ever on the alert, ready to sound an alarm and rouse into action those who have been ignorant of the dangers that threaten them—until, of course, they are informed of those dangers by the newspaper. At least, that's what their names indicate. Richard Steele's *Guardian* of 1713 was such a paper, with its strong pro-Whig vigilance, and many more newspapers have followed with militant-sounding names. Some papers see their names as synonymous with guards, well armed with loaded words, who patrol society's malevolent precincts sniffing out evildoing and calling attention to it; these include *Sentinel, Monitor, Watch,* and *Town Crier.* Other names embody the alarm itself, some sign or sound that will stir the reader out of somnolence. Among names of this kind are *Signal, Voice, Call, Alert, Clarion,* and *Bugle.*

Sentinel

Far more newspapers are named *Sentinel* in the United States of America today than in the United Kingdom, Canada, Australia, or New Zealand. Might that indicate that Americans have always been more wary of the possibility of attack than other English-speaking nations? A *sentinel* is a sentry, one who watches or keeps guard, from the French word *sentinelle,* Italian *sentinella,* Old Italian *sentina,* and ultimately the Latin *sentire,* "to watch, perceive through the senses."

Americans at first seemed to prefer the spelling *centinel,* perhaps influenced by the Spanish *centinela,* and there was a 1784 newspaper in Boston called the Massachusetts *Centinel and Republican Journal,* which took up the adoption of the U.S. Constitution as its principal cause, later changing its name to the *Columbia Centinel.* Other newspapers of that name followed: the *Centinel of the North-Western Territory* in 1793 in Cincinnati, Ohio; the *Centinel of Freedom* in 1796 in Newark, New Jersey; the Connecticut *Centinel* in 1802; and the *Northern Centinel* in Burlington, Vermont, in 1810. Finally in 1823 came the Utica *Sentinel,* with an "S," which remained the prevailing U.S. spelling.

On the other side of the Atlantic, there was not total indifference to security, as manifested by the Glasgow *Sentinel* in 1809; the Preston (Lancashire) *Sentinel* in 1821; and the *Sentinel* in London in 1821, subtitled *A Constitutional, Colonial and Nautical Register.*

America is still vigilant today, with *Sentinel*s in Grand Junction, Colorado; Fort Lauderdale, Florida *(Sun-Sentinel);* Fort Wayne, Indiana *(News-Sentinel);* Knoxville, Tennessee *(News-Sentinel);* Milwaukee, Wisconsin *(Journal Sentinel);* and Orlando, Florida. Just to be on the extra-safe side, there are also several newspapers patrolling the country under the name of *Sentry.*

Monitor

A monitor is something like a sentinel in its capacity as an alarmist—but packs more moral authority. The Latin *monere* means "to advise, warn, or admonish." A *monitor* is defined as "one who warns of faults, informs of duty, gives advice and instruction."

A London publication called the *Monitor*—one of the many pro-Whig periodicals issued by Richard Steele, abetted, as usual, by his friend Joseph Addison—appeared for a few issues in 1714.

The first Sunday newspaper in London was Mrs. Elizabeth Johnson's *British Gazette and Sunday Monitor* in 1779. It later dropped the *Gazette* and became simply the *Sunday Monitor,* a blue-nosed sounding entity if ever there was one. In the manner of modern tabloid newspapers, however, Mrs. Johnson's admonitions combined moral righteousness with ample bits of juicy gossip. George Crabbe in his satirical commentary "The Newspaper" took the *Monitor*'s measure when he wrote in 1783:

Then lo! the sainted MONITOR is born,
Whose pious face some sacred texts adorn:
As artful sinners cloak the secret sin,
To veil with seeming grace the guile within;
So moral Essays on his front appear,
But all is carnal business in the rear;
The fresh-coin'd lie, the secret whisper'd last,
And all the gleanings of the six days past.

In 1789 a newspaper called the *Moniteur universel* appeared in Paris, positioning itself in opposition to further change after the Revolution. In 1814 Napoléon himself was a contributor of political articles to the *Moniteur.*

Influenced by that Paris newspaper, the *Monitore Napolitano* was founded in Italy in 1796 and edited by Countess Eleonora de Fonseca Pimentel, who corresponded with Goethe and Voltaire. Her editorial cause for the *Monitore* was the "sacred words of freedom and equality" inspired by the French Revolution, which she hoped to see emulated in the Republic of Naples.

The first newspaper published in New Orleans was *Le Moniteur de la Louisiane,* begun in 1794 and published in French until 1814. There was, no doubt, much to monitor in those early days of a rakishly cosmopolitan city that had no shortage of revelers.

Today the best-known newspaper named the *Monitor* is undoubtedly the *Christian Science Monitor,* founded in 1908 by Mary Baker Eddy, who had previously established the Christian Science religion. At the age of eighty-six, she became embroiled in a long-lasting public feud with Joseph Pulitzer's New York *World.* By then famous for the religious views expressed in her best-selling books, Eddy became a target for Pulitzer's paper, which decided that she was mentally incompetent and incapable of managing her affairs; the *World* urged a lawsuit by her relatives. The case against her was ultimately dismissed, and the following year she founded the *Monitor* with the lofty goal "to injure no man, but to bless all mankind."

The *Monitor's* moral foundation was clear from the beginning. It was intended as a protest against the kind of "yellow journalism" practiced by Pulitzer, Hearst, and other newspaper barons. In 1910 the *Monitor* sponsored a series of "clean journalism" meetings. Probably no newspaper has ever had its name so carefully chosen. In 1883 Eddy had written: "Looking over the newspapers of the day, one naturally reflects that it is dangerous to live, so loaded with disease seems the very air. These descriptions carry fears to many minds, to be depicted in some future time upon the body. A periodical of our own will counteract to some extent this public nuisance; for through our paper we shall be able to reach many homes with healing, purifying thought."

Eddy insisted that the words *Christian Science* should precede *Monitor* in the paper's name. According to her biographer Robert Peel, "The designated title was an identification of the paper with the promise that no human situation was beyond healing or rectification if approached with sufficient understanding of man's God-given potentialities. Nor did the 'good news' of Christianity involve the prettification of bad news, but rather, its confident confrontation."

The *Monitor* is a general newspaper with only one daily article devoted to Christian Science and is noted for the excellence of its world news coverage. Ironically—in view of Eddy's bitter hostilities with Joseph Pulitzer, who later founded the Pulitzer Prizes—the *Monitor* has won at least five of those prestigious awards.

Watch

The Anglo-Saxon word *wæcce* means "a state of being awake." From it we get the noun *watch,* which can mean not only a gold-plated Rolex, but also a state of alertness for the purpose of guarding or protecting, like a sentinel. The Telluride (Colorado) *Watch* is very much in that tradition. Established in 1996, the paper, its purpose, and its name are encapsulated in very few words by publisher Seth Cagin: "We thought it was unusual, succinct, accurate. When we started the paper, there were TWO bad papers in town so we wanted to emphasize vigilance."

No question, Mr. Cagin could win prizes for succinctness.

Town Crier

The position of town crier can be traced back at least to the England of 1066, when William the Conqueror, never one to be self-effacing about his achievements, employed a number of individuals to go from town to town and let people know about his conquest. (After all, most people would want to know who had conquered them.) This was centuries before the printing press, so written notices would have been painstakingly done by hand, and most of the populace were not able to read them anyway. The scheme worked so well that the office of town crier was permanently instituted in hundreds of villages. Whenever there was important news, a messenger would relay it to the town crier, who would ring a bell. The townspeople would gather in the square, and after lots of shouting "Oyez, oyez" ("Listen, listen" in French), the town crier would let the people know about a plague, or a fire, or a royal execution.

Newspapers did not seem to get the idea of using *Town Crier,* or sometimes just plain *Crier,* as a title until the nineteenth century, when such a paper appeared in Birmingham, England, in 1861. A few years later Liverpool had a *Town Crier* and then London had one, too. By 1900, when actual town criers had vanished except as ceremonial offices, every town in England seemed to want a newspaper of that name, and they popped up in Bristol, Hull, Macclesfield, Guildford, Folkestone, Aldershot, Gravesend, Canterbury, Cheltenham, Cambridge, St. Ives, and heaven knows where else. Today most *Town Criers* are in the United States, and they are usually community newspapers that shy away from plagues, fires, and royal executions and concentrate on anniversaries, Little League ball games, and school plays.

Signal

Signal, from the Latin *signum* ("visible symbol or sign") is a word in use only from the end of the sixteenth century and may be any one of several media—flags, bells, hand signs, beacons, and fires among the possible mechanisms. It now means "a sign, token or watchword agreed upon in advance as the occasion of some action."

One of the first recorded uses of *Signal* for a newspaper title was the New York *Evening Signal,* founded in 1839 as an antidote for "respectable people" to the scandalous, crime-ridden, sex-drenched pages of the New York *Herald,* a paper operated with personal flamboyance by James Gordon Bennett. So intent on sounding the alarm for moral reform was the *Signal* that it referred to Bennett as an "obscene vagabond," a "polluted wretch," and "a venomous reptile." Somehow he and the *Herald* survived the *Signal*'s attack.

Another early *Signal* was in Michigan in the lakeside community of Port Sanilac on the shores of Lake Huron, where the Sanilac *Signal and Huron County Advocate* was published in 1858. The "signal" in question may have referred to a log shanty near the lake, used for the manufacture of wooden shingles, which served as a landmark for boatmen from the 1840s. An actual kerosene-burning lighthouse was in Port Sanilac in 1886, and in 1924 it was electrified, providing a conveniently bright beacon for bootleggers to unload contraband liquor from Canada. The *Signal* presumably was no longer around by that time to sound any alarms to federal revenue authorities.

Today there are newspapers with *Signal* in their names in Baldwin City, Kansas; Carnegie, Pennsylvania *(Signal Item-Star);* Crowley, Louisiana *(Post-Signal);* Santa Clarita, California; and Weiser, Idaho *(Signal American)*.

Voice

Most newspapers with the name *Voice* are qualified by being the "voice *of* something or other." The word goes all the way back to the Sanskrit *vâc*, meaning "sound or speech." Its original meaning, "the sound uttered by living beings," by the fourteenth century also meant "wish, choice, or opinion," and, by extension, the person who expresses those views. More often than not, a *Voice* newspaper is associated with the views of some specific group, labor union, religious organization, or ethnic affiliation. Among the first was the *Voice of the People* in 1831 in London. The *Voice of Jacob* in London in 1841 was subtitled *A Fortnightly Publication for the Promotion of the Spiritual and General Welfare of the Jews*. The *Voice of India* was a newspaper in Bombay in 1883. Beginning in 1914 there were numerous incarnations of the *Voice of Labour* in London and Dublin. The *Voice of the World Citizen* had a brief run in the 1960s in London. The *Voice Universal* in Southwick, England, purported to speak for just about everyone, at least as long as it lasted, from 1958 to 1971.

Among the most notable papers of that name today is the *Village*

Voice, a news weekly emanating from Greenwich Village in New York City, one of whose founders was the iconoclastic novelist Norman Mailer. Precisely whose "voice" the newspaper speaks with is not clear, but with characteristic Lower Manhattan modesty it does call itself the "premier expert on New York's cultural scene" and "the authoritative source on all that New York has to offer." All right, already!

Call

From an Old English word, *ceallian,* meaning "to talk or prate," the Middle English word *callen* was defined as "to utter loudly and forcibly, so as to be heard at a distance." The noun *call* is "a shout, a cry for help, or a summons." From the sixteenth century it could also mean a signal, as on a bugle, urging action. It was in this sense that the name was used for newspapers in the nineteenth century.

In 1856 the *Daily Morning Call* was founded in San Francisco—not to urge action, however, but to maintain the status quo. Despite its rousing name, it was a conservative, proestablishment antidote to the San Francisco *Bulletin,* the "fighting journal" founded the previous year to oppose corruption in city government. Mark Twain (known then as Samuel Clemens) was a reporter for the *Call* in 1864, but his style was too rambunctious, and he was fired after four months on the job.

The *Call* had its hands full trying to keep the lid on dissension. A literal "shoot-to-kill" attitude pervaded San Francisco's rough-and-tumble journalism. The *Bulletin's* crusading was so effective that its publisher and editor, a man with the unusual name of James King of William, was shot to death in 1856 by the editor of the Sunday *Times,* James Casey, whom King had exposed as having served time in Sing Sing for grand larceny. In 1879 Charles de Young, who with his brother, Michael, had founded the San Francisco *Chronicle* in 1865, was fatally shot by the son of a political enemy named Isaac Kalloch. Then, in 1886, the *Chronicle's* Mike de Young was shot (though not fatally) by Adolph Spreckels because of defamatory allegations made against Spreckels's father, Claus, the sugar tycoon. In an ironic twist of fate four years later, Adolph's brother, John D. Spreckels, acquired the *Call,* which by that time had reversed field and become a feisty, in-your-face newspaper, a gadfly to the older muckraking *Bulletin* and a continuing bitter rival of De Young's established *Chronicle.*

Spreckels sold the *Call* in 1913 to the Hearst chain, and in 1919 it merged with the *Bulletin,* later merged again as the *News-Call-Bulletin,* then ceased to exist in 1960, when it was folded into the San Francisco *Examiner,* which in turn bit the dust as a daily in 1999.

While San Francisco's *Call* was heard in the morning, New York's was an *Evening Call,* a Socialist newspaper from 1908 to 1923. England's Willesden *Call* was established in 1913, and a London *Call* in 1914.

Today's Allentown (Pennsylvania) *Morning Call* is a descendant of an earlier paper known as the *Critic,* founded in 1883. In 1894 the publishers decided a new name was needed and had a contest with a five-dollar gold coin as a prize for the schoolchild who submitted the winning entry. The new name was announced on January 1, 1895. The winner is not identified in any records, and thus the reasons for choosing the *Morning Call* are unknown.

There's also a *Call* in Woonsocket, Rhode Island, a *Times-Call* in Longmont, Colorado, and a *Caller-Times,* founded in 1883, in Corpus Christi, Texas.

Alert

The newspaper that comes closest to sounding an alarm every time you look at its front page must be the *Alert* in Chetek, Wisconsin. *Alert,* which means "an alarm to prepare for action," has an interesting etymology, originating with the French phrase *à l'erte,* which the French got from the Italian *all'erta,* meaning "on the watch," an *erta* being a watchtower or raised structure, related to the Latin *erigere,* "to erect." The Chetek *Alert* is a weekly, not a daily, so if its readers are alerted to something requiring prompt action, it may be a few days before they actually get around to it. That must be okay with the people of Chetek, since the *Alert* has been around since 1882.

Clarion and Bugle

From the Latin *clarius* ("clear"), a *clarion* is "a kind of trumpet with a shrill tone"—or the word can mean "the sound of such a trumpet." Even though a trumpet is the preferred instrument of the archangel Gabriel to alert the world to its impending demise, and Joshua used something like a bugle at the battle of Jericho, and trumpet calls have re-layed information in armies since medieval days—not many newspapers think of themselves as musical instruments of any kind—even though most of them have plenty of brass. It is odd that there are no journalistic *Trumpet*s or *Cornet*s to speak of, only a few *Clarion*s, and even fewer *Bugle*s outside the pages of fiction.

There was a *Clarion* in Grand Haven, Michigan, in 1858, and one in London from 1891 to 1934, and various others throughout England, Australia, South Africa, and the United States up until the present day, but the name is not found among many major daily newspapers anymore. The largest-circulation *Clarion* is the *Clarion-Ledger* in Jackson, Mississippi, and there are others in Geneseo, New York; Palestine, Texas; Hancock, Kentucky; and on the Kenai Peninsula, Alaska.

A *bugle,* from the Latin *buculus* (also the root of the word *bovine*), originally meant "a young bullock, steer or wild ox," and the musical *bugle,* short for *bugle-horn,* was developed in the fourteenth century, originally made from the horn of an ox. The bugle was first used as a hunting horn, and thereafter became widely used for giving military signals. As a newspaper title, a *Bugle* in Council Bluffs, Iowa, tooted its own horn in 1858, and there was one in London from 1907 to 1922. Today there's one in Camp Verde, Arizona, but the most famous *Bugle* is a fictional one—to which Spider-Man, also known as freelance photographer Peter Parker, sells his pictures.

9

Let There Be Light

"Give light, and the people will find their own way" has been the motto of Scripps-Howard (now just Scripps) newspapers since 1927. It is accompanied by a logo picturing a lighthouse. The origin of the quotation is not clear—some say it is a paraphrase of a line in Dante's *Purgatorio;* others think it came from Euripides—but all agree that it first appeared in newspaper print in 1922, also with a lighthouse drawing, over a column called "Turning on the Light" by Carl Magee, the crusading editor of the Albuquerque (New Mexico) *Tribune.*

Newspapers typically believe that "turning on the light"—to eliminate the ignorance of darkness—is one of their primary missions, and some of them express that commitment in luminous names, from the plain and simple *Light* itself to various other sources of illumination, both celestial—*Star, Sun, Aurora, Comet, Meteor, Globe, World, Planet, Orrery*—and man-made—*Beacon, Pharos, Headlight, Searchlight, Spotlight, Flare, Mirror,* and *Reflector.*

Light

Other than the *Man in the Moon* (which surely emanates a very pale sort of light), a short-lived anti-Cromwell paper in 1649, the appearance of light-related newspapers is mostly a phenomenon of the nineteenth century. The word *light* itself is a good old Anglo-Saxon word, coming from *lēoht,* related to the Greek *leukos,* meaning "bright" or "white." The *Banner of Light* was "a weekly journal of romance, literature and general intelligence" in Boston, Massachusetts, in 1858. The London *Light* had a wide range of interests, describing itself in 1880 as "an illustrated political, theatrical, musical, comical, satirical, sporting and society journal." In 1889 came the *Northern Light and Islington Star*—providing its illumination in two ways, as did the *Sun-Light* in Liverpool in 1891.

Perhaps the foremost modern newspaper called the *Light* was a long-time daily in San Antonio, Texas, which ceased publication in 1992 after a 111-year history. The original appearance of the *Light* was announced in an occasional paper called the San Antonio *Surprise,* which explained that it would be a lively daily devoted to the issues of interest to San Antonio and reported that "the *Evening Light* would be visible January 1, 1881 . . . and will grow brighter and stronger with each issue." It was first published six days a week, appropriately enough at the office of the Texas *Sun.* In 1924 the *Light* became a Hearst paper and continued until 1992 when Hearst bought the rival San Antonio *Express-News* and decided to extinguish its own *Light.* Other *Light*s still shine in Point Reyes, California, and Waxahachie, Texas.

Star

Far more popular luminaries are the *Star* and the *Sun,* which are among the top ten most frequent names among English-language newspapers. *Star* is from the Anglo-Saxon *steorra,* loosely speaking "any of the luminous bodies seen in the skies," but more precisely, "a self-luminous celestial body (other than comets, meteors and nebulae), as distinguished from reflective bodies such as planets and moons." The nearest star to the Earth is the Sun (Anglo-Saxon *sunne*).

The word *star* is rich with connotations that reinforce an image of superiority, knowledge, and stability. Early human beings believed that illustrious individuals reappeared in the sky as stars after death. It was a star in the East that led the Magi to the infant Jesus. In astrology, the "stars" are a major influence in a person's destiny. The North Star, or Polaris, has been the mariners' guide for millennia, and Shakespeare's Julius Caesar compares his own steadfastness to it:

> But I am constant as the Northern Star,
> Of whose true-fixed and resting quality
> There is no fellow in the firmament.

Since the mid-nineteenth century the word *star* has been used to refer to one who "shines" in society, art, industry, or science. Little wonder, then, that newspapers found it such an appealing word to put at the top of their pages.

The name *Star* appeared on newspapers in the late eighteenth century, among the first being the *Northern Star* in Belfast in 1792, the *Oriental Star* in Calcutta and the *National Evening Star* in Dublin, both in 1793; the *Union Star* in Dublin in 1798; and the *Star* in London in 1801.

In the United States, the *Morning Star* appeared in Newburyport, Massachusetts, in 1794; the *Western Star* in Stockbridge, Massachusetts, in 1789; the *Western Star* in New York in 1812; and the *Republican Star* in Easton, Maryland, in 1821.

The Anniston (Alabama) *Star,* which was established around 1900, waxes downright poetic about its name. On the publisher's Web site, Chris Waddle, vice president for news, rhapsodizes:

> The symbol of the "star" worked its way out of the human mind 6,000 years ago in the Fertile Crescent. The Sumerians made it a common sign as they became the first of human kind to commit thoughts to a hand-held medium. For Sumer the print was cuneiform on wet clay. For us the method is wet ink on newsprint, and, in time to come, the crackle of electron on computer screen. . . . When a Southerner lies down to sleep on a camping trip in the woods, the stars twinkle through the branches and tree limbs just barely beyond reach, it seems to dreamy eyes. . . . The universe seems to blend as though guiding stars might be the shiny fruit of those trees rooted in the same earth where we lie.

At what might be considered the opposite end of the literary spectrum, Nobel Prize–winning novelist Ernest Hemingway practiced his craft at another *Star,* the noted daily in Kansas City, for six months in 1916–1917. He credited that newspaper's stylebook with helping to shape him as a writer. This excerpt from the paper's no-nonsense manual sounds as if it might have come from a Hemingway novel: "Use short sentences. Use short first paragraphs. Use vigorous English. Be positive, not negative." Kansas City's *Star* was founded in 1880 with a sale price of two cents and an emphasis on chatty local news. The other Kansas City papers sold for a nickel, inspiring poet Eugene Field, managing editor of the rival *Times,* to versify:

> Twinkle, twinkle, little Star,
> Bright and gossipy you are;
> We can daily hear you speak
> For a paltry dime a week.

Today *Star*s also twinkle in many towns and cities, including Toronto, Ontario; Johannesburg, South Africa; Beirut, Lebanon; Tucson, Arizona; Casper, Wyoming *(Star-Tribune);* Fort Worth, Texas *(Star-Telegram);* Honolulu, Hawaii *(Star Bulletin);* Indianapolis, Indiana; Minneapolis, Minnesota *(Star Tribune);* Lincoln, Nebraska *(Journal-Star);* and Newark, New Jersey *(Star-Ledger).* Londoners have their choice of *Stars:* the *Daily Star* is a right-wing tabloid, but the *Morning Star* is a red one— the reincarnation and hotly debated renaming (in 1966) of the former *Daily Worker,* a publication of the Communist Party. The *Star* of Hope, Arkansas, is a daily published in the hometown of former president Bill Clinton, and Merced, California, promises twenty-four-hour, day-and-night illumination with the *Sun-Star.*

Sun

Sun is hardly less redolent of superlative connotations than *star.* More than a source of light, whose absence is the definition of night, the sun was worshiped as a deity from the earliest ages of humanity, and it has been specifically associated with both Apollo and Christ. Poets have used it as a symbol of brightness, glory, splendor, and power. The majesty implied in the word was appropriated by *Le Roi Soleil,* Louis XIV, the Sun King.

By the late eighteenth century, *Sun* was in use for newspaper titles. A *Sun* rose in London in 1794. The *Rising Sun* was a newspaper in Keene, New Hampshire, in 1795, and a *Sun* saw the light of day in Pittsfield, Massachusetts, around 1800.

The first New York *Sun* was established in 1833, not to be confused with the fiercely political daily of right-wing persuasion that was started in 2002. The original *Sun* somehow survived an 1835 hoax in which it printed an article purporting that people and animals had been found living on the moon. The paper was taken over in 1868 by the noted editor Charles A. Dana and became noted for its pithy style. Eugene Field, an admirer of Dana, wrote a tribute to him, which ended: "You'll need no epitaph but this: 'Here sleeps the man who run / That best 'nd brightest paper, the Noo York Sun.'"

A *Sun* city editor, John B. Bogart, coined one of the most famous newspaper adages of all time: "When a dog bites a man, that is not news; but when a man bites a dog, that is news." In 1897 the *Sun* also originated the famous Christmas essay, "Yes, Virginia, There Is a Santa Claus." The morning edition of the *Sun* ceased to shine when it was acquired by the *Herald* in 1920. The evening edition merged with the *World-Telegram* in 1950, and the new paper became known as the *World-Telegram & Sun* until 1966.

One of London's popular tabloids is the *Sun,* and Ottawa, Toronto, Vancouver, Calgary, and Winnipeg all have their own, and of course *Le Soleil* is in Quebec. In Australia, Sydney has the *Sun-Herald,* Melbourne reverses the order with the *Herald Sun,* and Brisbane basks in a plain old *Sun.*

The Baltimore *Sun,* founded in 1837, is one of the leading U.S. *Sun*s and has as its motto "Light for All." H. L. Mencken and Ernest Hemingway both wrote for the Baltimore *Sun,* although probably not in collaboration.

Other major *Sun* newspapers can be found in Chicago *(Sun-Times)* and are spread across the Sun Belt from San Bernardino, California; to Las Vegas, Nevada; to Fort Lauderdale, Florida *(Sun-Sentinel).*

Aurora

Before it can shine, the sun also rises, and the moment that it does so is known as dawn. The Greek goddess of dawn is Eos, and her Roman counterpart is Aurora, most often pictured rising from the ocean in a chariot with her rosy fingers dripping with dew.

These early-rising ladies symbolize not only first light, but also the beginning of a new enterprise, and that was the reason *Aurora* was chosen by Benjamin Franklin Bache as the name of his cantankerous Philadelphia daily paper, founded in 1790 at the dawn of the new American Republic. Bache, who inherited his printing equipment, his acerbic tongue, and his shrewd commercial instincts from the famous grandfather for whom he was named, called his paper the *Aurora General Ad-*

vertiser. Its logo was the emblem of a rising sun and its motto, in Latin, *Surgo ut prosim* ("I rise that I might serve"). The *Aurora's* idea of serving was taking potshots at presidents George Washington and John Adams, the Federalist Party, and the Congress. Bache delighted in reporting on congressional infighting, which sometimes culminated in spitting and fisticuffs, and on such steamy subjects as Alexander Hamilton's adulterous affair with a convicted swindler's wife. Bache's journalistic archenemy was William Cobbett, who published a paper called *Porcupine's Gazette,* in which he labeled the *Aurora* a "vehicle of lies and sedition" and Bache himself an "infamous scoundrel."

Canada's Labrador City *Aurora,* one of the few newspapers anywhere still to bear that name, commemorates not the dawn but the aurora borealis. Also known as the northern lights, this is a spectacular electromagnetic phenomenon that produces a vivid display of colors in the sky and is believed to be caused by high-speed electrons and protons emanating from the sun, which are drawn magnetically to the earth's polar regions, then collide with air molecules to produce luminosity. Boreas was the Greek god of the north wind. According to *Aurora* editor Michelle Murphy, Labrador City provides an excellent view of the aurora borealis.

The English-language newspaper that greets the sunrise in Karachi, Pakistan, does not deal in Greek or Latin names. Called simply *Dawn,* it was established in 1947 at the same time the nation gained its independence. The same company, however, does publish a marketing magazine that is known as *Aurora.*

Comet and *Meteor*

Comet and *meteor* are words that refer to celestial illumination—and are also associated with swift movement—but despite these assets, for some reason they have not become widely used for newspaper titles. In the case of the *meteor* (from the Greek *meteôron,* "something high in the air") also known as a shooting star, with the larger ones called fireballs, perhaps its lack of popularity derives from the fact that even though it generates much heat and light and enters the earth's atmosphere at high velocity, it usually dissipates itself in hot air before reaching the ground. But comets (Greek *komētes,* "long-haired," because comets often have long tails), have luminosity, speed, and permanence. Some comets are even periodicals, coming again and again, just as a newspaper would like to do. There's a *Comet* in Thibodeaux, Louisiana, others in Hertfordshire and Surrey, England, and there's a *Meteor* in Madisonville, Texas—and that's about it.

Globe

Globe, from the Latin *globus* ("round body") was in use by the sixteenth century to refer to a spherical planet, and more specifically the Earth. The Globe Theatre, built in 1599, in which Shakespeare was a partner, had a painted sign depicting Hercules supporting the Earth. When Prospero in *The Tempest* refers to the "great globe itself," Shakespeare primarily had in mind the Earth, but also the rounded shape of the theater. While not a source of light in itself, Earth, like all planets, reflects the light of the sun. The connotation of *Globe* as a newspaper title includes both the light it reflects and the all-encompassing geographical extent of the Earth.

There was a newspaper called the *Globe* in London by 1803; in Washington, D.C., in 1830; in Toronto by 1844; in San Francisco in 1858. The Boston *Globe,* which remains that city's leading newspaper, was established in 1872. The Toronto *Globe & Mail* is one of Canada's most respected newspapers. St. Louis, Missouri, for many years was noted for the *Globe-Democrat,* but that paper ceased publishing in 1986.

The Joplin (Missouri) *Globe,* founded in 1896, takes a stab at the meaning of its name in its mission statement: "The *Globe*'s mission remains the same—to be an essential part of people's lives by providing valuable information on what's happening in their world."

World

The meaning of *world* is a little further removed from the concept of light. Etymologically it comes from the Germanic words *wer* ("man") and *ald* ("age"), so that in a strict sense it means the "age" or "life of man," or in other words "human existence in its earthly state." In this Old English sense, it has been used in this way since at least the ninth century. But in a broader sense, *world* is taken to mean not only the earth, but the heavens, and the universe—indeed, the whole of creation.

There was a weekly publication called the *World* in London in 1753, that title appearing next to a woodcut of a man looking at a globe representing Earth. Its colophon indicated that it was sold, appropriately enough, at an establishment known as the Globe in Pater-Noster Row.

There was a newspaper called the *World* in Calcutta, India, in 1797, and, alluding to the emergent nations of the Western Hemisphere, a *New World* in Philadelphia, also in 1797. In 1827 the *World* was created in London and in 1840 in Dublin. In 1843 the *News of the World* was established in London as a Sunday paper of the lurid persuasion and still is to this day. The largest American dailies with the name are the Omaha (Nebraska) *World-Herald* and the Tulsa (Oklahoma) *World.*

The New York *World* was founded in 1860 and acquired in 1882 by newspaper tycoon Joseph Pulitzer. It capitalized on its name with many circulation-building stunts, the most famous of which was a voyage around the world in 1889 by newswoman "Nellie Bly," racing against the record of Jules Verne's hero Phileas Fogg in *Around the World in Eighty Days.* Traveling by ships, trains, rickshaws, sampans, horses, and donkeys, Bly (the pen name of Elizabeth Cochran) made it in 72 days, 6 hours, 11 minutes, and 14 seconds.

Planet

Inasmuch as the celestial bodies *Star, Sun, Globe,* and *World* are all commonly used newspaper names, you might wonder why more *Planet*s have not been appropriated from the solar system. Good question. The *Daily Planet,* of course, is well-known, but primarily as a fictional newspaper in the fictional city of Metropolis, where Clark Kent, alias Superman, is a reporter.

Since 1972 a real newspaper called the *Planet* has been published in the real city of Metropolis, Illinois. When the Illinois legislature, for reasons that only a Chamber of Commerce could appreciate, declared Metropolis the "official hometown" of Superman, the Metropolis *News* obligingly became the *Planet.* Since then at least two other honest-to-goodness *Daily Planet*s have appeared: one in Telluride, Colorado, and one in Berkeley, California.

Other real newspapers named the *Planet* appeared in London from 1837 to 1844 and again from 1907 to 1911; in Richmond, Virginia, from

1883 until 1996; in Birmingham, England, in the 1960s; and in Sutton and Epsom, England, in the 1980s. In 1996 the *Planet on Sunday* was published in England for only one issue. There are still weekly *Planet*s in Newburyport and Wenham, Massachusetts; Honolulu, Hawaii; and Tampa, Florida.

Orrery

Not content with one globe, world, or planet, there was briefly a newspaper in Boston that incorporated the whole solar system. From October 1794 until October 1796, the *Federal Orrery* was published by Robert Treat Paine (Jr.), a poet, lawyer, and theater buff, and son of a signer of the Declaration of Independence. Paine named his paper for a device that had been commissioned earlier in the eighteenth century by the Earl of Orrery, whose name was then affixed to it. It was a model composed of globes representing the sun, the moon, the earth, and all the known planets, arranged in approximate scale to each other and mechanically animated to make orbital movements.

In 1767 David Rittenhouse, the Philadelphia clockmaker who succeeded Benjamin Franklin as president of the American Philosophical Society, made an orrery that became widely known. The American radical Thomas Paine refers to an orrery in *The Age of Reason,* written in 1794–1795, and appends a note to describe it thus: "It is a machinery in clockwork representing the universe in miniature: and in which the revolution of the earth round itself and round the sun, the revolution of the moon round the earth, the revolution of the planets round the sun, their relative distances from the sun, as the center of the whole system, their relative distances from each other, and their different magnitudes, are represented as they really exist in what we call the heavens."

Ironically, the *Federal Orrery*'s founder was also named Thomas Paine at the time he edited the paper, but in 1801 he changed his name to that of his father in order to have a "Christian" name and not to be confused with his more famous namesake, the radical patriot, essayist, and Deist. Some historical accounts still make that confusion between the two Tom Paines.

Beacon

Man-made light sources also provide newspapers with images of illumination for their names. *Beacon* is probably the most popular. The word's origin is Old High German *bouhhan* and Middle English *bekene* ("signal"). It came to have the meaning of giving light, especially as a warning or as guidance, as in a lighthouse.

The *American Beacon and Commercial Diary* appeared in Norfolk, Virginia, in 1815, and a *Beacon* was published in Edinburgh in 1821 and in London in 1822. The name has continued in use for numerous papers in England, the United States, Canada, New Zealand, and Barbados. The name is frequently used in seaport communities, and nothing is more natural than the *Beacon*s of Mobile, Alabama; Palacios, Texas; Boca Grande, Florida; Santa Barbara, California; and Warwick, Rhode Island. But the best-known paper using the title is probably inland Akron, Ohio's *Beacon Journal.*

Pharos

One type of beacon is a *pharos,* another word for lighthouse, named for the island of Pharos, off Alexandria, Egypt, where King Ptolemy II ordered a lighthouse constructed in 280 BC. It turned out to be one of the Seven Wonders of the Ancient World, which was regrettably destroyed in the fourteenth century. There was a Macedonian *Pharos* (in Greek) in the 1880s, and today Logansport, Indiana, gets its daily news in the *Pharos-Tribune.*

Headlight, Searchlight, and Spotlight

Other light-oriented newspapers are in Bainbridge, Georgia *(Post-Searchlight);* Redding, California *(Record Searchlight);* Scappoose, Oregon *(Spotlight);* and Deming, New Mexico, a mining community, where the *Headlight,* dating back to the 1880s, is so named for the lamp affixed to a miner's hat.

Flare

It may be written with great flair, but the name of a weekly in Hobbs, New Mexico, is the *Flare,* a nineteenth-century word of unknown origin, that means a "sudden outburst of light." It appeared in 1948, was a daily paper for a few years in the 1950s, then returned to weekly status. It was founded by Agnes Kastner Head, after a dispute with the established Hobbs *News-Sun,* which would not run ads for her husband's candidacy for mayor. Mrs. Head said to heck with that and started a rival paper, naming it for a Phillips Petroleum gas flare that, emulating the star of Bethlehem, had guided her to Hobbs several years earlier. And oh yes, her husband was elected. Today there is a community center in Hobbs named for Agnes Head, who served in 1969 as a delegate to the state constitutional convention and died at age eighty-eight in 1992—but the former mayor seems forgotten. The *Flare* was bought in 1996 by its old nemesis, the *News-Sun.*

Mirror and Reflector

Reflected light represented by a *mirror* is widely used for newspaper names, perhaps alluding to Hamlet's advice to the Players, in which he describes the purpose of the theater: "to hold, as 'twere, the mirror up to nature; to show virtue her own feature, scorn her own image, and the very age and body of the time his form and pressure." Come to think of it, that might do very nicely as the mission of a newspaper. *Mirror* comes to English from the French *miroir* ("looking-glass") and ultimately from the Latin *mirare* ("to wonder"). But one of its early meanings, probably the one newspaper owners had in mind, was "something that gives a true representation, or in which the truth may be seen," like the omniscient looking glass of the haughty queen in the Grimm tale of "Snow White," who asked: "Mirror, mirror on the wall / Who's the fairest of them all?"

In 1779, Edinburgh had a paper called the *Mirror,* and in 1798 London had one called the *Mirror of the Times.* There was also a *Mirror* in London by 1804; in Waterford, Ireland, by 1808; and in Hartford, Connecticut, in 1809.

When drawings and then printed photographs became practical, *Mirror* came into its own as a graphic name to indicate that the news would be not only reported but illustrated. In 1904 the *Daily Mirror* in London became the first newspaper exclusively illustrated by photographs. In 1910, it had its first royal photo scoop with a picture of King Edward VII lying in state (after his death, of course).

Today's London *Mirror* is a mass-circulation tabloid that once sold seven million copies in a single day, a feat it accomplished by a policy of enormous headlines on such major news stories as those on a recent page 1: MADONNA HORSE FALL HORROR and HOW I LOST FIVE STONE, the "exclusive" account of Jack Osbourne (Ozzy's son). (For American readers: a "stone" is a unit of weight equivalent to fourteen pounds.) That is presumably how one holds, as 'twere, the *Mirror* up to nature in this day and age.

New York also had a tabloid *Daily Mirror* at one time, whose management estimated its editorial content was 10 percent news and 90 percent entertainment, but evidently it was not entertaining enough, and it succumbed in 1963. Today more sedate and perhaps even more entertaining, *Mirror*s can be found in the United States in such places as Gilmer, Texas; Arapahoe, Nebraska; Tonganoxie, Kansas; and Sooke, British Columbia.

Akin to a *Mirror* is a *Reflector,* and newspapers of that name are in Battle Ground, Washington; Norwalk, Ohio; and Greenville, North Carolina.

10

"Advertisements—the Life of a Paper"

Benjamin Franklin received a letter in 1767 from his friend and sometime publishing partner James Parker, who was lamenting over the travails he was experiencing in the newspaper business. Parker complained, "I get but few Advertisements yet, which are the Life of a Paper." There really was no need to explain this fundamental publishing principle to Franklin; he had begun his profitable career with the Pennsylvania *Gazette* in 1728, and by midcentury it was always loaded with ads. The first page of the issue of January 2, 1750, for example, is virtually all advertising for such goods as blankets, rugs, petticoats, breeches, cloaks, writing paper, handkerchiefs, garters, gloves, snuffboxes, inkpots, knives, forks, wineglasses, cinnabar, cochineal, clove oil, olive oil, almond oil, licorice, cordials, elixirs, balsamic tinctures, opium, cubebs, female pills, pencils, anchovies, capers, lemons, rum, molasses, coffee, cocoa, pepper, nutmeg, lace, necklaces, passenger tickets to London—and, as one advertisement put it with cavalier ennui, "a great many other things too tedious to mention."

Franklin called this paper the *Gazette,* but given its contents, he might as well have called it the *Advertiser,* a name that was becoming increasingly popular in the eighteenth century. The expression of political views may have been the prime reason for the establishment of the earliest newspapers, but then, as now, making money was always high on the list of publishers' motivations. During the late seventeenth and early eighteenth centuries, newspapers became less political and more commercial. Among the first papers in London to run paid advertisements was the *City Mercury,* whose aim was to help restore businesses in the wake of the Great Fire of 1665. No journal could have sounded more business-friendly than the twice-weekly publication that boosted the London economy in 1713 under the title *British Merchant, or Commerce Preserv'd*. Other newspapers followed suit in devoting space to advertising, with names that included the straightforward *Advertiser,* and also, as time went on, *Enterprise, Commercial, Exchange,* and even such blatant badges of brazen ballyhoo as *Bonanza, Budget, Budgeteer, Cash-Book, Drummer, Pennysaver,* and *Trader.*

Advertiser

Typical of this new breed of merchandising vehicles was the *Daily Advertiser,* which lasted in London from 1730 to 1807. It offered advertising space for books, medicines, physicians, houses, and various other goods and services, along with a moderate quantity of political, commercial, and social news.

From around 1700 in Germany, there had been newspapers with primarily commercial purposes published under the name *Anzeiger,* the German word for *Advertiser.* The word came into English from the French *avertir,* or sometimes *advertir,* meaning "to give notice to." Another of its meanings, which would be of less appeal to the advertisers themselves, was "to warn." Its Latin root, *advertere,* means "to turn to." An *advertiser* can refer either to the business paying someone to help it hawk its wares—or to the medium that does the hawking, in this case a newspaper. It wasn't long before a number of English and Irish newspapers found the word *Advertiser* in the title was useful to remind businessmen of the old adage:

> The codfish lays ten thousand eggs,
> The homely hen lays one;
> The codfish never cackles
> To tell you what she's done.
> And so we shun the codfish,
> While the lowly hen we prize,
> Which only goes to show you that
> It pays to advertise.

The Dublin *Daily Advertiser* was published in 1736, followed by the Sherborne (Dorset) *Mercury and Weekly Advertiser* in 1737, and the Belfast *News-Letter and General Advertiser* in 1738. By the 1760s the

Public Advertiser was the most popular newspaper in London, with daily circulation in the tens of thousands.

In the New World, the concept of selling advertising in newspapers was immediately popular, and the Pennsylvania *Journal and Weekly Advertiser* was established in 1742 by William Bradford III, grandson of William Bradford I, a printer who, with William Rittenhouse, founded the first paper mill in America, in Philadelphia in 1690.

Bradford's *Advertiser* was followed in 1748 in Boston by the *Independent Advertiser,* which was the organ of a political club founded by Samuel Adams at the age of twenty-six, almost thirty years before he organized the Boston Tea Party to protest the British tea tax. Adams, who was also working in his family's brewery while editing the newspaper, published it only for a year—but you can still buy beer with his name on the bottle (although you should discreetly overlook the fact that this particular Samuel Adams brand has only been around since 1985).

More *Advertiser*s followed in both England and the Americas, including the Bath *Advertiser* in 1755; the New London (Connecticut) *Summary, or the Weekly Advertiser* in 1758; the Pennsylvania *Evening Post and Daily Advertiser,* the first daily newspaper in the New World, printed in 1783 in Philadelphia; the New York *Daily Advertiser* in 1785; the *General Advertiser* published by Benjamin Franklin Bache (Franklin's grandson) in Philadelphia in 1790; and the Boston *Daily Advertiser,* founded in 1813.

In 1784 the Pennsylvania *Packet & Advertiser* devoted more than 60 percent of its space to advertising. After 1800 advertising accounted for 90 percent of some papers. The word *Advertiser* was in the titles of five of the eight American daily papers in 1790, in twenty of twenty-four in 1800, and in twenty-one of forty-two in 1820, according to Paul Starr in *The Creation of the Media: Political Origins of Modern Communication.*

During the early years of the nineteenth century, the most prosperous New York papers were the *Commercial Advertiser,* the *Mercantile Advertiser,* and the *Daily Advertiser,* according to journalism historian Frank Luther Mott. Mott says, "The word 'Advertiser' was no misnomer in these titles, for mercantile papers sometimes appeared with nearly all of their space given to commercial announcements. Dull as these newspapers now seem to the general reader, they led the field in circulation through much of this period."

In Australia, the Sydney *Gazette and New South Wales Advertiser* was published as early as 1803, and in 1840 the New Zealand *Advertiser* was added to the list.

Nowadays, of course, virtually every newspaper is an "advertiser," whether or not its name indicates that fact, since paid advertising is how newspapers derive most of their revenue. The word *Advertiser* is still the third most frequent newspaper name in Great Britain, where it can be found in Buxton, Cardigan, Guildford, Harrowgate, Maidenhead, Norfolk, Suffolk, Essex, Perth, Rugby, and St. Albans, among many others—but it is seen less often in Canada and the United States, where the largest papers of that name are in Montgomery, Alabama, and Honolulu, Hawaii. The Montgomery paper was founded in 1829 as the *Planters' Gazette.* The Honolulu *Advertiser* was founded (as the *Pacific Commercial Advertiser*) in 1856 by Henry Whitney, whose parents were missionaries. The main news story in the first issue was the wedding of King Kamehameha IV, but true to its name, most of the front page was devoted to advertisements—fifty-two in all.

Enterprise

From the French *entre* ("between") and *prendre* ("to take"), an *enterprise* in English is an "undertaking, especially a project that requires activity, courage, and energy, or a bold, arduous, momentous or hazardous attempt"—just as most business ventures demand, right? *Enterprise* seems to be more apt as a name for papers in the New World; the United States and Canada have the lion's share.

The earliest newspaper of that name listed by the British Library is the Saginaw (Michigan) *Weekly Enterprise* in 1858. In the same year in the mining boomtown of Virginia City, Nevada, the *Territorial Enterprise* was founded. It gave Samuel L. Clemens (before he became known as Mark Twain) his first job as a newspaper reporter. He worked at the *Enterprise* from 1862 to 1864, writing humorous sketches and local news stories.

By 1861 the Kansas City (Missouri) *Enterprise* was being published, followed by the Manchester (Michigan) *Enterprise* in 1867; the Gore Bay (Ontario) *Enterprise* in 1877; the Beaumont (Texas) *Enterprise* in 1880; and the West Berlin (New Jersey) *Enterprise* in 1892. There are many more today, mostly in midsized American towns and cities, the largest in circulation being the Riverside (California) *Press-Enterprise.*

Commercial

Commercial comes from the Latin *com-* ("with" or "pertaining to") and *mercis* ("commodities, or merchandise") and it means "occupied with or pertaining to trade or business activity." It was used as a noun in the nineteenth century meaning "a traveling salesman," and in the twentieth century, it became a common term for a paid announcement on radio and later television.

Noah Webster was the founder and editor in 1793 of a daily New York newspaper known as the *American Minerva,* in honor of the Roman goddess of wisdom. Webster, already well known for the publication of his "blue-backed" speller, a grammar, and a reader, gave up the editorship in 1797. The paper almost immediately changed to a double-barreled mercantile name, the *Commercial Advertiser*—apparently shifting its primary interest from wisdom to business. The *Commercial Advertiser* endured for more than a century, and Webster himself not quite that long, although he did have time to edit and publish the first comprehensive American dictionary in 1806, with an expanded version in 1828, and a new translation of the Bible in 1833.

The *Wall Street Journal* of its day, the *Commercial Bulletin* was a newspaper in Boston, Massachusetts, beginning in 1865, specializing in post–Civil War news as it affected business interests. There was also a New Orleans *Commercial Bulletin* during this period, with a variety of news items, not only those that dealt with business but also world news under the heading "By Telegraph" and local news called "City Intelligence." The Pittsburgh *Commercial*—with the word used as a noun— was published from 1863 to 1873, and the Cincinnati *Commercial* also flourished during this period.

The most famous newspaper today with *Commercial* in its name is the distinguished Pulitzer Prize–winning Memphis (Tennessee) *Commercial Appeal,* which has a colorful history. One of its ancestors, the Memphis *Weekly Appeal* (later the *Daily Appeal*) was founded April 21, 1841, by Henry Van Pelt, a supporter of Martin Van Buren, who had lost the presidency of the United States to William Henry Harrison. Van Pelt believed that the Harrison camp had run a dirty campaign, and his newspaper was founded as an "appeal" to the "sober second thought of the people—never wrong and always efficient," which became the motto of the *Appeal.* The paper's politics were Democratic and strongly secessionist.

In 1858, an even more vigorous and extreme Democratic paper was founded called the *Avalanche.* When Union troops occupied Memphis in 1861, the plucky *Appeal* staff boarded the last train south, crating up its presses and taking them to a series of other cities in order to continue publishing; the name of the *Avalanche* was suppressed, along with its policies, and it continued to be published in Memphis as the duller-sounding *Unionist Bulletin* until after the Civil War.

In 1889 the Memphis *Commercial*—again standing alone, with nothing to modify—was founded by a group of well-heeled Memphians to provide support for a candidate who had the misfortune to lack any other newspapers in his camp. The corporate name of the publisher was the Memphis Commercial Publishing Company, and so the paper was called the *Commercial.* In 1890, the *Commercial* bought the *Appeal-Avalanche,* the latter two papers having merged the previous year. Thus was born the *Commercial Appeal,* restoring its name's adjectival function; the name *Avalanche* was deemed superfluous (or perhaps just too inflammatory) and generously consigned to the use of other cities in the United States (for more on this, see Chapter 14).

There are *Commercial*s doing business today in Pine Bluff, Arkansas; Danville, Illinois *(Commercial-News);* Vincennes, Indiana *(Sun-Commercial);* Leesburg, Florida; South Windsor, Connecticut *(Commercial Record);* and Cleveland, Mississippi.

Exchange

Exchange—which originally meant a place where merchants, brokers, and bankers meet to do business—is not a widespread name for a newspaper, but there are a couple. One of them, in Scotland County, North Carolina, the Laurinburg *Exchange,* takes its name so seriously that it charges $1.75 for one day's admission to its Web site. Hoot mon!

Bonanza

Spanish for "good weather" from the Latin *bonus* ("good"), *bonanza* was first used in American English in 1844 to mean "an especially rich lode of gold or silver ore," and then, by extension, any kind of "prosperity, profitability or abundance." It also has a phonemic affinity with the Italian *abbondanza* ("abundance"). The North Lake Tahoe (California) *Bonanza* has been helping merchants become prosperous and make life more abundant for its readers since 1970.

Budget and *Budgeteer*

The French word *bougette* ("leather bag, or wallet") comes from the Latin *bulgus,* a Gaulish word meaning a "bulge or pouch." Now, of course, the word means a statement of estimated expenses and revenues, for a government, a business, a household, or an individual. It is also used by editorial workers to mean the amount of space to be devoted to news versus advertising in an edition of the newspaper.

In Douglas, Wyoming, the *Budget* has been the weekly newspaper since 1886. It was established as *Bill Barlow's Budget* by a journalist, Wyoming state legislator, and Douglas mayor whose real name was Morris (or sometimes Merris) C. Barrow and his wife, Minnie. Barrow had once worked for the Laramie *Boomerang.* Starting in 1904, Barrow included in the *Budget* a monthly supplement called *Sagebrush Philosophy,* whose front cover carried the carpe diem motto "Live, Laugh and Love—There'll Come a Time When You Can't."

The town of Douglas, incidentally, is also the home of Douglas Herrick (for whom the town was not named—that was U.S. senator Stephen A. Douglas), who created the "jackalope," a mythical animal that is a cross between a jackrabbit and an antelope. Although it doesn't really exist, President Ronald Reagan somehow had the stuffed head of one mounted on the wall of his ranch house.

In Duluth, Minnesota, there is a paper called the *Budgeteer-News* (a *budgeteer* is "one who makes a budget"), and in this case the name probably refers to the reader to whose budgetary needs the paper's advertising is directed.

Cash-Book

A *cashbook* is just what it sounds like: a bound volume in which all monetary expenses and receipts are written. When the Missouri *Cash-Book* was established as a newspaper in 1871, it could not have stated more bluntly that it was a mercantile tool as much as a source of information. Greg Dullum, a member of the paper's current staff, provided an explanation of the name, drawn from William H. Taft's book *Show-Me Journalists: The First 200 Years.* Taft quotes a no-nonsense memo by the *Cash-Book*'s first editor, Walter C. Malone:

> Our selection of a name was made for two reasons. First, a stand-ing advertisement of the principle on which we intend to conduct our business. Experience has taught us that there is but one name given under Heaven whereby a newspaper can be made to pay and that is CASH. The other reason is its originality or oddity. We have world's doings recorded in numerous Day-Books transferred to countless Ledgers with the requisite number of Indexes. But until now, no "Cash-Book" to indicate by its balances that there is a com-munity sufficiently intelligent and willing to support its newspapers as it does the merchants, mechanics, lawyers, doctors, and others with CASH. Therefore, we (and you) make the Cash-Book.

After a couple of mergers, the most recent in 1977, the paper is now the Jackson *Cash-Book Journal,* a name that would warm the iciest cockles of an accountant's heart.

Drummer

The *Drummer* is an unabashed tub-thumping huckster, an adjunct of the Wright County *Journal-Press* in Buffalo, Minnesota. Circulation fig-ures suggest that the tail wags the dog: the *Drummer* distributes 50,000 (free) copies each week, while the actual newspaper that provides the news items that are served up sparingly with the *Drummer*'s ads has 5,850 (paid) subscribers. The *Drummer*'s logo is a colorfully uniformed bass drummer, but don't let that festive refugee from a marching band fool you—a *drummer* is also a vendor who goes about the countryside figuratively (at one time literally) beating a drum to attract a crowd for products to be sold, or, in other words, a traveling salesman (or, of course, saleswoman).

Pennysaver

A newspaper that would be dear to the heart of that old founding fa-ther, aphorist, and unabashed salesman, Benjamin Franklin, is the *Pen-*

nysaver. After all, that's a penny earned. The name *Pennysaver* is borne by newspapers—or to put it more accurately, shopping flyers salted lightly with news items—all over upstate New York, and in other places, too. It would not be surprising had Franklin been the founder of a paper with this name, although the lineage for its usage seems to date back only to the 1940s, when merchants decided that instead of individually mailing sales letters to customers, they could save a penny (or maybe even two) by combining them into one publication. They presumably meant to imply that the readers could also save a pretty penny. One of these papers, the *Pennysaver & News,* is in Le Roy, New York, a town doubly distinguished as the home of Jell-O and of the stringless bean.

Other New York *Pennysavers* are in Skaneateles, Manlius, Seneca Falls, Marathon, Moravia, Clinton, Owego, and Hamilton. They do get around and can also be perused in West Volusia, Florida; Racine, Wisconsin; and Dickinson, North Dakota.

Trader

Trade, from the Old High German word spelled the same way, originally meant "track or course," and hence, "a pursuit, or a business," and hence, "the exchange of commodities either in barter or for cash." A *trader* thus is a person who engages in that activity, and the newspapers of that name encourage the activity by devoting themselves primarily to advertising space. Apart from the many publications devoted to specific commodities (automobiles, cycles, fish), there have been newspapers bearing the name since the mid-nineteenth century. There was a Mississippi *Free Trader* in 1858, and a *Scottish Trader* in Glasgow in 1898. London had a newspaper curiously known as the *Amateur Trader,* subtitled "A General Advertising Medium," from 1896 to 1916 (when perhaps it turned pro).

Today, although *Traders* are mostly shopping supplements to regular full-service newspapers, you will find publications of that name in Fayetteville, North Carolina; Westchester County, New York *(Patent Trader);* Torrington, Connecticut *(Foothills Trader);* Chestertown, Maryland *(Tidewater Trader);* and Warragul, West Gippsland, Australia.

11

Flora and Fauna

Relatively few kinds of plant life have appeared on newspaper nameplates. The journals do not seem to have found suitable titles in the rose,
the daisy, the oak, the elm, the yellow squash, or even the Edenic Tree of
Knowledge. Among the few examples of flora to be found are the *Acantha, Leaves* of various species, and the *Pine Cone.* By contrast, the animal kingdom is generously represented by a wide range of creatures,
from tiny insects to galumphing mammals, including *Beaver, Bee, Wasp,
Mosquito, Cricket, Beetle, Coyote, Eagle, Grizzly, Hippo, Rhino, Pacer* (a
type of horse), *Porcupine,* and *Roadrunner*—although it must be admit-
ted that neither the *Cricket* nor the *Beetle,* whose name pops up on a paper known as the *Beetle and Wedge,* actually refers to any kind of animal.

Acantha

An *acantha* (the Greek word for "thorn") is a spine or prickly fin, of
the kind found in abundance, for example, on the acanthus plant. The
Acantha in Choteau, Montana, is a weekly newspaper founded in 1893
in Dupuyer, Montana, and it prides itself on being prickly. As the publisher explains, the original owners founded the newspaper to act as a
thorn in the side of those who wanted the county seat of the new Teton
County to be in Choteau, thirty miles south of Dupuyer. Naturally, the
newspaper favored Dupuyer and campaigned relentlessly for it. Despite
the editorial writers' best efforts—or, who knows, perhaps because of
them—Choteau was chosen. Realizing that if you can't lick 'em, it
might be the better part of valor to join 'em, the paper departed Dupuy-

er and set up shop as the Choteau *Acantha,* taking gleeful delight in remaining thorny in its coverage of county officials ever since.

Leaf and *Leaves*

Leaf, a word that comes directly to us from the Anglo-Saxon *lēaf,* and before that, from a Sanskrit word, *lumpati,* meaning "the stripping or peeling off of something," at its simplest means "an outgrowth from the stem of a plant." Adam and Eve relied on the fig leaf, Canada venerates the maple leaf, and Clarksville, Tennessee's daily *Leaf-Chronicle* memorializes a product that in the nineteenth century made Clarksville the world's leading market for dark-fired, high-nicotine tobacco. The paper resulted from the 1890 merger of the Clarksville *Chronicle,* purportedly Tennessee's oldest newspaper, founded in 1808, and the Clarksville *Tobacco Leaf.*

Other newspapers commemorate leaves of which the surgeon general is more likely to approve, such as the Elm Grove (Wisconsin) *Elm Leaves;* the Oak Park (Illinois) *Oak Leaves;* and the River Forest (Illinois) *Forest Leaves.*

Pine Cone

Above a beautiful Pacific Coast beach, the town of Carmel-by-the-Sea, California, is nestled in a pine forest. Hence, its newspaper, founded in 1915, is called the Carmel *Pine Cone.* In 1986, fed up with red tape over building codes and zoning laws, Clint Eastwood ran for mayor of Carmel and was elected with 72 percent of the vote. He served one two-year term. Carmel has no parking meters, street addresses, or door-to-door mail delivery. It does have forty wineries and Doris Day.

Longville, Minnesota, is also situated in the midst of pine forests, and while it does not boast of movie stars among its citizenry, it does have a weekly newspaper called the *Pine Cone Press-Citizen,* not to mention weekly turtle races during the summer.

A *pinecone* is defined as a "mass of ovule-bearing scales, also known as a *carpellate strobile.*" Now wouldn't that make a dandy name for a newspaper?

Beaver

Beavers are North American rodents that can grow as large as a hundred pounds and live as long as ten years. The name *beaver* comes from the Sanskrit word *babhru,* meaning brown, which is the usual color of the critters. They are noted for building dams in streams, in order to surround their homes with protective moats. Valued for their fur, they are widely regarded as pests because of damage caused by flooding cultivated lands, gnawing trees, and burrowing underground. Nonetheless, despite this major nuisance factor—or maybe because of it—*Beaver* has been chosen as the mascot for the Oakville, Ontario, hockey team and as the name of the community's triweekly newspaper.

Bee

Although *Bee* at first may seem an odd name for a newspaper, it has been popular from at least the eighteenth century, and when you stop to think about it, it's easy to understand why. From the Anglo-Saxon word *bēo,* a *bee* is an insect with many characteristics that most newspapers would be elated to have. Even though there are more than twenty thousand species of bees, we are most familiar with the honeybee and the bumblebee, which are splendid role models for journalists. First, a bee generates lots of "buzz"—always busy, moving constantly from one place to another, just as the avid reporter is constantly on the move covering a news beat. In the course of the bee's activity, it engages in cross-pollination, which is vital to much plant life—just as the spreading of news items is vital to a free society. Many kinds of bees are also known to be great communicators, able to convey sophisticated information to each other. And, of course, some bees make honey, which could be compared to a newspaper's entertainment sections, or maybe to its advertising profits. Perhaps most telling of all, bees sting—and most newspapers like to think they have the same needling ability when hard-hitting editorials are called for.

New London, Connecticut, had a *Bee* in the late 1790s, founded by supporters of Thomas Jefferson. The *Bee* attacked the "stand-up" law of 1801, which called for standing up or showing hands to vote, a practice that intimidated pro-Jefferson Democratic Republicans who might wish to vote against the Federalists, who were in power. The Federalists, however, had an antidote for this *Bee*'s sting and jailed its editor for violating the Sedition Act.

L'Abeille de Nouvelle Orleans (the New Orleans *Bee*) was a noteworthy newspaper that lasted from 1827 to 1925. At first only in French, it published an English edition until 1872, when competition from other English-language papers in New Orleans caused it to revert exclusively to French again. The *Bee* briefly also had a Spanish edition, *La Abeja.*

In 1857 James McClatchy founded the Sacramento *Bee,* the first in what was to become a chain of California *Bee*s, with others in Fresno and Modesto. In a 1991 Sacramento *Bee* article, the name was explained by quoting an editorial that ran in the paper's first issue: "The name of The *Bee* has been adopted as being different from that of any other paper in the state and as also being emblematic of the industry which is to prevail in its every department."

In other words, McClatchy promised a paper that would be as busy as a bee. In 1943, the paper's management commissioned Walt Disney himself to create a logo for the paper. Disney's creation still appears on all three *Bee*s' nameplates—a perky black-and-gold bug named "Scoopy," with huge eyes that are suspiciously like those of Donald Duck. The papers also urge their readers to *"Bee* informed."

England has been slower to jump on the *Bee* bandwagon. In Lincolnshire, there was a Stamford *Bee* in 1830, and London had a *Bee Hive* in 1872. But most of the *Bee*s have been American, such as the Omaha (Nebraska) *Bee* in 1871 and the Amherst (New York) *Bee,* founded in 1879 and now part of a colony of suburban New York *Bee*s in Cheektowaga, Depew, West Seneca, Lancaster, Clarence, East Aurora, Orchard Park, and Kenmore-Tonawanda.

A number of *Bee*s buzz in California, including the Soledad *Bee,* the Brisbane *Bee-Democrat* (who knew that bees had political affiliations?), and the Lake County *Record-Bee.* Others include the New Berlin (Illinois) *Bee;* the Newtown (Connecticut) *Bee;* the *News-Bee* in Morristown, New Jersey; the *Register & Bee* in Danville, Virginia; the Bonner County *Daily Bee* in Idaho; and the Summit County *Bee* in Utah, whose official state symbol just happens to be a beehive (commemorating the industriousness of the Mormons who founded the state).

In the Texas town of Beeville there is a newspaper, founded in 1884 as the *Bee,* which has nothing to do with the insect. Like the town itself, it commemorates Barnard E. Bee, who between 1836 and 1841 was a very busy Bee—successively secretary of the treasury, secretary of state, secretary of war, and an ambassador for the fledgling Republic of Texas. The Beeville paper is now known as the *Bee-Picayune.*

In Arkansas there is a town named in 1897 for a Dutch coffee merchant, Jan de Geoijen, whose name no one could either spell or pronounce, so the residents just gave up and called the town De Queen. In the town there is a newspaper founded in 1897 and still published as a weekly whose *raison de nom* is neither the insect nor a public figure; its only excuse is an atrocious but inevitable pun—De Queen *Bee.*

Wasp, Mosquito, Cricket, and Beetle

In the insect world, at least a couple of others have flitted their way into newspaper names. Around 1800, Harry Crosswell in Hudson, New York, published a journal of vituperative political commentary called the *Wasp.* And there's a paper called the *Mosquito,* in Carlisle, Massachusetts, an area known for an abundance of the bloodsucking insects. It is unlikely that the *Mosquito* will become quite so popular on nameplates as the more useful *Bee.*

The *Cricket* in Manchester-by-the-Sea, Massachusetts, which began publication in 1888, has nothing to do with an insect of any kind. Founded in 1629, the village was originally known as Jeffrey's Creek, and a resident was known as a "Creekite"—a word that devolved into "Cricket." Hence, the newspaper's name. As Australian pundit Eric Shackle points out in one of his informative online essays, Manchester-by-the-Sea had an even earlier newspaper with a pseudo-insect name, the *Beetle & Wedge,* whose name actually includes no living creature at all, but refers to a device used for splitting logs.

Coyote

The Murdo (Wyoming) *Coyote,* a weekly newspaper, was established in 1904 by William Williamson, a lawyer who later became a judge and six-term Republican congressman. Kelcy Nash, who is now the editor, is unsure of why Williamson chose that name but suggests it was probably because the area around Murdo teemed with the critters (coyotes, not congressmen). Nash points out that the local high school teams are also nicknamed the Coyotes, which you must admit is a better name for a football team than, say, the Gazettes (or even the Gazelles, for that matter).

A *coyote,* from the Nahuatl *coyotl,* is a species of wolf *(Canis latrans),* also known as the prairie wolf, which abounds on the western plains of North America. A coyote can run thirty-five miles per hour and will eat almost anything—now that does sound like a football player—but prefers a nice juicy small to mid-sized mammal or fowl, a trait that makes it a menace to sheep ranchers and chicken farmers. Despite bounties placed on them, resulting in thousands being killed each year, the coyote population has increased, so that there are even more of them today than there are readers of the *Coyote.*

Eagle

The watchful eagle is the most apt bird for the name of a newspaper, and it has stood the test of time. In the seventeenth century there were papers named *Dove, Kite, Screech-Owl,* and *Vulture,* but the *Flying Eagle* of 1652 is the name that had staying power, even if the paper itself did not. A Puritan journal that railed against the celebration of Christmas, it was not successful, and after only five issues, it folded its wings with the hope that it would swoop back in the future with "more heavenly intelligence."

The eagle was the emblem of the Ptolemies of Egypt and of the armies of Rome and of Napoléon, so when in 1782 it was chosen as the symbol of the United States of America—over the objections of Benjamin Franklin, who favored the turkey—it spawned a series of American newspapers who wished to personify not only the sharp-eyed ferocity of the bird itself, but also the patriotism that it represented.

Among them was the Brooklyn *Daily Eagle,* founded in 1841. In its first issue, it pledged to be "vigilantly zealous for equal rights both great and small, particular and general," and, further, to "contend for everything that is right" and "submit to nothing that is wrong." The poet Walt Whitman became its editor in 1846 and was fired two years later; he then headed for New Orleans, Louisiana, where he worked on a paper called the *Crescent*. The Brooklyn *Eagle* was published continually for 114 years, closed in 1955, but now has been revived and operates as a community paper.

Elsewhere *Eagle*s still soar in Wichita, Kansas; Cheyenne, Wyoming *(Tribune-Eagle);* Bryan–College Station, Texas; and Reading, Pennsylvania.

Grizzly

Since 1941 the weekly Big Bear *Grizzly* has been the only newspaper in Big Bear Valley, California. The paper is almost a daily, since it also publishes the Big Bear *Shopper* each Thursday and the *Grizzly Weekender* (haven't we all had weekends like that?) on Saturday. The grizzly (the animal, not the newspaper) is a large and powerful bear *(Ursus horribilis)*. Though their fur is mainly yellowish brown, some of these bears have silvery tips on their fur, which makes them *grizzly* (from the French *gris,* or "gray"). Occasionally an encounter with a grizzly may turn out to be *grisly,* but let's not go there.

Hippo and Rhino

"New Hampshire's largest weekly newspaper" is the superlative claim of the *Hippo,* which publishes editions in Manchester and Nashua. "We chose the name," says publisher Jody Reese, "because it sets us apart from traditional community newspapers. We wanted to be able to define ourselves as something new and different from what people expected from a weekly newspaper. I think it has worked wonderfully." The publishers apparently confined their choice of names to zoo animals, and Reese speculates about an alternative name: "Why *Hippo* and not *Rhino*? Well, *Hippo* is easier to spell and evokes positive feelings."

Rhinos must exude less negativism in the South, or maybe the spelling skills are simply superior in North Carolina, where the *Rhino Times* can be found weekly in Charlotte and Greensboro. The *Rhino Times* doesn't claim to be the largest anything, but its nameplate does carry a picture of a fierce-looking rhinoceros and promises "All the Rumors Fit to Print."

For what it may be worth, *hippopotamus* derives from two Greek words that mean "river horse." The hippo is a cousin of the hog, enjoys wallowing in the water and, reminiscent of the panda in a best-selling book, eats shoots and leaves. The *rhinoceros* also has a Greek name, from *rhinos* ("nose") + *keras* ("horn") and is also herbivorous, but unlike the hippo, the rhino has a horn (or sometimes two) on his nose. It should be noted that despite the etymology of their names, neither animal is ordinarily found in Greece, Africa being the more likely habitat, and, in the case of the rhino, India, Malaysia, and Sumatra as well.

Pacer

The Savage *Pacer* in Minnesota might suggest an especially ill-tempered father-to-be in a hospital waiting room, or perhaps a department store floorwalker with a chip on his shoulder. The real origin of the name is actually much more interesting than either of those bogus scenarios.

A *pacer* in this sense is a horse that runs in a gait in which the legs move in lateral pairs, with the horse being supported alternately by its right and left legs. The most famous pacer in harness-racing history was Dan Patch, a sports superstar in the early twentieth century whose name was better known than that of Michael Jordan or Tiger Woods today. Dan Patch was the first horse ever to run a mile in less than two minutes. His best official time was 1:55.25, set in Lexington, Kentucky, in 1905. But he shaved a quarter-second off that record on September 8, 1906, in an unofficial race at the Minnesota State Fairgrounds—a mark that stood until it was tied in 1938 by a horse named Billy Direct and surpassed in 1960 by Adios Butler, at 1:54.3.

Dan Patch was trained in a stable owned by Marion Willis Savage in Hamilton, Minnesota. Both Savage and Dan Patch fell ill on the same day, July 4, 1916, and died shortly afterward within a day of each other. In the horse owner's honor, the town of Hamilton changed its name to Savage, and in 1994, when a weekly newspaper was established in Savage, it was called the *Pacer,* in memory of Dan Patch.

Porcupine

William Cobbett was an Englishman who came to Philadelphia in 1793 and began to write virulently anti-American pamphlets, which he signed with the pseudonym "Peter Porcupine." A porcupine, from the Latin *porcus* ("pig") + *spina* ("spine"), as we all know, is a rodent (described by *Webster's New International Dictionary* as "large, or rather large") with sharp, stiff spines mixed in with its hair—sort of like Clay Aiken of *American Idol*. Cobbett likened himself to this creature, not because he thought of himself as a large or rather large rodent, but because he regarded his views as prickly, like its spines. He founded a newspaper in 1797 called *Porcupine's Gazette and United States Advertiser,* which was prickly indeed. In one issue it complained that the purging-and-bleeding methods used by Dr. Benjamin Rush in treating yellow fever "have contributed to the depopulation of the earth." Rush sued Mr. Porcupine and won a judgment of five thousand dollars, the equivalent of about seventy-five thousand dollars today. Cobbett had to borrow and beg from friends to come up with the money and soon left for England.

In London in 1800 Cobbett started another newspaper, which he named simply the *Porcupine.* It lasted only a few issues. Cobbett himself, however, lasted much longer and went on to publish the *Political Register,* which included the text of speeches made in Parliament, and to serve a two-year jail sentence for more of his prickly "treasonous libel." In 1812 financial trouble forced him to sell the *Register* to its printer, a man named Thomas Hansard, who wasted no time in putting his own name on what remains to this day the definitive source of who said what in the House of Commons, now known as *Hansard's Parliamentary Debates.*

The indefatigable Cobbett returned to America with the idea of digging up the remains of patriot Tom Paine in New York City and bringing them to England for reburial in Paine's native soil. The remains, which by this time consisted only of a bag of moldy bones, were somehow lost when Cobbett arrived at Liverpool in 1819.

Liverpool, by odd coincidence, was the site of another *Porcupine,* founded in 1860 by Hugh Shimmin, a bookbinder whose obituary in the pages of his newspaper in 1879 likened him to Cobbett in his "fearless denunciation of what he believed to be rotten and wrong in social and political affairs." The obituary made no mention of Tom Paine's bones.

Any newspaper named for a prickly rodent is likely to be edited by someone of similar disposition—and that was also true of the Los Angeles *Porcupine,* founded in 1877 by Horace Bell. Bell had come to California in 1852 and was a gold miner, a lawyer, a Union officer in the

Civil War, a vigilante ranger who pursued Mexican bandits, and the editor of a newspaper in which he wrote of his daring feats.

The *Porcupine,* which railed against injustices in the Los Angeles barrios, lasted until 1899. Bell, who practiced law into his eighties, collected many of his *Porcupine* articles into a book called *Reminiscences of a Ranger.* Before his death, in 1918, he wrote to his children: "Someday Los Angeles will be a great city. I will not live to see it, but you will . . . and it will extend from the mountains to the sea." Not to mention to Anaheim and Disneyland.

Roadrunner

"Beep! Beep!" That's how moviegoers of a certain age remember the Warner Brothers Looney Tunes cartoon character known as Road Runner, the eternal nemesis of Wile E. Coyote, created in 1949 by Chuck Jones. The real-life roadrunner *(Geococcyx californianus)* is a bird in the cuckoo family, largely earthbound, which got its common name for running at great speed (actually only about fifteen miles per hour, which may be fast for a bird, but is no match for a Harley-Davidson or even for a coyote).

The *Valley Roadrunner,* in Valley Center, California, began publishing in 1974, and as editor David Ross tells it, was named thanks to a seemingly irrelevant suggestion: "The original owner, Van Quackenbush, was tossing about for a name to give it, and considered the usual suspects, such as *Chronicle* or *Times.* However, his father, who owned a canning factory, saw something around in his factory that made him suggest the *Roadrunner.*"

Well, it's fortunate that the elder Mr. Quackenbush didn't see cockroaches or rats in his cannery.

12

Myth-ellaneous

For the naming of constellations, NASA missions, and General Motors cars, the Greeks (mythological ones, of course) have frequently had a word for it. The same is true for newspapers. While one of the earliest widely used names, *Mercury,* drew its inspiration from the Romanized name for the Greek messenger god, Hermes, other papers have gone straight to the characters and symbols of Greek myth, including *Aegis, Argus, Atlas, Echo, Palladium, Phoenix,* and *Zephyr* (and *Breeze*).

Aegis

Aegis is a Greek word of uncertain origin that was the name of a symbol ascribed to the god Zeus, and later to Athena, having significance as a long-life charm. It may have been related to the word *aigos,* or "goat," and was described by Homer as a shaggy ornament with golden tassels. It was also depicted as a hairy breastplate surrounded by serpents and topped with the terrifying head of a Gorgon. Why, you may ask, is there a newspaper in Bel Air, Maryland, named for a hairy, snake-infested breastplate? The paper was founded in 1856 as the *Southern Aegis and Harford County Intelligencer,* simplified in 1905 to the *Aegis.*

The answer is that the word *aegis* came to mean "a shield or protection." The publishers of the *Aegis* said that the paper was intended to protect the interests of the residents of the county. Recently some thought was given to adopting the plainer name of the *Shield,* but in view of the name's antiquity and uniqueness, the publishers decided to stick with *Aegis.*

In Barron, Wisconsin, the *News-Shield* has been protecting readers since 1876—although, one assumes, not *from* the news, as its name might suggest.

Argus

Argus was a monster in human form with a hundred eyes, some of which were always wide awake. With so many eyes to go around, Argus was chosen by Zeus's wife (and sister), Hera, to guard Io, a priestess whom she had jealously changed into a cow and who needed watching. That's why *argus* means "one who is always watchful and vigilant"—although you might not think so when you know the end of the story: Hermes put all of Argus's eyes to sleep by telling tedious stories, and then killed him, or perhaps merely bored him to death—who knows? Hera then took his eyes and used them to decorate the peacock's tail. Poor Io, without someone to watch over her, was tormented by a gadfly all the way to Egypt.

Undeterred by Argus's checkered reputation as a vigilant guardian, Thomas Greenleaf founded the New York *Argus* in 1795, and another *Argus* sprang up in Albany in 1813. The *Argus of Western America* was established in Frankfort, Kentucky, in 1816. There are or have been *Arguses*, mostly with their eyes wide open, in Bradford and Brighton, England; Newport, South Wales; Dundalk, Ireland; Guyra and Wagin, Australia; Denver, Colorado; Memphis, Tennessee; Carlsbad, New Mexico; and Portland, Oregon.

An argus is also a type of Asian pheasant *(Argusianus argus),* and the Sioux Falls (South Dakota) *Argus-Leader* is in an area noted for an abundance of pheasants, which also happen to be the state bird. Tempting though it is to make a connection between bird and newspaper, the South Dakota pheasant, alas, is not an argus, but the Eurasian ring-necked pheasant *(Phasianus colchicus).* The *Argus* was established in 1881, the *Leader* in 1883, and the two merged in 1887.

Atlas

Atlas, which pops up now and again as a newspaper title, derives from a Greek mythological explanation of how the world is suspended. Atlas was a god in charge of the pillars that supported the earth; later he was demoted to a mere Titan and given the less desirable chore of holding the earth on his head and hands—and you know what a drag that can be. Hence the word came to mean the bearer of a great burden. In the sixteenth century the geographer Gerhard Mercator published a collection of maps which had an image of Atlas holding the earth on its cover; thereafter the word was also used to mean any collection of maps.

As a newspaper title, *Atlas* denotes the means by which the world is brought to its readers. In 1826 a London newspaper appeared with the title of the *Atlas: For India, China, and the Colonies.* In 1844 a weekly journal in Sydney, Australia, bore the name *Atlas,* and from 1856 to 1865 Albany, New York, had a *Daily Atlas and Argus.* At least one paper with that ancient name has survived since 1846: the Monmouth (Illinois) *Daily Review Atlas.*

Echo

Echo is a Greek word (*echos,* "sound") that in English means "the repetition of a sound caused by the reflection of sound waves." In Greek mythology, Echo was the personification of this phenomenon, a nymph who had a really rough time in life. First, she ran afoul of Zeus's wife Hera, who put a curse on her so that she could say no words except by repeating what she heard others say. If this wasn't problem enough, the poor thing fell in love with the self-absorbed Narcissus, who was so uninterested in her, or in anything but himself, that Echo pined away until nothing was left of her but her voice. It's hard to understand why the word *echo*—either as an image of something parroted from another source, or as a hapless disembodied forest sprite—would make a suitable name for a newspaper, but there were and are dozens, if not hundreds, of them.

The name can be explained for some newspapers established in tandem with another, like the Liverpool *Echo,* which in 1879 was a cheaper evening companion to the morning Liverpool *Daily Post,* whose news items it rehashed. Other *Echo*es, however, have stood alone. Among the first was the *Echo or Edinburgh Weekly Journal* in 1729. The *Echo* of London came along in 1868, and many more followed. In 1884 came the first issue of the South Wales *Echo,* which calls itself the "voice of South Wales."

You will find an *Echo* resounding in dozens of other cities, including Basildon, Bournemouth, Brighouse, Darlington, Dorset, Essex, Exeter, Gloucester, Lincoln, Northampton, Southampton, and Sunderland in England; Airdrie, Amherstburg, Haliburton, Invermere, and Pincer Creek in Canada; Dublin, Enniscorthy, Gorey, and New Ross in Ireland; Byron Bay, Kununura, and Lismore in Australia; Alexandria and Ely, Minnesota; Fairfield, Ohio; Leavenworth, Washington; Naples, Florida; and several other cities in the United States.

Palladium

Another Greek mythological source of newspaper names, although not a very frequent one, is *Palladium.* There was a New England *Palladium* in the 1790s and a Nebraska *Palladium* in the 1850s, and today you'll find a *Herald-Palladium* in St. Joseph, Michigan, and a *Palladium-Item* in Richmond, Indiana.

The word means "safeguard or protection." Like the Argus, however, the Palladium has its drawbacks as a symbol of a reliable defender of the people. The Palladium was a statue of the goddess Pallas Athena and was reputed to provide protection for the city of Troy as long as it stood in place. During the Trojan War, Ulysses and Diomed removed the statue, and Troy was defeated.

Phoenix

The *phoenix* is a crimson-and-gold bird in ancient Egyptian myth that lives for several hundred years, then destroys itself in a fire made of cinnamon twigs, only to rise again from its own ashes, youthful and refreshed—the original "extreme makeover." The word *phoenix* has a circuitous etymological route into English. The Egyptians called this fabulous bird a *benu* and associated it with the sun god Ra, investing the bird with the symbolism of the rising sun: resurrection and rebirth into future life after death.

The Greeks heard about the *benu,* and naturally they wanted one, too. As words have a way of doing, it got twisted in translation and also conflated with the Greek word *phoinix,* which meant "purplish crimson," the bird's color. (The same root word spawned *Phoenicia,* which is what the

Greeks called Canaan, because it was famous for producing a purple dye.) When the Romans took over the word, they spelled it *phoenix,* and it also became a Christian symbol of resurrection. In use in England by the ninth century, it was sometimes anglicized into *phenix* or *fenix,* but the older spelling has remained standard. The word also came to mean anything of "unique or singular excellence, a paragon."

In that sense it was a popular eighteenth-century title for newspapers, including the Liverpool *Phoenix or Ferguson's Weekly Gazette* by 1794. There was a London *Phoenix* in 1808, and the first American Indian newspaper, the *Cherokee Phoenix,* was founded in New Echota, Georgia, in 1826. The Bristol (Rhode Island) *Phoenix* was founded in 1837 and is still going strong, not yet having found it necessary to immolate itself. Muskogee, Oklahoma's *Phoenix* was started in 1888, and the Saskatoon, Saskatchewan *Phoenix,* founded in 1902, is now the *Star-Phoenix.* There is also a *Phoenix* in Phoenixville, Pennsylvania—but not in Phoenix, Arizona, where it would probably be a *Phoenix* too frequent.

Zephyr and *Breeze*

Zephyr comes from the Latin *zephyrus* and before that from the Greek *zephyros,* and it originally meant the "west wind," or sometimes the "god of the west wind." Etymologists think it's probably akin to the Greek *zophos,* which meant the "dark side," which would be the west, of course, since that's where the sun sets.

Nowadays a zephyr can be any kind of gentle breeze, no matter what direction it comes from, and the newspapers that use it for their names in Galesburg, Illinois, and Moab, Utah, both seem to have their tongues in their cheeks. (Maybe they're trying to whistle in the wind.) Neither of them appears to be a "gentle breeze" of a newspaper; both are alternative news sources to the regular dailies, Galesburg on a weekly basis, Moab on a more leisurely, but nonetheless agitated, bimonthly schedule.

The Galesburg *Zephyr* calls itself "the world's first public access newspaper," by which it apparently means that anybody can submit a news story or opinion article. As the *Zephyr* points out with alacrity, however, that doesn't mean it will necessarily be published.

Moab's *Canyon Country Zephyr* seems even crankier about what news items it will print, with a motto that claims it has been "hopelessly clinging to the past since 1989." Its principal editorial anathema is tourism, the source of undesirable recreational development in the Moab area, about which it promises "all the news that causes fits."

If *Zephyrs* are reputedly gentle, *Breezes* are a different matter. The word has nothing to do with Greek mythology; it comes from the French *bise,* later *brise,* and it means a "cold, dry wind from the north or the east." That's what it was intended to mean, at any rate. People now toss around the word *breeze* even more freely than *zephyr,* and it doesn't really matter which way the wind is blowing, or how hard.

But at least the *Daily Breeze* in Torrance, California, and another in Cape Coral, Florida, come by their names honestly. After all, both cities are virtually on the beach, albeit on opposite coasts.

The Torrance *Breeze* was founded in 1894 by a druggist named "Doc" (aren't they all?) Barkley, who is reputed to have said, with questionable lyricism but unassailable logic: "I'm going to start a newspaper tomorrow and call it the *Breeze,* because the breeze always blows here." At first the *Breeze* blew only for Redondo Beach, but then, like any self-respecting gust of wind, it gathered strength and spread itself farther to other Pacific Ocean beach communities.

Breezes in Cape Coral actually blow, not from an ocean, but from the euphonious Caloosahatchee River, although the Gulf of Mexico is just a seashell's throw away.

13

The Wheel and Other Inventions

As one of the great human inventions, the wheel is among the most historic, ranking right up there with the airplane, the computer, the television, and the Xbox. For reasons that in some cases you might not expect, a number of newspapers have adopted the names of various human-made devices, although, inexplicably, no one has yet published a paper called the *Electric Blanket*. Among names related to inventions and mechanical processes are the *Anvil, Boomerang, Brand, Camera, Derrick, Dial, Flume, Hot Blast, Hub, Locomotive, Pendulum, Phonograph, Reaper, Rocket, Shuttle, Tomahawk,* and, of course, *Wheel.*

Anvil

The Hondo (Texas) *Anvil Herald,* a weekly newspaper since 1886, owes its origins to one of those frequent disputes about a county seat. The towns of Castroville and Hondo City vied to be the seat of Medina County, and Castroville won the election. Castroville supporters staged a celebration featuring the firing of anvils, a pastime (that for some unimaginable reason seemed amusing) in which anvils are blown into the air by charges of gunpowder. The newspaper was founded just after the election and was named the Castroville *Anvil* as a weird kind of homage to that explosive event.

Six years later, there was another election, and this time Hondo City became county seat. In 1903 the owner of the Castroville *Anvil* bought the Hondo *Herald* and merged the two papers as the Hondo *Anvil Herald.*

Incidentally, it must have been quite a feat to launch those anvils, which are typically a hundred or more pounds in weight. The word comes from the Old English *anfilt,* probably related to the Latin *pellere* and Swedish *filta,* "to strike," and now means a forged iron block used by smiths, farriers, and other craftsmen as a base on which to pound metal into shape.

Boomerang

You might expect to find a newspaper named the *Boomerang* in Australia, if you found one anywhere. The word is an English modification of a word in the Dharuk language of the original inhabitants of New South Wales, and it means "a throwing stick." It is primarily a club with a sharp edge that can be thrown to make unusual arcs, attacking its target from a different direction than the one from which it is thrown. Some boomerangs return to their starting points, and these are regarded as toys; the weapon or "war boomerang" does not return (or if it does, you're in serious trouble).

The newspaper in Laramie, Wyoming, called the *Daily Boomerang,* is not known to return to its starting point when tossed by a carrier. Instead its name was a tribute to a mule owned by the paper's founder, American humorist Bill Nye (not the "science guy," another guy). Nye's mule was named Boomerang because the loyal creature followed him everywhere he went, and although he would chase it away, it always returned like a boomerang. We are indebted also to Nye for assuring us that "Wagner's music is better than it sounds."

Brand

For a town of only about fifteen thousand people, Hereford, Texas, is famous for a good many things. It's known as "the town without a toothache," owing to the natural occurrence of fluoride in its drinking water; it's also called the "Windmill City," since that healthful water is pumped out of the ground by a collection of more than four hundred windmills; it's the home of the National Cowgirl Hall of Fame and Western Heritage Center; and it has what is billed as the largest all-girl rodeo in the United States (and probably the world). For reasons difficult to explain, it once aspired to be known as the "Athens of the Panhandle." Named for the breed of white-faced English cattle that were imported there in large numbers in the 1890s, Hereford had a newspaper, founded in 1901, with the sensible name of the Hereford *Reporter.* Some while later, the Hereford penchant for coining clever sobriquets must have overpowered the publisher, and he changed the name to the *Brand*—a word that comes from the Old Norse *brinna* ("to burn") and refers to the infernal device that burns a mark of ownership into the hides of those white-faced cows for which the town was named.

Camera

The *Daily Camera* in Boulder, Colorado, got its unusual name from Frederick P. Johnson and Bert Ball, who founded it as a weekly in 1890. The title reflected their goal to publish more illustrations than any other newspaper. A similarly named paper, the Ile *Camera,* has been a weekly in Grosse Ile, Michigan, since 1945. *Camera* is a Latin word that means "chamber," and its usage for a picture-taking device came about from the invention of the *camera obscura,* a darkened chamber with an aperture through which light projects an image of external objects. And, as they say, the *Camera* never lies.

Derrick, Gusher, and Producer

Derrick began its life as a word in the early seventeenth century, thanks to Thomas Derrick, who around the year 1600 was the industrious hangman at Tyburn, the site of executions in London since the twelfth century. Derrick became famous for the diligent pursuit of his profession: more than three thousand people—from saintly martyrs to common criminals—were given the opportunity to meet their maker through his efforts. Aiming to increase his productivity, Derrick devised a contraption from which twenty-three of his unfortunate clients could be hanged simultaneously. It was such a handy device that shipbuilders began to use it to hoist their vessels, and referred to it as a *derrick,* which must have made old Tom as proud as a royal peacock. By the eighteenth century, *derrick* was commonly used to refer to any kind of crane to support something heavy.

With the advent of the oil industry beginning in 1859 in Pennsylvania, the word was used to mean the framework over an oil well used to support drilling equipment. Oil-field terminology, and not *derrick*'s original macabre meaning, explains the newspaper founded in 1871 in Oil City, Pennsylvania, and called the *Derrick*. Its files are a rich source of information about the early days of the oil industry and were used extensively by Ida Tarbell, who in 1904 invented investigative journalism with her muckraking magazine series "The History of the Standard Oil Company," in which she endeavored to show that the business practices of tycoon John D. Rockefeller Sr. constituted inverse proof of the maxim that "nice guys finish last."

The petroleum industry has created other newspaper names. In 1912, Oklahoma experienced the first of several oil booms, and the town of Drumright sprang up overnight near two cattle ranches where oil was discovered. A newspaper was founded in March 1913 and, following Oil City's precedent, called itself the Drumright *Derrick*. When the *Derrick* lost its identity after being acquired in the 1970s by a publisher in another city, Drumright felt the need of a new newspaper, and in 1989 the Drumright *Gusher* erupted on the scene. A *gusher*, as you will know if you remember James Dean ecstatically dripping with gooey slime in the movie *Giant*, is an oil well with attitude—resulting in a very large natural flow. The word comes from the Middle English *guschen*, meaning, as you might expect, "to flow spoutingly."

Less ostentatious quantities of black gold are expressed by the title of the newspaper in Seminole, Oklahoma, which was founded during the oil boom of the 1920s. The Greater Seminole field was among several that gave the United States an oil surplus in the mid-1920s. Seminole became a boomtown, noted for its remarkable profusion of "producers," that is, wells that yielded commercial quantities of oil. Karen Anson, managing editor of the Seminole *Producer*, reports that her newspaper was named to commemorate these lucrative oil sources. After all, who'd read a paper called the *Dry Hole*?

Dial

It is well known that on September 14, 1898, in Room 19 of the Central Hotel in Boscobel, Wisconsin, two traveling salesmen got the idea of putting a Bible in every hotel room in the world, thereby initiating the

Gideon Society. What is not so well known is why Boscobel's weekly newspaper, founded in the 1870s, is called the *Dial*. In fact, that's the "great mystery of Boscobel," according to editor David Krier.

The name of the town itself is also a great mystery; the Wisconsin Historical Society provides six explanations, the best and least probable of which is that an early settler belled his cow with a particularly mellifluous ding-dong, known as "Boe's cow bell." (The original Boscobel is a historic house in Shropshire, England, probably derived from French or Italian for "beautiful woods.")

Although *Dial* is an unusual name for a newspaper today, there have been a good many previous *Dial*s, including the *Southern Dial* in Montgomery, Alabama, from as early as 1858; the St. Albans *Dial,* in the same year, in England; the *Dial* in London in 1860; the Clerkenwell *Dial and Finsbury Advertiser,* 1862; and a newspaper that didn't want to exclude anyone from its readership, the ecumenically named *Dial: A Journal for Everybody,* in Portsmouth, England, in 1880.

From the Latin *dies* ("day"), *dial*'s earliest meaning was "an instrument used to tell the hour of the day by means of the sun's shadow on a graduated surface"; that is, a sundial. Etymologically, the name *Dial* is related to *Journal*. Some of the nineteenth-century *Dial*s, possibly the one in Boscobel, were named in homage to the famed Transcendentalist religious and literary magazine founded by Ralph Waldo Emerson and Margaret Fuller. In its first issue, May 4, 1840, it explained its name: "The DIAL, as its title indicates, will endeavor to occupy a station on which the light may fall; which is open to the rising sun; and from which it may correctly report the progress of the hour and the day."

Flume

The Fairplay *Flume* (and try to say that three times fast) is a weekly in Fairplay, Colorado. The town was founded in 1859 by gold miners who wanted everyone to have an equal chance at staking a claim; hence "Fairplay." The *Flume* also had its origin in mining. A *flume* (Latin *fluere,* "to flow") is an inclined artificial channel through which water flows · from a distance for power, irrigation, or transport purposes, and it is used in gold mining for the movement of ore.

The *Flume*'s editor, Robin Kepple, explains: "We understand the

Flume acquired its name due to the vast amount of mining in Fairplay and Park County. In Fairplay's case, a flume was used to channel rocks, minerals and tailings from one place to another in the endless pursuit of gold. Some folks believe the name *Flume* was selected because the newspaper helps 'channel' information."

Hot Blast

The town of Anniston, Alabama, was created as a model-city of the "New South" in 1873, built upon the growing importance of Alabama's iron mills. The Woodstock Iron Company installed a forty-ton blast furnace, which gave Anniston its raison d'être. In 1883 Woodstock's chief and Anniston's founder, Samuel Noble, decided the town needed a newspaper, and he turned to the Atlanta *Constitution*'s managing editor, Henry Grady, for advice. Grady had become nationally known for promoting the industrialization of the "New South" and was the prime mover in positioning Atlanta ahead of its Georgia rivals, Augusta, Macon, Savannah, and Athens. Inspired by the blast furnaces of the Anniston iron foundries that sent sparks flying skyward, Grady felt that the editorials of a newspaper should explode with good ideas in the same way, sending their own sparks into the community. He suggested the new paper be called the *Hot Blast.*

In 1887 it became a daily, and in 1900 it merged with the newly established Anniston *Star.* For a while it continued to be known as the *Hot Blast,* then the *Star and Hot Blast,* and eventually just the *Star.* Perhaps the management feared readers might confuse the *Hot Blast* with hot air.

Hub

Hub is an impenetrably mysterious word, whose origins are uncertain. Dictionaries will only hint enigmatically that it may be related to the earlier *hob,* the "raised part of a fireplace," but they are at a loss explain why by 1649 it meant "the central part of a wheel from which the spokes radiate," and in 1858 it was metaphorically used by Oliver Wendell Holmes to refer to "a center of important activity." At any rate, in 1888 the Kearney, Nebraska, newspaper was dubbed the *Hub,* and its publishers have been more than satisfied with the name ever since. Says the *Hub*'s Web site: "The word is short and strong, conjuring many positive images. By definition, it means being at the center of things, exactly where a good newspaper and its website belong." The wagon wheel hub, it is suggested, also symbolizes the journey of pioneers who passed through Kearney on their way to settle the West, and the term relates to Kearney's view of itself as a center of commerce, education, and health care for Nebraska.

Locomotive

The *Locomotive* has been the weekly newspaper of the Nebraska village of Lawrence (population about three hundred) since the 1880s. In those days, reports publisher Allen Ostdiek, six or seven daily trains powered by steam locomotives came through the town. Lawrence was situated on two railroad branch lines, the Burlington & Missouri and the Missouri Pacific, so *Locomotive* was an apt name for the paper. The railroads lasted until late into the twentieth century—one track was pulled up one hundred years to the day it was laid—but no trains stop at Lawrence now. Still, the *Locomotive* chugs on. Do you suppose Chattanooga ever had a paper called the *Choo-Choo*?

Pendulum

The pendulum-regulated clock, which made possible a minute hand and a second hand, and thereby caused timekeeping to be much more accurate, was invented in 1656. East Greenwich, Rhode Island, was incorporated in 1677 and named for Greenwich, England, home of the Royal Observatory. The U.S. Naval Observatory in Washington, D.C., was officially designated in 1854—and that was the same year that William Sherman (another one, not the general who was to march through Georgia) took over a failing newspaper in East Greenwich. The paper was called the Kent County *Atlas and General Advertiser,* but not for long.

Sherman lived in nearby Wickford and was reluctant to move to East Greenwich, so he published his paper in one town one week, and in the other the next. He called it the *Pendulum* because it was on a "swinging schedule," moving from town to town each week. His motto, which might raise eyebrows these days, was "to swing for all." According to current publisher David Dear, Sherman stopped swinging in 1858 and moved to East Greenwich permanently, but the name stuck.

The word is from the Latin *pendulus,* meaning "hanging," and a clock's pendulum regulates the inner workings by moving back and forth, thanks to gravity and momentum.

Phonograph

The Abbotsford (Wisconsin) *Tribune-Phonograph* was established in 1863, but Thomas A. Edison did not invent the phonograph until 1877! What's going on here? Did the Wisconsinites have a time machine that enabled them to peer into the future? Not really. What people today call a *phonograph*—that is, people born before 1980, who remember having one—was a device that Edison patented to record and reproduce sounds through the vibration of a paper-thin metal diaphragm connected to a metal stylus, which cut a groove on a roll or disk of hard wax or soft metal. Voilà, a phonograph record!

There was, however, another kind of phonograph that existed before Edison's invention, in plenty of time to provide a name for the *Tribune-Phonograph.* It also makes more sense as a newspaper title than Edison's record player. From about 1820 the word *phonograph* was used to describe the written symbol for a sound, as opposed to an *ideograph,* the written symbol for an idea. This symbol was later more commonly called a *phonogram.*

Please don't expect an explanation of why the *Tribune-Phonograph*'s logo is a wind-up phonograph of the type that used to be called a Victrola, which didn't appear until after 1900. There is also a *Phonograph-Herald* in St. Paul, Nebraska, which has been using that name since the 1880s.

Reaper

Reap is an Old English word, related to *ripe,* which means "to cut crops with a scythe," or more generally to gather in the harvest. A *reaper* is a person or thing that reaps and refers especially to a mechanical de-

vice patented by Cyrus McCormick in 1834. But when you capitalize
reaper and put *The* in front, you get Death personified.

This is not to suggest that the Richfield (Utah) *Reaper* has anything
to do with the Grim One. The name no doubt stemmed from the agri-
cultural history of the community, situated in fertile soil from which its
name was derived. Actually, it doesn't seem to bother the local populace
that the weekly paper might be mistaken for a memento mori, since the
Reaper has been merrily flourishing since 1888, when it succeeded the
less funereal *Advocate.*

Rocket

A *rocket,* from the Italian *rocchetto,* was originally "a bobbin, spool
or distaff to hold thread to be fed to a spinning wheel." By the seventeenth century, the word was also used to mean a tube (shaped like a
distaff) filled with combustible material, the ignition of which propelled
the tube high in the air, usually bursting aloft and releasing a shower of
sparks, which invariably caused *ooh*s and *aah*s and occasional singed
eyebrows in onlookers. These devices were used for pyrotechnic dis-
plays (as they still are), for signalling, and (as patriots know from singing
about the "rockets' red glare") for explosive weapons.

The Wyalusing (Pennsylvania) *Rocket* was founded in 1887, and it is
said that the name was suggested by a young girl who was impressed by a
fireworks display on American Independence Day. Well, it makes a suitably
patriotic story, anyway. The paper has been owned since 1894 by the family of David Keeler, the current publisher of the *Rocket-Courier,* formed in
1968 by the merger of the *Rocket* and the rival Wyoming County *Courier.*

The weekly *Blowing Rocket* in North Carolina does not actually commemorate an incendiary device. It's really just an extension of the name
of the town in which it is published—Blowing Rock, named for its location on a cliff that creates a strong updraft.

Shuttle

Britain's Kidderminster *Shuttle,* in a Worcestershire town not far from
Birmingham, was first published in 1870, having been named as a trib-

ute to the town's carpet-making industry, which was like cars in Detroit or cheese in Cheddar. In those days thread was fed into the carpet looms for weaving from handheld devices called shuttles. The Severn Valley Railway Authority has recently made plans for a *second* Kidderminster Shuttle—a light-rail connection with the nearby town of Bewdley. So now *Shuttle* readers may also be Shuttle riders.

Tomahawk

The *Tomahawk* in Mountain City, Tennessee, was established in 1874 as the mundane-sounding Taylorsville *Reporter.* Of course, the city sounded mundane, too, and it changed its name the same year as the newspaper, 1885, when Roderick Random Butler persuaded the people that Mountain City was more appropriate for a town at 2,429 feet of elevation. Not one to hold back when it came to renaming, he also convinced the citizens of nearby Smith's Mill to change their town's name to Butler, which happened to be his name, too.

Before the arrival of English settlers, the area had been the hunting ground of Cherokees, Creeks, and Yuchis. *Tomahawk,* a word of Algonquian origin, is an axe used as a weapon. Originally the tomahawk had a wooden shaft with a head of stone or copper, but later iron was used.

With a dandy name like that for the paper, you have to wonder what possessed the new owner in 1915 to change it to the Johnson County *News,* which you must admit is pretty blah. The paper changed hands again in 1956, and the new publisher could hardly wait to change it back to the *Tomahawk.*

Wheel

The origin of the name of the *Western Wheel* in Okotoks, Alberta, brings a spate of speculation from a former owner and from its office manager. Bruce Klippenstein, who was the third owner of the community paper founded in 1976, isn't sure about why it was named, but he has no shortage of suggestions, based on punning with the word *wheel.* Among his ideas: the editor was (or wanted to be thought of as) a "wheel" in the community; the events of life turn around as a wheel turns; the newspaper is the "spokes-person" for the community; and the newspaper covered "wheel people" and "wheel estate." (Groan.)

Fortunately, office manager Sandy Manske was able to elicit the actual origin of the name from a staff member who has been with the paper since its founding. She says that *Western* came from the fact that the original owner was from Ontario in eastern Canada and wanted to be associated with his new home in the west. *Wheel* originates from the fact that the town of Okotoks is in the middle of its surrounding readership area and disseminates the news in all directions, like spokes on a wheel.

14

Location, Location, Location

It doesn't take much deduction to ascertain that the *Oregonian* in Portland, the *Oklahoman* in Oklahoma City, the *Tennesseean* in Nashville, the *Scotsman* in Edinburgh, and the *Australian* in Sydney, to cite just a few in this category, get their names from the places in which they are located. Names like these are so obvious that no further explanation is needed. Other site-specific newspaper titles, however, are derived less directly from their locales, and elucidation of them may be not only necessary, but also possibly amusing or even surprising. Among them you can find such appellations as *Ark, Avalanche, Cake, Centennial, Charter, Coaster, Crag and Canyon, Crescent, Epitaph, Gondolier, Gringo and Greaser, Hillbilly, Ileach, Irrigator, Nugget, Oran, Outpost, Pilot, Pinnacle, Piper, Pirate, Sachem, Vidette, Visitor,* and *Wanderer.*

Ark

The *Ark,* a newspaper in Tiburon, California, has been published weekly since 1973 and was at first housed in an actual ark, which had been moved out of San Francisco Bay onto dry land, says editor Marilyn Kessler. She does not describe the ark in any detail, but we can be reasonably sure that it was not filled with pairs of every beast, bird, and thing that crawls on the ground (well, possibly just a few tiny ones in the unswept corners). A century ago, rich San Franciscans kept boats, which were known as arks, as summer getaways at nearby Tiburon across the bay. These were modified versions, with added superstructures, of nineteenth-century flat-bottomed riverboats that were also known as "broadhorns" and used to carry produce. Tiburon still has an area known as Ark Row made up of a group of these old arks now on dry land.

In addition to this floating type of ark, popularized by Noah, there was also the famous Ark of the Covenant, in which Moses placed the stone tablets containing the Ten Commandments. As Kessler and her co-publisher, Barbara Gnoss, recount, confusion with this biblical ark has caused the paper some difficulties. The newsroom was once visited by a woman purporting to be "Cleopatra, Queen of the Nile," who, because of the Old Testament association of the paper's name, had selected the *Ark* to publish an article she had written containing news that would "shake the world." One reason—perhaps not the only one—that the *Ark* couldn't publish the article was that Cleo had written her revelation in ancient hieroglyphics, difficult for most newspapers to set in type.

Avalanche

An *avalanche,* influenced by the French *avaler* ("to descend") and the Late Latin *labina* ("earth slide"), is a large mass of snow, ice, rock, or earth descending suddenly down a mountain or over a precipice.

The Memphis *Daily Avalanche* was established in 1858 as a strongly prosecessionist newspaper, and its founders undoubtedly thought of it as a powerful natural force casting its weight, like an avalanche, upon the political turmoil prior to the Civil War. It was later absorbed into the rival *Appeal* and finally merged with the *Commercial Appeal.*

The proximity of modest mountains to Crawford County, Michigan, and the Big Bend area of Texas no doubt explain the Crawford County *Avalanche,* founded in 1879, and the Alpine (Texas) *Avalanche,* founded in 1891.

But the name of the Lubbock *Avalanche-Journal,* situated in the flatlands of the Llano Estacado ("staked plain") of Texas, has no such topographical explanation. The newspaper's publisher justifies the name in this way: On the morning of Friday, May 4, 1900, residents of the fledgling Lubbock settlement woke to discover that overnight, the community had become the home of a weekly newspaper, the *Avalanche,* published by John Dillard, a Lubbock lawyer, and Thad Tubbs, a professional gambler. Dillard had shrouded the newspaper in secrecy until its debut, hoping to surprise the readership "suddenly, like an avalanche hits." In 1926 it was sold to a rival paper and became the *Avalanche-Journal.*

Cake

The town of Banbury, in Oxfordshire, England, has been famous since at least 1550 for its "Banbury cakes," oval pastries filled with biscuit crumbs, allspice, eggs, butter, and spiced dried fruit such as currants, raisins, and citrus peels. They are similar to Eccles cakes from Lancashire. The cakes were first made in the thirteenth century with abundant fruits brought by Crusaders returning from the Middle East.

Banbury is also famous for a nursery rhyme beginning "Ride a cock horse to Banbury cross . . . " One version of this rhyme, dating from the eighteenth century, mentions the Banbury cake:

> Ride a cock horse to Banbury cross,
> To see what Tommy can buy,
> A penny white loaf,
> A penny white cake,
> And a two-penny apple pie.

The more famous version of the nursery rhyme omits reference to the cake and goes:

> Ride a cock horse to Banbury cross,
> To see a fine lady upon a white horse,
> Rings on her fingers and bells on her toes,
> She shall have music wherever she goes.

Dictionaries are all a little skittish about explaining what a cock horse is, one venturing that it might be a stallion, that is, a male (cock) horse, or perhaps an especially proud, high-spirited one. Others say it is a child's rocking-horse, or perhaps refers to a position, such as a child riding on an adult's knee, analogous to being on horseback. Another opinion is that "cock horse" refers to two people riding astride the same horse. Still others suggest a "cock horse" is a spare horse kept at the bottom of a hill to assist coaches. Everyone seems to agree that by transference the phrase "on a cock horse" has come to mean "in a jubilant mood."

The Banbury cross was an actual religious symbol erected in 1478 in the market square, where bread (or maybe cake) was distributed to the poor. By 1600 Banbury was, by one contemporary account, "far gone in Puritanism," and the reformers pulled the cross down. Another was erected in 1859, by which time Puritan fervor had considerably diminished, to celebrate the marriage of Queen Victoria's daughter Victoria Adelaide Mary Louisa to Friedrich Wilhelm of Prussia—if, indeed, a marriage that produced the kaiser who led Germany into World War I could be regarded as a cause for religious celebration.

The Banbury *Cake* is a free tabloid newspaper established in 1973 by its parent company, the Oxford *Mail*. Can the Boston *Cream Pie* be far behind?

Centennial

Settlement of South Dakota began in earnest in 1873, the year that the railroad finally reached the territory and rumors of fabulous gold deposits spread. Gold fever led to the establishment of the town of Deadwood, named for dead trees found in the canyon in which the city was built, and home to Calamity Jane, who lived there, and Wild Bill Hickok, who died there in a poker game in 1876, shot in the back while holding what became known as the "dead man's hand"—two black aces, two black eights, and an unspecified fifth card. In 1973, a new newspaper was established in Deadwood, and having a lot of history to commemorate during the last hundred years, it was called the Lawrence County *Centennial*.

Charter

On August 9, 1941, four months before the United States entered World War II, President Franklin D. Roosevelt and Prime Minister Winston Churchill issued a joint document known as the Atlantic Charter. The two world leaders drafted this manifesto aboard the U.S.S. *Augusta,* anchored in Placentia Bay, Newfoundland. *Charter* comes from the Latin *charta* and originally meant "a map," but it came to be used for a written instrument issued by a sovereign power granting rights to the people. The Magna Carta (also spelled Charta) of June 15, 1215, is a well-known example. The Atlantic Charter was regarded as a postwar blueprint, pronouncing that "all of the nations of the world, for realistic as well as spiritual reasons, must come to the abandonment of the use of force." So much for the best-laid plans of mice and men.

Fast-forward to 1997. The lofty goals of the Atlantic Charter may not have been quite realized, but in Placentia, the announcement of the construction of a nickel smelter in the area, with an expected population increase, led to the establishment of a new weekly newspaper. Recalling the historic events of a half-century earlier, its founders called it the *Charter.*

Coaster

Coast and, by extension, *coaster* come from the Latin *costa,* meaning "rib or side." *Coast*'s primary meaning as a noun is now the "side of the land facing the sea," or, in other words, the seashore. A *coaster* can be either "a vessel that coasts," that is, glides through the water along the land, and, through transference of meaning, anything that moves smoothly, or it could be "a person who lives by the seacoast."

The *Coaster* is a weekly newspaper in Asbury Park, New Jersey, a noted seaside resort, known for its association with Bruce Springsteen and for a Cole Porter lyric comparing it—or, more precisely, contrasting it— to Granada. Even though the shoreline city was once the home of a noted roller coaster called the "Galaxy," the fact that the *Coaster* also serves Ocean Township and Neptune pretty well proves that its name is literally littoral.

The Harbour-Breton *Coaster* in Newfoundland is similarly situated, in a deep-sea fishing port at water's edge in an area known as the Coast of Bays.

The case of the Fort Bend *Herald and Texas Coaster* in Rosenberg, Texas, requires further expatiation, since Rosenberg is about fifty miles from the nearest seacoast, that of the Gulf of Mexico. But the Texas "Gulf Coast" is generously defined to include a broad swath of land ranging as far as Houston and beyond. The *Herald and Coaster* was originally two papers, the Rosenberg *Herald* and the Texas *Coaster,* published in nearby Richmond, which obviously thought of itself as a coastal town. They merged in 1958 as the Richmond-Rosenberg *Herald-Coaster,* but in 2005 the paper changed its name once again, to the Fort Bend (County) *Herald and Texas Coaster,* indicating that even though its readers may not be able to dabble their toes in the water, still they are proud denizens of the third coast.

Crag & Canyon

Banff, Alberta, is a city flanked on all sides by the Rocky Mountains. Spectacular scenery spreads in every direction. Complementing this vista is the weekly newspaper called the *Crag & Canyon*. *Crag* is from the Gaelic *creag* ("rugged rock"). *Canyon* is from the Spanish *cañon* ("tube"), which in turn came from the Latin *canna* ("reed"), related to the English word *cane*. A canyon is "a deep valley with high slopes."

Crescent

Appleton, Wisconsin, boasts of having been home to the magician Harry Houdini and the novelist Edna Ferber. Houdini, whose real name was Erik Weisz, moved there from Budapest in 1878, when he was four years old, and left when he was thirteen. Ferber, whose real name was Edna Ferber, moved there in 1897, when she was twelve, and stayed long enough to work as a reporter for the Appleton *Daily Crescent* for three dollars a week, before being fired and moving on to New York, *Show Boat,* the Pulitzer Prize, the Algonquin Round Table, and *Giant.* The *Crescent* had been around since 1853 and was named for a big bend in the Fox River that swept around its office building. It is now the *Post-Crescent.*

New Orleans, which is nicknamed the "Crescent City" owing to a similar bend in the Mississippi River, had a *Daily Crescent* in the nineteenth century for which Mark Twain and Walt Whitman wrote. Defiance, Ohio (the town, not the folk-punk band of that name from Bloomington, Indiana), sits on a crook in the Maumee River and has a newspaper known as the *Crescent-News.*

The word *crescent* comes from the Latin *crescer* ("to increase") and referred initially to the increasing moon's shape. It was later a symbol of the goddess Artemis (Diana), and then of Byzantium, specifically the Turkish Empire and the spread of Islam. Today it can refer to anything crescent-shaped, like the flaky roll the French call a *croissant,* or an artfully curved row of houses in a snazzy subdivision, or all those river bends.

Epitaph

Epitaph is a word of great finality, and we all look forward in happy expectation to the laudatory phraseology that will be inscribed upon the monument beneath which we take our final slumber. Don't we? But surely it's the last name on earth (in every sense) that you would think suitable for a town's newspaper. That is, until you know the town is Tombstone, Arizona—which, come to think of it, is the last name on earth that is suitable for a town.

Tombstone, a silver-mining boomtown, was founded in 1879, and from its earliest days it was known as a dangerous place with more than its share of violent killings. Tombstone was where Wyatt Earp and Doc Holliday took on the McLaurys and the Clantons in the iconic Gunfight at the O.K. Corral. Tombstone, which oxymoronically calls itself "the town too tough to die," is also the home of the legendary cemetery known as Boot Hill.

In 1880 John P. Clum established the *Epitaph,* proclaiming that "No Tombstone is complete without an *Epitaph.*" The word comes from the Greek *epi* ("upon") + *taphos* ("tomb"). Nowadays the *Epitaph* tradition is carried on by students of the University of Arizona Department of Journalism with a semimonthly publication. More timely items can be found in the weekly Tombstone *News,* but no longer in the *Tumbleweed,* which ceased publication in 2006 after eighteen years.

Gondolier

Venice, Florida, "the Shark Tooth Capital of the World," is an archipelago on the Gulf of Mexico whose topography must have put the city's founders in mind of Venetian canals. In fact, it has an architectural review board that ensures that buildings are all designed in northern Italian Renaissance style—a neat trick, one would think, for McDonald's or Taco Bell. Since that other Venice, the one in Italy, is famed for its gondolas—long, flat-bottomed boats propelled through the canals by straw-hatted tenors singing "O Sole Mio"—what else could the newspaper have called itself but the Venice *Gondolier*?

Gringo and Greaser

Offensive both to Anglo-Americans and to Hispanic Mexicans, the name *Gringo and Greaser* was given to a semimonthly newspaper published in 1883–1884 by Charles L. Kusz in Manzano, Mexico, eighty miles from Santa Fe, in what is now the U.S. state of New Mexico.

Gringo is a word used disparagingly by Spanish-speakers in referring to English or Americans. It originated in the eighteenth century in Spain as a corruption of *griego* ("Greek"), with the intention of referring to any kind of stranger who spoke an unintelligible language. The first Mexican usage of *gringo* is recorded in an 1849 journal by J. W. Audubon (John James's son), who complained about being called one. *Greaser* is a pejorative term used by Anglos for a Latino, presumably in reference to dark, oily hair or a diet rich in fats.

Kusz, himself a "gringo," was also the postmaster, a hotelier, rancher, surveyor, and immigration official, as well as being an ornery cuss, who used his newspaper to decry powerful politicians whom he accused of stealing land grants. The paper might have lasted longer if Kusz had been able to—he was shot to death (some say by cattle rustlers who feared exposure in the paper) as he ate supper in his office on March 27, 1884.

Hillbilly

Hillbilly, formed from the words *hill* ("an elevation of land") + *billy* ("a chap or a fellow"), has been used since around 1900 to mean a backwoods person, usually in the mountains of the southern United States. It is more often than not used contemptuously—especially by city slickers—to indicate a person of little education or breeding. But the name is worn proudly by the West Virginia *Hillbilly,* a weekly in Richwood, West Virginia.

Richwood is also known as the "Ramp Capital of the World," a ramp being a wild leek *(Allium tricocum)* that when fried in bacon grease is especially favored by hillbillies in West Virginia. Jim Comstock, late editor of the *Hillbilly,* once printed his newspaper with ink infused with the smell of ramps in order to provide the aroma of home to subscribers who had left Richwood. The Post Office was not charmed.

Ileach

The *Ileach* is an English-language newspaper, although the name is Gaelic, meaning a native of the island of Islay, one of the Inner Hebrides off the western coast of Scotland. *Islay* is pronounced "EYE-lay" and

Ileach is pronounced "EE-lakh." (Be sure to clear your throat on the second syllable.) Besides its newspaper, Islay is noted as the home of seven single-malt Scotch whiskey distilleries: Laphroaig, Ardberg, Lagavulin, Caol Ila, Bunnahabhain, Bruichladdich, and Bowmore. They are best pronounced before sampling.

Irrigator

Newell, South Dakota, sits in an area of 57,068 acres that are irrigated by the Belle Fourche River Dam project, which was initiated in 1905. The system comprises 94 miles of irrigation canals, 450 miles of irrigation laterals, and 232 miles of drains, including 7 miles of closed pipe drains, providing water for land to grow mainly alfalfa and corn. *Irrigation,* from the Latin *ir* ("in") + *rigare* ("to water") means "supplying with water, especially through artificial channels to increase the fertility of land," and it is so important to the arid farmland around Newell that not only is its newspaper called the Butte County *Valley Irrigator,* but the high school mascot is also an Irrigator. Go, Irrigators!

Nugget

The Nome (Alaska) *Nugget* holds no surprises in the origin of its name. In 1900, when it was founded, Nome was filled with gold miners, all of whom were feverishly looking for exactly that—gold *nuggets,* a nineteenth-century word coined as a diminutive of a southwestern dialectical term, *nug,* meaning "lump." It's probably those very same miners who inspired another Nome newspaper published about the same time and known as the *Hell Whooper.*

Across the state, near the Yukon Territory, the town of Eagle (population 146) once had a newspaper whose name defies explanation: the *Buzz Saw and Bladder.* It's better not to inquire any further about that one.

Oran

In a speech in the provincial legislature in Halifax, Nova Scotia, one of its members complained of something he had seen "in the Oran." Premier John Buchanan interrupted. Legislators waited expectantly for his views on the issue. But, instead, he had a more fundamental question: "What's an Oran?"

In the Canadian community of Inverness, the *Oran* is the weekly newspaper, founded in 1976 as several mimeographed sheets stapled together. Today it is a more conventionally printed newspaper, and in keeping with the ethnic makeup of its community, *Oran* is Scottish Gaelic for "song." *Inverness,* by the way, is Gaelic for "at the mouth of the Ness River," and it is a city in the Scottish Highlands for which its Canadian counterpart is named. The Ness River flows into Loch Ness, home of a noted monster.

Outpost

An *outpost,* formed from *out* ("beyond certain bounds") + *post* ("a fixed place"), is a remote settlement, the usage having been derived from the military troop sent some distance from a halted unit to stand guard; by extension, the word has come to mean an advanced position in thought or research. David Crisp founded the weekly Billings (Montana) *Outpost* in 1997 as "a free and independent newspaper." He says he intended the name to evoke some sense of the West and also to signal his commitment to being an early warning of trouble, a first line of defense for the public's right and need to know. One thing the *Outpost* feels the public needs to know is in its slogan: "Our goal is to make money so we can put out a newspaper, not the other way around."

Pilot

Pilot, which comes from the Greek word *pēdon,* "blade of an oar," has a primary meaning of "helmsman, or one employed to steer a vessel." Maritime practice demands that a ship of a certain size take on a pilot familiar with local waterways to steer it into each port that it visits, whether on an ocean, a river, or a lake. Gilbert and Sullivan aficionados will recall that it was only faulty hearing that prevented the pair's famous seaside operetta from being about a group of *Pilots of Penzance.*

By extension, *pilot* began to refer metaphorically to anyone skilled in navigating through difficult situations, and, hence, a director, a guide, or a leader in any field. Both meanings of the word coalesce in most of the newspapers called the *Pilot,* since, with few exceptions, they all have been near navigable waters, and they all have offered guidance (whether expert or not) to their readers. Aircraft also have pilots today, but the airborne variety seems to have inspired very few newspapers.

Historic *Pilot*s have been published in London in 1808; Dublin in 1828; Preston (Lancashire) in 1831; Edinburgh, 1838; Tynemouth, England, 1839; Boston, Massachusetts, 1858; Dover, England, 1860; the Isle of Wight, 1873; Port Kennedy, Australia, 1897; and many other towns and cities too tedious to mention.

Today you may still read the Norfolk *Virginian-Pilot,* the Curry *Coastal Pilot* in Brookings, Oregon; the Hancock County *Journal-Pilot* in Carthage, Illinois; the *Daily Pilot* in Costa Mesa, California; the Glen Cove (New York) *Record-Pilot;* the Walker (Minnesota) *Pilot-Independent;* the Jackson (Minnesota) *County Pilot;* the Oyster Bay (New York) *Enterprise-Pilot;* the Plymouth (Indiana) *Pilot News,* and other *Pilot*s in Redding, Connecticut; Seven Points, Texas; Southport and Southern Pines, North Carolina; Steamboat Springs, Colorado; Whitefish, Montana; and Lewisport, Newfoundland. (Some readers may consider this list also too tedious to mention.)

Pinnacle

Hollister, California, is thirty miles north of the Pinnacles National Monument, a series of giant rock spires ranging up to twelve hundred feet in height, testifying to nature's awesome power along the rupture line of the San Andreas Fault. Because of its location, Hollister has the bravura to call itself the "Earthquake Capital of the World." Despite this constant peril—the entire downtown was destroyed by a quake in 1989—the residents are sufficiently calm and self-possessed to publish and read a weekly newspaper. Its managing editor, Dennis Taylor, reports that it is named the *Sunday Pinnacle* in tribute to the nearby natural phenomena.

A *pinnacle,* which comes from the Latin *pinna* (the same word on which *spine* is based), was first used to mean "an architectural piece ending in a pointed spire, used in Gothic construction to give added weight to a buttress." It later came to signify any tall structure, architectural or natural, that tapers to a pointed top, such as a mountain peak. From there, it was just a slight leap for *pinnacle* to mean the highest point of success.

Piper

Since the Middle Ages, Scottish Highlanders have been convinced that the sounds produced by bagpipes scare the daylights out of their military opponents. Those who didn't run away in fright were surely rendered dysfunctional by the maddeningly monotonous hum of the drones shrilly counterpointed by the weird, earsplitting wail of the melody chanter. It is no wonder that after the English defeated the Scots in 1745 at the Battle of Culloden, they wasted little time in outlawing, upon pain of death, the playing of bagpipes, which they quite sensibly regarded as instruments of war.

The bagpipe ban was lifted in 1782, owing to the fact that Scottish soldiers, now on the English side against the French, found it difficult to fight with much enthusiasm without that eerie caterwauling ringing in their ears. In 1794 the fourth Duke of Gordon formed a regiment known as the Gordon Highlanders, who became legendary for their bagpiping, and also, of course, for their fighting. Two of the regiment's battalions are the Deeside and the Donside, named for areas that lie on the banks of the Dee and Don Rivers.

Banchory, an Aberdeenshire town that lies between the Dee and the Don, publishes both a Deeside and a Donside edition of its newspaper, which is called—get your earplugs ready—the *Piper.*

Differences between the Deeside and Donside *Piper*s may be difficult for outsiders to discern—but then there has always been some confusion between the two areas, even by the Scots. The story is told of Lieutenant Colonel P. W. Forbes of Corse, who commanded a battalion of the Gordon Highlanders in the 1950s and for whom a favorite bagpipe march is named. When asked if his home in Corse was on Deeside or Donside, he replied it was difficult to tell: "When I piddle outside my front door I simply dinna know whether it runs into the Dee or into the Don."

Pirate

Penwith, a Cornish name which means "at the end of the headland," is the westernmost part of Great Britain, in a region of Cornwall that includes St. Ives, famous as the destination of the traveler who met the man with seven wives and an uncountable number of sacks, cats, and kittens. Penwith (not to be confused with Penrith—Cumbric for "red hill—far to the north in Cumbria) also includes Penzance ("holy headland"), a fact that should provide all you need to know about the origin of the name of the Penwith *Pirate*. Gilbert and Sullivan's operetta *The Pirates of Penzance* had its premiere on December 31, 1879, in New York and opened in London in 1880.

In the 1830s the Aberdeen *Pirate* flourished, its name recalling no musical-comedy villains, but the real McCoy—Scottish privateers who roamed the seas from the fifteenth century or earlier, among whom were Robert Davidson, William Eddy, Neal Patterson, and the most famous of them all—Captain William Kidd (whom no one ever thought of nicknaming Billy the Kidd).

Sachem

The Grand River *Sachem* has been the weekly newspaper in Caledonia, Ontario, since 1856. It was founded by the appropriately named journalist Thomas Messenger, who had previously published a newspaper called the *Sachem* in Cayuga. Messenger gave the *Sachem* a motto adapted from a line by the eighteenth-century poet William Cowper: "He is a free man whom the truth makes free and all are slaves besides."

Sachem is a word of Algonquian origin used to refer to a leader of some North American Indian tribes. Unlike a chief, who was usually chosen for his skill in battle, a sachem was noted for wisdom, and the duties of the office included dispensation of justice, reception of tribal guests, supervision of ritual activities, and—most aptly for its use as a newspaper name—bringing news back to the tribe from meetings with other tribes. Grand River is home to the Six Indian Nations: the Cayuga, Mohawk, Oneida, Onondaga, Seneca, and Tuscarora.

As a publisher, Messenger was so devoted to his duties that he himself acquired the nickname "Sachem." The newspaper is still housed in the building he erected in 1865.

Vidette

Usually spelled *vedette,* from the Latin *vedere* ("to see"), this word means "sentinel or outpost." J. W. Walsh, the founder in 1883 of the Montesano (Washington) *Vidette,* was asked why he chose that name for his paper. He replied, "Because the name is a French term for the forward point, or outer perimeter guard, of the main body of troops," and at the time of its founding, the *Vidette* was the westernmost newspaper in the United States. The first issue also referred to the word's meaning as a military sentinel on the frontier. An editorial proclaimed: "We are here. We mean business. And we mean to stay." And so it has, unlike the Elmira (New York) *Vidette,* which was first issued by William Murphy in 1816, but is no longer with us. There is a small paper called the *Star and Vidette* in Grand Valley, Ontario.

Visitor

The Morecambe *Visitor* in the Lancashire seaside resort was started by a printer named Charles Bingham, who moseyed over from Bradford, Yorkshire, around 1840 to take the sea air on his doctor's orders. Glen Cooper, editor of the *Visitor* nowadays, reports that dozens of hotels and guesthouses opened in Morecambe at that time, since the railway had just arrived and brought with it trainloads of tourists from the smoky mill towns of West Yorkshire, looking for a few days of fresh air.

Bingham was a resourceful chap, and he decided that he could make a few bob while breathing the salt air, so he began to compile lists of all the tourists in town, which he sold to the merchants back home in Bradford and also in Leeds. Presumably such a list—which Bingham labeled "The Visitor"—served the same marketing purpose that computer cookies do today when you visit a Web page for Caribbean cruises, cut-rate pharmaceuticals, or possibly other less wholesome merchandise that you would really prefer to keep secret: that is, to allow merchants with similar goods and services to inundate you with spam urging you to buy more of the same.

The sea air must have done Bingham good, because he was frisky enough to expand his paper and hustle some advertisements for it. Figuring that it would increase readership, he then added national and local news and—presto!—a newspaper called the Morecambe *Visitor* was created. It's been going ever since.

Wanderer

In the nineteenth century, Mattapoisett, Massachusetts, was a major shipbuilding town, where whaling ships that sailed from New Bedford were built. They included the *Acushnet,* which was the ship that Herman Melville sailed on and used as the model for the *Pequod* in *Moby-Dick.* The last whaler built in Mattapoisett—the *Wanderer*—was built in 1878 and continued to sail until 1924, when it anchored off Martha's Vineyard to wait out a storm—which turned out not to be a great idea, and the ship was smashed to smithereens on the rocks. According to Kenneth J. Souza, news editor of the *Wanderer,* the paper was named in commemoration of that historic event, although surely it has no wish to meet the fate of its namesake. A *wanderer* is "one who moves about without a fixed course," rooted in the Anglo-Saxon *wandrian,* which in turn comes from an earlier word, *windan,* meaning "to turn."

15

Oddities

The most fascinating newspaper names are often those whose meanings are not obvious—or perhaps they are obvious and for that very reason seem to be extremely peculiar titles for newspapers. These oddities often harbor intriguing backstories lurking behind such unusual names as *Alibi, Almanac, Bazoo, Bunyip, Cabinet, Casket, Chad, Chronotype, Eccentric, Exponent, Expositor, Eye* (and *Hawk Eye*), *Favorite, Fishwrapper, Handkerchief, Hour, Iconoclast, Ishmaelite, Jimplecute, Laconic, Optic, Pantagraph, Picayune, Potpourri, Quill, Solid Muldoon, Speaker, Tab, Topper, Traveler,* and *Triplicate*—all of which are (or at least were at one time) actual newspapers with actual readers.

Alibi

Alibi, from the Latin *alius,* means "elsewhere, in another place." From its use as a legal term in criminal cases, it has come to be used for any kind of excuse, sometimes one that is not altogether believable. The *Alibi* is a weekly "alternative" newspaper in Albuquerque, New Mexico, originally published as *NuCity.* It changed its name after a Chicago newspaper called *New City* persuaded *NuCity* that the similarity between the two was a little too close for comfort. Under those circumstances, perhaps *Alias* ("another name," from the same Latin root) might have been more appropriate for the retitled paper.

Almanac

Where can you find out when the next Year of the Monkey will occur on the Chinese calendar? One good source would be an *almanac,* which today generally refers to a book of assorted facts related to the calendar, the weather, geography, tides, astronomy, and any number of arcane topics. *Almanac* began life, believe it or not, as a place where camels kneel down. It comes from a Spanish Arabic word, *almanâkh,* composed of *al* ("the") + *ma* ("place") + *nâkha* ("kneel down"), and originally referred to a camp or settlement, where the ships of the desert could rest. Possibly becoming confounded with the Latin word *manacus,* a sundial depicting the figures of the Zodiac, *almanac* later meant "climate," then "a calendar of recurring events," and, finally, a "book of useful information."

It was primarily in the last sense (and not as a camel stop) that three housewives intended the word when they put out the first edition of the *Country Almanac* in 1965 in a kitchen in Portola Valley, California. The paper's contents basically included reports on births, deaths, schools, civic organizations, and government decisions in their community. Today the *Almanac,* having become citified and lost its "country" designation, is a weekly newspaper based in Menlo Park.

Bazoo

The poet Walt Whitman in his 1892 collection of essays, *November Boughs,* refers to a newspaper in Missouri called the *Bazoo.* It was in Sedalia in the 1870s. Whitman cites the name as an example of eccentric slang words of the American West. But as a former editor of the Brooklyn *Eagle,* he could have looked much closer to home and found a *Bazoo* in Elmira, New York, as early as 1877, as well as another in Tahlequah, Oklahoma, in 1888, and a short-lived (one issue) military paper in Arkansas in 1862 known as the Batesville *Bazzoo* (note the two z's in this one). The Elmira *Bazoo* was later changed to the prim and proper Elmira *Herald.*

Webster's New International Dictionary is not brave enough to provide an etymology for *bazoo,* but it comes up with three choices for its meaning: "a kazoo," slang for "loud, boastful talk," or slang for "the mouth." Of the three possibilities, either "mouth" or "loud, boastful talk" would be the most likely one that the namers of a newspaper might have had in mind. Indeed, Helen Sampson of the Chemung Valley *Reporter* (in the county in which the Elmira *Bazoo* once flourished) speculates, "Names of newspapers were selected to tell something about the newspaper. An exception may have been the *Daily Bazoo* of 1877. Whether it was meant to be a musical instrument, or had another meaning, a loud and boastful fellow, no one seems to remember."

Bazoo has other possible meanings, of varying degrees of propriety. Richard A. Spears in his *Slang and Euphemism* dictionary says *bazoo* has been in use in the United States since about 1900 (although it clearly must have been earlier) and offers two meanings, only one of which would be remotely suitable as a newspaper's name (a family newspaper, at any rate). The first definition, according to Spears, is a "jeer," synonymous with a "raspberry." The second meaning is a reference to female genitalia. Spears relates the word to *wazoo,* which also has two meanings: the "mouth" (with no salacious connotations), or "any unnamed [anatomical] area that can be tantalizingly hinted about" (most frequently, experience would indicate, the lowest portion of the alimentary canal).

The online Urban Dictionary thinks a *bazoo* is a substandard motorcar of the type that elicits rude comments from observers. Going further afield, one finds that Bazoo is a dance band from Thailand, known among the cognoscenti for its album *Phee Faa Party.* A bazoo (blue in color) is also a sort of moped with modifications that is mentioned in a children's book by Laurie B. Clifford. The *Oxford English Dictionary* has no truck at all with the word, leading one to conclude that it is entirely a New World phenomenon.

Bunyip

South Australia is the home of a most unusually named newspaper, the *Bunyip,* first published in Gawler in 1863. "What is a bunyip?" you ask, and it's a reasonable question. Well, the first thing you have to know is that the paper's founders were members of something called the Honorable Fraternity of Humbugs, established during the 1860s, the bylaws of which included the following purpose: "The object of this Association is the open advocacy of Humbug, in contradistinction to its secret practice in most other Societies. . . . The Society shall be presided over by three officers, the chief of whom shall be entitled Arch Flam, the second Bouncible Bam, and the third Surprising Sham." (If that doesn't make sense, don't worry, it's not your fault.)

The *Bunyip* was founded as the journal of this arcane society, and the choice of name was explained: "Why the *Bunyip*? Because the *Bunyip* is the true type of Australian Humbug! Go where you will in Australia, the poor benighted black fellow, if he wishes to astonish you with unheard of marvels, or strike you with supreme terror, raises before you the shadow of the mysterious Bunyip—ever near, ever promising to appear, but ever eluding sight and grasp."

Evidently the Bunyip was a mythical amphibious monster, analogous to the sea serpent of European lore, and in reality probably some species of alligator or crocodile that inhabited the inland swamps. Over the years, the paper became less the satirical lampoon that it was intended to be and more the general-interest weekly newspaper that it is today.

Cabinet

The word *cabinet,* from the Italian *gabbia,* and ultimately from the Latin *cavea,* originally meant "a cage or a basket." In more common English usage by the sixteenth century, it could be one of two things: a small chest or repository for valuables and documents, or a small room used for consultations with advisers to government officials.

In 1802, when Joseph Cushing founded a newspaper called the *Farmer's Cabinet* in Amherst, New Hampshire, it is not clear in which sense he intended the word. A 1797 paper in New Hampshire had been called the *Farmer's Museum,* and the newer paper may have been conceived as a source of valuable information and sage advice, instead of the "old news" that might be regarded as artifacts of the past in a "museum." Today the paper is known simply as the *Cabinet* and serves the area around Milford, New Hampshire.

Casket

Americans coin euphemisms by the carload, and above all else, they prefer neatly manicured words for anything connected with death. British novelist Evelyn Waugh lampoons this tendency in *The Loved One,* in which a California *cemetery* is a *memorial garden,* an *undertaker's assistant* is a *mortuary hostess,* and a *coffin,* of course, is a *casket.* (Never mind that *cemetery, undertaker,* and *coffin* are themselves earlier euphemisms for *graveyard, gravedigger,* and *burial box.*)

The name of the Antigonish *Casket,* a Nova Scotian newspaper, must seem especially bizarre to Americans. Actually *casket*—of uncertain etymology but probably from the French *cassette*—meant "a small ornamented box for jewels or letters" before it was hijacked to be used as a receptacle for a cadaver. Surely publisher John Boyd had a jewel box in mind in 1852, when he founded the *Casket,* for he gave the paper this motto: "Liberty: choicest gem of the Old World and fairest gem of the New." Of course, the *Casket* does include obituaries as well.

Chad

The 2000 United States presidential election made most Americans familiar with the word *chad*—collectively, small confetti-like pieces of paper (or, as now used, one such piece) produced by punching a larger piece, as in a computer punch card. The election depended on whether the computerized Florida voting machines had malfunctioned by leaving some of the punched-out chads "hanging," thereby causing votes to be miscounted. The word *chad* has been in use only since 1947, and dictionaries have not yet caught up with its etymology. A number of theories have been suggested, none of them very convincing.

One is that it is a back-formation, predicated upon a machine known as a "Chadless keypunch," a device invented by an apocryphal Mr. Chadless that purposely kept a U-shaped punched-out piece hanging to the card by a hinge; the assumption is that Mr. Chadless's name was misconstrued to mean that the machine produced no "chad," which then became the name for the punched-out pieces. Trouble is, there never was a Mr. Chadless, as far as anyone can tell, and the "chadless" keypunch machines were called that precisely because they produced no chad. So the chad came first. Another theory says that *chad* is an acronym for "card hole aggregate debris." It is also suggested that it's a corruption of *chaff* and *chips,* or an archaic Scottish word for "gravel."

Such speculation is all irrelevant in the case of the British newspaper known as the Mansfield *Chad*. It got its name in 1952 by combining the first two letters of the merged *Chronicle* and *Advertiser.* The *Chad* is clearly a better choice than the *Adch* would have been.

Chronotype

In Rice Lake, Wisconsin, the weekly paper is the *Chronotype,* but editor Sam Finazzo says no one knows why it was named that or by whom. Founded in 1874, the paper echoed the name of the Boston *Daily Chronotype*. That paper, established in 1846 by Elizur Wright, briefly employed the legendary editor Charles A. Dana before he was lured by Horace Greeley to the New York *Tribune* in 1847.

The word *chronotype* does not seem to exist in any dictionaries, except as a technical term in the jargons of both linguistics and neuroendocrinology. Neither of these seems likely as a newspaper title. The best anyone can come up with is that *Chronotype* is a portmanteau word coined from the Greek *chronos* ("time") and *type* (also of Greek origin) in reference to the printed word. It would mean something like "timely words." That's probably as good an explanation as anyone needs—or is likely to get.

Eccentric

Leave it to Eric Shackle, who has a Web page devoted to newspapers' eccentric names, to come up with a newspaper actually called the *Eccentric*. He notes that it is a chain of community newspapers headquartered in Birmingham, Michigan. In the 1870s the town's bachelors formed an exclusive group known as the Eccentrics, supposedly modeled after London's Reform Club, whose antics they knew of through Jules Verne's novel *Around the World in Eighty Days*. In 1878, two of the Birmingham club members, George Mitchell and Almeron Whitehead, founded a weekly newspaper, and they saw no reason not to call it the *Eccentric*.

The *Eccentric*'s Web site explains its mission in this way: "Because we publish community newspapers, we think about community journalism in a fundamentally different way than our bigger competition. They consider themselves to be independent from the stories and communities they cover, swooping in to write the unusual or sensational and then dashing off to cover something else. We regard ourselves as both accurate journalists and as caring citizens of the communities where we work."

How eccentric is that?

Expositor and *Exponent*

Since it comes from the Latin *exponere,* "to put out," that is "to expose, explain or expound," a newspaper called the *Expositor* could be expected to have an ideological agenda. That was certainly the case with the Nauvoo (Illinois) *Expositor,* published only one time, on June 7, 1844. Founded by a group of men who accused Mormon leader Joseph Smith of trying to seduce their wives, the *Expositor* had only a single issue, which began a chain of events that resulted in the murder of Smith and his brother and in the ultimate relocation of the Mormons from Illinois to Utah.

Smith, sometimes known as the Prophet, was an avid exponent of polygamy, who carried his belief in plural marriage to unusual extremes by occasionally propositioning other men's wives. One of them was Jane Law, whom Smith urged to give him "half her love," magnanimously encouraging her to confer the remainder on her husband. William Law demurred at the desirability of this domestic arrangement, and with several friends also opposed some of Smith's other doctrines; consequently, these men were expelled from Smith's church.

Law, his brother Wilson, and five others founded the *Expositor* with the express purpose of attacking Smith with "the truth, the whole truth and nothing but the truth." As editor Sylvester Emmons wrote in the first (and only) issue: "We are earnestly seeking to explode the vicious principles of Joseph Smith and those who practice the same abominations and whoredoms." Smith thought those words unkind and unseemly, and since he was also president of the Nauvoo City Council, he ordered the presses of the *Expositor* destroyed and all remaining copies of the paper burned.

Law and his group accused Smith of violating the U.S. Constitution, and the governor of Illinois agreed. Smith and his brother Hyrum (that's the way he spelled it) were jailed in Carthage to await trial. But two hundred angry anti-Mormons felt that it might take too long to bring Smith to justice, so they broke into the jail and shot Joseph and Hyrum dead.

Another *Expositor,* in Brantford, Ontario, was founded in 1852 and has a much less lurid past, at least as far as anyone knows. It has happily managed to publish a good many more issues than the Nauvoo paper, in a city noted as the place where Alexander Graham Bell set up the first operable telephone in 1876.

The Seaforth *Huron Expositor* also flourishes in Ontario, as does the Sparta *Expositor* in Tennessee. Similar in meaning and stemming from the same Latin root is the *Exponent,* exemplified in Clarksburg, West Virginia's *Exponent-Telegram* and Culpepper, Virginia's *Star-Exponent.*

Eye and *Hawk Eye*

The Arcata *Eye*—in its own words, "the mildly objectionable newspaper for Arcata, California"—has a nameplate featuring a close-up view of an eyeball. Presumably it is keeping an amused watch over the happenings in this California town "behind the redwood curtain." Founded in 1996, the *Eye* promises "scintillating news stories" plus the "tactile pleasure of big, crinkly pages and real newsprint on your hands." The *Eye* is famous for its funky police reports, which have been collected in book form and sometimes are written as limericks:

> Fun Bunchers smoked pot on the track
> Where, sadly, trains won't soon be back.
> The dizzy doke smopers
> Like affable dopers
> Agreed it was time that they pack.

The first *Eye* on record was in London in 1833, followed by others in 1885 and 1935. London also had papers called the *Eye-Opener,* the *Eye-Witness,* and the *Bull's Eye.* Tralee, in County Kerry, Ireland, has the weekly *Kerry's Eye* to look over things.

If the *Eye*s are watchful, the *Hawk Eye* in Burlington, Iowa, must be even sharper-sighted. *Hawk-eyed,* of course, means "having vision as keen as a hawk's" (which is reputedly very keen, enabling the birds of prey to spot snakes, rodents, and various small mammals from a great height and snare them for supper). The Burlington *Hawk Eye,* however, is not named for the bird, and certainly not for Hawkeye Pierce of *M*A*S*H,* who came from Maine, anyway. The reason for the paper's name is convoluted.

Two Burlington men, Judge David Rorer and newspaper publisher James Edwards, proposed the name as a sobriquet for Iowans—but for different reasons. Judge Rorer had come across the name in James Fenimore Cooper's *The Last of the Mohicans,* published in 1826. Hawkeye, the nickname of central character Natty Bumppo, was a brave and resourceful pioneer.

Meanwhile, Edwards, publisher of the *Iowa Patriot* in Burlington, had befriended Sac Indian chief Black Hawk, who had moved to Iowa in 1833 after being defeated in a war against the United States and then released from prison. As a tribute to his heroic friend, Edwards changed the newspaper's name to the *Hawk-Eye and Iowa Patriot,* and also proposed "Hawk-Eyes" as a nickname for residents of the Iowa territory.

For whichever reason, the name "Hawkeye" was adopted by territorial officials in 1838, eight years before Iowa became a state. The University of Iowa borrowed the name for its mascot, which since 1948 has been represented by Herky (short for Hercules) the Hawk. The Burlington daily has since shortened its name simply to the *Hawk Eye,* which also was the name of a paper in London in 1880.

Favorite

It shows real self-confidence for a newspaper to call itself the *Favorite*—but you have to admit that it's easily justified when it's the only paper in town. In Franklin, Kentucky, the *Favorite* has been a weekly paper since 1857. In Bonham, Texas, the *Daily Favorite* first appeared in 1892. Any paper named the *Favorite* must be the envy of many others, with news printed under a title from the Latin *faverere,* meaning "to regard with especial esteem or good will." Former speaker of the U.S. House Sam Rayburn, whose exploits were often featured in his hometown paper, was the Bonham *Favorite*'s favorite son. The Franklin *Favorite* still publishes, but the Bonham paper must have fallen into some disfavor, as it closed in 2002, to be replaced by two weeklies with more mundane names, the *News* and the *Journal.*

Fishwrapper

Talk about truth in advertising! Many newspapers have been referred to as "fishwrappers"—or worse—but the monthly newspaper in Port Clinton, Ohio, on the shore of Lake Erie, actually puts it in the nameplate. Filled mostly with fishing and boating news, the *Fishwrapper* pluckily acknowledges its fate—unlike other newspapers in its corporate group with good, staunch names like *News-Herald, Gazette, Tribune,* and *Sentinel,* whose ultimate use is probably exactly the same. There have been newspapers in Alaska with similar names: the double-duty *Fishwrapper and Litter Box Liner* in Kodiak and the *Sun and Salmon Wrapper* in Juneau.

Handkerchief

In 1831 there was a London newspaper that called itself the *Political Handkerchief* for the reason that it was printed on calico in order to avoid and to protest a tax on paper. Ten issues were published by Henry Berthold until the killjoys at the British Stamp Office got around to deciding that cloth with printing on it was subject to all the same regulations that applied to newspapers. The vendors who sold it were imprisoned, and the readers were forced to keep their noses clean with something else.

Hour

The *Hour* has been keeping Norwalk, Connecticut, up to the minute since May 6, 1871. Its first issue addressed the reasons for its name in nebulous, vaguely apocalyptic terms that were probably not any clearer to readers at that time than they are today. Publisher Brainard W. Maples wrote:

> When we had decided to commence the publication of this paper, our first perplexity was for a name. Like young parents, we have been puzzled what to christen our offspring. A name must be appropriate, expressive, and in harmony with the object which it is intended to imply. Our paper will give an epitome of the occur-

rences of The Hour, making thereon such comments as may seem called for and proper. With The Hour come our duties and our responsibilities, to The Hour they are confined, and within The Hour must be completed. Beginning with time and continuing to eternity, The Hour embraces all that is of interest to humanity here and affords the opportunity to prepare for the hereafter. The Hour is our theme, our opportunity, and our limit, and we have selected it as a name. Our duty now is to make THE HOUR a pleasant, useful Hour, that may not pass unheeded or unread.

More circumbendibus than that would truly be a superfluity.

A short-lived religious newspaper called the *Hour* was published in London from 1873 to 1876. The British Library also records a single issue of a newspaper in 1879 called the *Half-Hour,* which must have been written for speed-readers.

Iconoclast

The town of Crawford, Texas, gained fame as the locale of George W. Bush's ranch retreat; it also is the home of a weekly newspaper that probably never made it into any presidential press summaries. A racy-looking tabloid, it is called the *Lone Star Iconoclast,* and its editorial policy has often given Bush Republicans as much dyspepsia as its name suggests (Greek *eikôn,* "image" + *klastēs* "breaker"). Founded in 2000 —when it did endorse George W. Bush for president—and named in homage to an 1890s publication in nearby Waco edited by William Cowper Brann, the Crawford *Iconoclast* enthusiastically backed John Kerry, and not the local son, in the 2004 election. A virulent eruption of protest resulted.

As the publisher, W. Leon Smith, wrote in an editorial: "We expected that perhaps a few readers might cancel subscriptions, and maybe even ads, but have been amazed at a few of the more intense communications, some of which bordered on outright personal attacks and uncalled-for harassment. . . . Too, some individuals are threatening innocent commercial concerns, claiming that if they advertise in *The Iconoclast,* they will be run out of business. We consider this improper in a democracy."

The life of an iconoclast can be tempestuous, as editor Brann of yesteryear learned. He ran articles highly critical of Baylor University, attracting international attention and culminating in a gunfight between Brann and a Baylor supporter named Tom Davis in downtown Waco. Like the gingham dog and the calico cat, the two men fatally wounded each other. (I wasn't there; I simply state what was told to me by the Chinese plate.)

Ishmaelite

"Call me Ishmael" is the famous opening line of Herman Melville's novel *Moby-Dick.* In that novel the narrator establishes himself as a latter-day version of the original Ishmael in Genesis, that is, an outcast from society.

Ishmael was the product of a dalliance between Abraham and Hagar, an Egyptian slave. When Abraham's wife, Sarah, later became pregnant (with Isaac), she started feeling a bit snarky and insisted that Hagar and Ishmael be sent into the desert, where they were about to die of thirst when, lo! an angel encountered them, produced a spring of water, and told Hagar that Ishmael would be the father of a great nation. Ishmael later married an Egyptian and fathered twelve sons and one daughter, who married Esau, his half-brother Isaac's son. Small world!

In Islam, incidentally, Ishmael as portrayed in the Koran gets a much better deal: in this version Abraham and Hagar were married to each other at the time of his birth, and he is regarded as one of the major prophets.

In the Judeo-Christian tradition, though, Ishmael is a man at odds with the world. Sidney Lewis, the fiery editor who founded the Sparta (Georgia) *Ishmaelite* in 1878, was also frequently at odds with the world. In christening his paper, he felt that *Ishmaelite*—although perhaps awkward to pronounce—was a name that represented the epitome of independence—a quality for which his paper became widely known.

Spartans don't seem bothered by the discrepancy that their newspaper is a Semitic name, even though the town's own nomenclature is of Greek ancestry, in honor of the Georgians who fought against the Indians, supposedly with the same tenacity that the ancient Spartans showed against the Athenians.

Jimplecute

Jefferson is a town with a storied past. Named in the 1840s for Thomas Jefferson, it is in an area of northeastern Texas that had been acquired by the United States in the Louisiana Purchase of 1803. The town's position on Big Cypress Creek, into which the Red River once flowed, made it a busy port, welcoming as many as five steamboats a week. In 1873 Jefferson suffered two setbacks: the river was reconfigured, making steamboat traffic impossible, and the newly completed railroad line bypassed the town.

Two notable institutions survived this reversal of fortune. One is the Excelsior House Hotel, founded in the 1850s, which has continued to play host to luminaries including Ulysses S. Grant, Oscar Wilde, and Lady Bird Johnson (though not all at the same time). The other is the town's influential weekly newspaper, founded in 1848, the Jefferson *Jimplecute,* known sometimes simply as the *Jimp.*

Even Vic Parker, publisher and editor of the *Jimplecute,* cannot swear to the meaning of the name, which has been lost in the dim mists of the past. But he gamely offers at least four possible explanations.

One tale has it that the newspaper's first editor-typesetter liked to take a nip or two as he worked, and on one occasion he dropped a handful of loose type on the floor. When he gathered it up on his composing stick, the random letters spelled "J-I-M-P-L-E-C-U-T-E." This explanation begs the question of why anyone would think it a good idea to name a newspaper based on a batch of pied type.

The second explanation is that the word is an acronym of the motto: "Joining Industry, Manufacturing, Planting, Labor, Energy, Capital (in) Unity Together Everlastingly." There are some problems with this explanation. Even though the motto now appears on the newspaper's nameplate, there is no evidence that it was there in the earliest issues. Moreover, its syntax is labored and unnatural, as though someone whose first language was perhaps Bulgarian had devised a "backronym"—a desperately contrived phrase whose initial letters could be coerced into spelling *Jimplecute.* One more objection: if that's supposed to be a motto for Jefferson, it's peculiar that it omits any reference to the town's most notable nineteenth-century economic activity: steamboat shipping.

The Bogeyman Theory is that a *Jimplecute* is a mythical creature invented to frighten superstitious slaves before and during the U.S. Civil War. This story describes the beast as a crouched animal with a forked tail and the mouth of a dragon, the head of an Indian, the body of an armadillo, and the front legs of a lion ready to spring, with a snake riding on its back. Well, if outback Australians named a newspaper after a mythical beast called a "Bunyip," it may just be possible that backwoods Texans might have done the same.

Parker himself favors the most rational explanation: that *Jimplecute* is a legitimate, though archaic, English word. He cites research by Fred Tarpley for his book *Jefferson: Riverport to the Southwest,* which suggests that the word, in slightly different forms, is slang for "sweetheart" or "slim" or "neat." The noun *jimp,* according to the *Oxford English Dictionary,* is of Scottish origin and dates at least to 1470, meaning "a minute or subtle point, a trifling distinction, a quirk, a tittle." *Webster's New International Dictionary* lists the word *jimpricute* (note only the slight difference in spelling) meaning "elegant, handsome, or neat" and ascribes it to "local U.S." usage. It's certainly reasonable to imagine that the paper was intended to be called the *Jimpricute,* and that tipsy typesetter just didn't spell it right.

Another *Jimplecute* was published in Spring Place, Georgia, from 1881 to 1903, but no one knows how it was named, either. J. Roy McGinty Jr., writing at the Murray County Museum Web site, reports that the origin of *Jimplecute* has long been the subject of conjecture. Edith Bullard, daughter of the paper's founder, Clarence Heartsill, says that the word meant "clean and neat"; she thinks her father may have just copied the name from its Jefferson counterpart, as he visited Texas around the time he started the Spring Place paper.

A newspaper with the variant spelling *Jimplicute* was published during much of the twentieth century in Scott County, Missouri.

Laconic

Laconia was a region of ancient Greece of which Sparta was the capital. Spartan discipline was noted for rigorous austerity, as everyone knows from the creepy story of the boy who let a fox he had stolen gnaw through his stomach rather than confess that he was concealing it under his tunic. Yecch! This austerity applied to the Laconians' use of language as well. They prided themselves on their concise dry wit, which the Athenians thought was so abrupt as to border on rudeness. Hence, the word *laconic* means "terse, using few words."

Schoolteacher Joseph Debnam of Snow Hill, North Carolina, undoubtedly prized terseness—although there is no reason to believe that he was also rude like the Laconians, or that he kept a fox under his tunic, for that matter. When Debnam gave up teaching in 1906 and founded a weekly newspaper, he named it the *Southern Laconic,* later known as the *Standard Laconic.* After Joseph's death in 1934, his widow, Birdie, became publisher and continued to write a column and sell subscriptions until she was eighty-nine. Their granddaughter, Betty Debnam, nurtured in the knowledge that brevity is the soul of wit, invented the *Mini Page,* that cute little section in the weekend newspaper that has educational stories, games, and puzzles for kids.

Optic

Optic is from the Greek *optikos,* "pertaining to sight," and though the word is an adjective, it was humorously used in the nineteenth century as a noun meaning "eye." With that in mind Russell A. Kistler founded the Las Vegas (New Mexico, not Nevada) *Daily Optic* in 1879, with a policy of providing vivid eyewitness accounts of political rallies, sporting events, church services, theatrical performances, and killings. The killings occurred with much frequency, and a momentous headline of July 1, 1881, announced: "The Kid Killed." The kid in question was William Bonney, otherwise known as Billy the Kid, who frequently did his dirty work in the region surrounding Las Vegas.

Another William, who turned out rather better, cut his journalistic teeth on the *Optic.* (Yikes! What an excruciating metaphor!) He was William Shawn, later of far-flung fame as editor of *The New Yorker* magazine.

The Mount Vernon (Texas) *Optic* came along later, founded in 1894; it was shortly merged with the older *Herald,* to view the world as the *Optic-Herald,* as it still does.

Pantagraph

The Bloomington (Illinois) *Pantagraph* was founded in 1837, but then it was called by the more conventional, if lengthy, title of the

Bloomington *Observer and McLean County Advocate.* Its founder was Jesse Fell, who later took in a partner named Charles Merriman, who must have realized that the paper's original name was a mouthful, so in 1853 he coined *Pantagraph,* from Greek roots that mean "write all things." Merriman said the name was "a perpetual injunction upon its editors to dip their pens fearlessly into all matters of human interest."

The *Pantagraph*'s motto is "Independent in everything, neutral in nothing." Fell lived up to this injunction, first by being the man who nominated Abraham Lincoln as U.S. senator from Illinois, and then by supporting Lincoln for president in a county composed of a majority of proslavery Southern emigrants. Lincoln won both the county and the presidency.

Picayune

The New Orleans *Times-Picayune* is among the most famous newspapers in the United States, and one reason is undoubtedly its goofy-sounding name. Look up *picayune* in the dictionary, and you will find that it means something "very small, or of the least value, petty, paltry, mean, narrow in outlook, contemptible, insignificant." Gosh, just the words you would pick to describe a newspaper you wanted people to read!

But there is, as you might have guessed, more to the story. The New Orleans *Picayune* was founded in 1837 by two newspapermen, Francis Lumsden and George W. Kendall, who arrived from points north with seven hundred dollars in their pockets and, having nothing better to do, decided to start their own paper. They called it the *Picayune,* because that was the price of a copy.

The picayune had been a Spanish coin in Louisiana and Florida worth about six and a quarter cents, but after the Louisiana Purchase the name was applied to the U.S. five-cent piece (also called a fippenny bit). Although the picayune was a Spanish coin, the word came from the French *picaillon,* a Piedmont coin of small value, adopted from the Provençal word *picaioun,* which was a diminutive of the Portuguese *picalho* ("money"). The *Picayune* was the first newspaper in New Orleans to cost less than a dime.

Kendall, a printer and humorist who had worked for Horace Greeley in New York, later became the world's first war correspondent, covering the Mexican-American War, and then pioneered as a sheep rancher in Texas and had a county named for him. Kendall's flippant commentary gave the *Picayune* a reputation as a sassy and amusing newspaper.

During the Mexican-American War in 1847, the *Picayune* sent small, swift boats to meet the slower steamers from Vera Cruz carrying news of the war's progress. The boats were equipped with typesetting facilities, and the paper was set and ready to go to press by the time the boats were back in New Orleans.

The paper merged with the *Times-Democrat* in 1914 to become the *Times-Picayune.* Among notable writers who worked there were Elizabeth Meriwether Gilmer, who, as Dorothy Dix, dispensed advice to the lovelorn of several generations; William Sidney Porter, who became famous in New York as O. Henry; and William Faulkner, who won a Nobel Prize for Literature (but not specifically for the copy he wrote for the *Times-Picayune*).

The *Times-Picayune* received worldwide attention during Hurricane Katrina in September 2005 for courageously continuing publication, either online or with other newspapers' equipment, after its own plant was flooded.

There is at least one other newspaper with the *Picayune* name. Early in 1890, two brothers, Carl and M. M. McFarland, established the Beeville (Texas) *Daily Picayune.* They had worked on the New Orleans *Picayune* and named their newspaper in homage to it. After a few years it merged with a rival paper to become the *Bee-Picayune.*

Potpourri

The *Potpourri* is a weekly newspaper published in the communities of Magnolia and Tomball, Texas. It is a fine name for a newspaper that publishes a miscellaneous variety of news items, once you master its customary French pronunciation and learn to live with its unsavory etymology. *Potpourri* means "mixture or medley," specifically an *olla-podrida,* which is a Spanish dish of meat and vegetables. *Potpourri's* roots are the French words *pot* ("pot") + *pourrir* ("to rot"). This reference to a rotten pot no doubt reflects the lack of refrigeration in the seventeenth century, when the first *potpourri* was stewed up, making good use of a bit of dubious meat whose glory days were long over. *Potpourri* also denotes a jar of flower petals and spices used to make your room smell sweet after you've cooked all that rotten meat.

Quill

Quill is a word that came into English around the late fourteenth century from the German *kiel* and originally meant "a hollow tube, like a reed." It later was used to refer to the stiff feathers on the wing or tail of a bird, or the spines on a porcupine or hedgehog, and by the sixteenth century to a writing implement made by sharpening and splitting the tip of a bird's feather, which was then dipped in ink like a pen. A quill came to symbolize the work of a scribe or a journalist. As a symbol, the word is used by the American high school journalism honor society Quill and Scroll; the magazine of the Society of Professional Journalists is known as the *Quill;* and the Quill Awards honor Canadian community newspapers.

There are at least two newspapers that are called the *Quill.* The West Plains (Missouri) *Daily Quill* was founded in 1885 as the *Weekly Quill.* It became a daily in 1903. The *Quill,* a weekly in Stronghurst, Illinois, was founded in 1926.

Solid Muldoon

The *Solid Muldoon* was a weekly newspaper in Ouray, Colorado, that was established in 1879. The name was originally coined as a character in a comic song by Ned Harrigan, of the team of Harrigan and Hart, pioneers of American musical comedy—and thereby hangs a tale, or actually two or three of them.

First performed by Harrigan in a Broadway revue in 1874, the song, "Muldoon, the Solid Man," made gentle fun of a fictional small-time Irish American politician named Michael Muldoon, who peppered his speech with highfalutin malapropisms and who had a fine opinion of himself, as the lyrics indicate:

> Go with me and I'll treat you dacent,
> I'll set you down and I'll fill the can,

As I walk the street, each friend I meet
Says: "There goes Muldoon. He's a solid man."

"Muldoon, the Solid Man" became one of Harrigan and Hart's most popular characters and appeared in numerous shows over the next few years.

So well known was the fictional Muldoon that when real-life strongman William Muldoon became famous as the world champion Greco-Roman wrestler, the media appropriated the phrase and called him "the Solid Muldoon."

There's yet another twist to the story before the *Solid Muldoon* became a newspaper. In 1877, a con man named George W. Hull, who had previously perpetrated the hoax of the "Cardiff Giant," created a new sensation that was eagerly accepted by a gullible public. Hull had spent three years fashioning his second "petrified man"—a five-hundred-pound, seven-and-a-half-foot figure, touted as the "missing link"—which was actually a Frankensteinish monster made of mortar, clay, rock dust, plaster, ground bones, blood, and meat. A confederate of Hull's, William Conant, who had previously learned a thing or two about hoodwinking the public while working for P. T. Barnum, "discovered" the body near Beulah, Colorado. It was soon dubbed "the Solid Muldoon" and exhibited throughout the new state of Colorado for fifty cents a look. Finally, it was revealed as yet another hoax.

Enter Colonel David F. Day, a Medal of Honor winner for heroism in the Civil War, who established a newspaper in Ouray. Well known for sarcasm and caustic wit, Colonel Day wanted to provoke plenty of attention for his new paper, so he named it after the phony fossil. The *Solid Muldoon* lost no time in vigorously attacking sacred cows, including elected officials, citizens' vigilante groups, socialites, and the Catholic Church. Libel suits were filed by the score.

The phrase *Solid Muldoon* has a distinguished literary life, quite apart from its use as a newspaper title. One of Rudyard Kipling's stories in *Soldiers Three,* published in 1888, was called "The Solid Muldoon," in an ironic allusion to a traumatized corporal. And, as Don Meade points out in his exhaustive study of Harrigan's song in "The Life and Times of 'Muldoon, the Solid Man,'" the pompous Irishman even earned a cryptic allusion in James Joyce's incomprehensible novel *Finnegans Wake.*

Here's the epilogue: "Solid Muldoon" songwriter Ned Harrigan's partner, Tony Hart, was committed to an asylum and died at age thirty-five. Harrigan continued to work in Broadway theater until his death at sixty-seven in 1911; his daughter, Nedda, married the director Joshua Logan. William "Solid" Muldoon, the wrestler, became a friend of Harrigan's and was New York State Boxing Commissioner from 1921 to 1923. A wooden plaque near Beulah, Colorado, purports to mark the site where the "Solid Muldoon" "fossil" is buried. Dave Day, founder-editor of the _Solid Muldoon,_ shut down the paper and moved to Durango, Colorado, in 1892, to establish the Durango _Democrat._ He wounded the editor of a rival paper in a shootout. After Day's death, his son, Rod, took over the _Democrat,_ and in 1922, Rod shot and killed the city editor of the Durango _Herald_ but was acquitted on the grounds of self-defense. In 1928 the _Herald_ and the _Democrat_ merged. In 1907 Rudyard Kipling was awarded the Nobel Prize for Literature. James Joyce, who never won a Nobel Prize, died in 1941, two years after the publication of _Finnegans Wake,_ which remains among the best-known, least-read books of literature.

Speaker

A tale of two cities can be told about how the Temiskaming (Ontario) _Speaker_ and the Hazleton (Pennsylvania) _Standard-Speaker_ each got their names.

In the Canadian parliament (certainly unlike the American Congress), the speaker is expected to preside over the House of Commons impartially, giving favor to no political party. In 1906 in the town of New Liskeard, the father-and-son team of E. F. and A. E. Stephenson chose the name _Speaker_ for their new paper because they wanted it to follow a nonpartisan policy. It was common in that era for Canadian newspapers to align themselves with either the Liberals or the Conservatives and to toe the appropriate party line.

In the case of Hazleton, Carl Christopher, executive editor of the _Standard-Speaker,_ traces the origins of the name to the _Plain Speaker,_ an afternoon daily that was founded in 1882. Clearly, its name indicated its aspiration to forthrightness. In 1961 the _Plain Speaker_ merged with the morning _Standard-Sentinel_ and became the _Standard-Speaker_ (instead of the _Plain-Sentinel_).

Tab

All around the world these days, increasing numbers of newspapers are squeezing their contents into a reduced size known as "tabloid." Well, you have to admit that it's a tempting alternative. Tabloids are cheaper to produce than traditional-sized papers, they demand fewer words to fill up their columns (hence, smaller staffs), and they appeal to younger readers who tend to grow bored after fifteen seconds on the same topic. Folded in the usual reading position, the tabloid—or "tab"—page is about eleven by fifteen inches, approximately one-half the size of the standard newspaper (which is called a "broadsheet"). Tabloids are easier to handle on a bus or subway and are sometimes called "straphangers' specials."

Some of the more prominent long-established tabloid newspapers include the New York *Daily News,* the New York *Post,* the Toronto *Sun,* and London's *Daily Mirror, Daily Star,* and *Sun.* But you'll soon be seeing more papers in that format. In the area around Boston, Massachusetts, there is a chain of some fifteen free weekly tabloid community papers, designed to appeal to younger readers, that are published under the name of *Tab.* Now owned by the Boston *Herald,* they include the Cambridge *Tab,* Brookline *Tab,* Needham *Tab,* Watertown *Tab & Press,* Framingham *Tab,* Natick *Bulletin & Tab,* and a number of others.

The name *tabloid*—meaning "tabletlike"—originated as a term trademarked in 1884 by the Burroughs Wellcome Company to refer to compressed and concentrated drug products. People loved the word, and it soon lost its medicinal meaning. *Tab* is now used to designate almost anything condensed—not only newspapers, but also Broadway shows abridged for Las Vegas stages, reduced-calorie colas, and movie stars of modest talent.

Topper

Topper is a word of many and varied meanings: a candle-snuffer, a cheater at dice, a logger who works high in the trees, a worker who puts lids on containers, a finisher of the upper parts of garments, a loader who piles boxes in tiers, the remains in a pipe bowl, a blow to the head, a funnier story than the previous one, anything superlative, or—as in the case of the Clinton (Wisconsin) *Topper*—a man's high hat, usually made of silk or beaver, worn with formal dress. The weekly paper was founded by a man who liked to stroll about town duded up like Fred Astaire, carrying a cane and wearing a top hat. (Whether he also tap-danced is not reported.) He carried his sartorial style over into the naming of his newspaper, whose nameplate originally pictured a jauntily tilted topper above the letter *T*—but it was dropped when a new publisher must have figured that such a logo was old hat.

The town, named for Dewitt Clinton, the governor of New York, was established in 1843 as a railroad and grain center and was among the first in its area to have running water, an amenity that is still celebrated each year with a Water Tower Festival.

Traveler

From about 1800, the word *traveller* (later Americanized as *traveler*) was commonly used as a short form of the full phrase *commercial traveller,* meaning "a manufacturer's sales representative who moves from place to place soliciting orders." In 1801 a London newspaper that reported items of interest to these itinerant vendors called itself the *Traveller* (later called the *Globe & Traveller*). An identically named journal was in Greenfield, Massachusetts, in 1811. By 1831 New York had a publication known as the *Traveller, and Spirit of the Times,* which was a journal aimed at fans of sporting events.

In 1825 the Boston *Traveller* was founded, as a bulletin of stagecoach listings. It evolved into the *Boston Daily Evening Traveler* and continued to publish until 1967, when it was merged into the Boston *Herald-Traveler,* then finally disappeared under the weight of additional merged titles.

The town of Arkansas City, Kansas, has a newspaper called the Arkansas *Traveler.* This combination of words comes from the well-known fiddle tune "Arkansas Traveler," derived from a popular nineteenth-century play. In the play, a traveler finds an Arkansas backwoodsman singing a song that begins: "Oh, once upon a time in Arkansas, / An old man sat in his little cabin door." In the lyrics, the man complains that his roof leaks, but it's raining too hard to repair it. He is advised to wait until a sunny day, but he replies that it would be pointless to do that, as the roof doesn't leak when it isn't raining!

In another version, approved by the Arkansas State Song Selection Committee in 1947, the beauties of the state are emphasized:

> On a lonely road quite long ago,
> A trav'ler trod with fiddle and a bow
> While rambling thru the country rich and grand,
> He quickly sensed the magic and the beauty of the land . . .

The University of Arkansas student newspaper is also known as the *Arkansas Traveler.*

Triplicate

In Crescent City, California, the *Daily Triplicate* traces its history back to 1879. At one time, confides its publisher, Teresa Tsalaky, it was three different newspapers, the Del Norte *Times,* the Coast *Times,* and the Crescent City *News.* In 1912 William McMaster consolidated the three into one newspaper and called it the Del Norte *Triplicate,* using a word based on the Latin *triplicare,* the actual meaning of which is "a third thing corresponding to two others of the same kind." Del Norte is a county in northern California that includes the city founded in 1854 and named because of its location on a sweeping, crescent-shaped beach.

The Elusive Ones

Origins of a few unusual names have proved elusive, and as we end this list of oddities, it is a source of unrelenting regret that inquiring minds must await a later investigation of them—or, *horribile dictu,* face the fact that we may never discover the inside stories of how the Yadkin *Ripple,* the Miller County *Autogram-Sentinel,* the Shawville *Equity,* the Benalla *Ensign,* the Millbrook *Roundtable,* the Council Bluffs *Daily Nonpareil,* the Eden *Magnet,* the Steinbach *Carillon,* the Carbonear *Compass,* and no less than three *Gleaner*s entered the world.

16

The *Brute*, the *Beast*, and Other Figments

In *Scoop*, Evelyn Waugh's savagely hilarious novel about British newspapering, a character named William Boot, a nature writer devoted to badgers and water voles, is hired (owing to mistaken identity) as a war correspondent by a London newspaper, the *Daily Beast*, to try to outdo the rival *Daily Brute*. The *Beast* and the *Brute*, of course, are not actual newspapers, but rather examples of Waugh's malicious wit in satirizing the incivility with which he characterized the entire London press.

The satire is just as trenchant in Waugh's *Vile Bodies*, in which the hero is a gossip columnist for a newspaper called the *Daily Excess*, owned by the high-handed Lord Monomark—an unmistakable parody of London's *Daily Express*, which was owned by the high-handed Lord Beaverbrook.

In *London Up to Date*, a satirical 1894 guide to the city by the flamboyant journalist George Augustus Henry Sala, a menagerie of prehistoric (and imaginary) creatures provide facetious newspaper names. Sala, who wrote for the *Daily Telegraph*, probably had that paper in mind as the fictitious *Morning Mammoth*. He adds,

> There are at least half a dozen daily competitors of the *Morning Mammoth* which all claim, and justly claim, an astoundingly large circulation. The *Daily Megatherium* sells, we all know, by millions. The circulation of the *Morning Plesiosaurus*, is phenomenally gigantic, and the same may be said of the *Panoeotherium*, the *Daily Anoplotherium*, and the *Morning Mastodon*. Other lights among these tremendous diurnals are the *Iguanodon* and the *Morning Dipsopoios*.

Not all novelists who invent fictional names for newspapers are as sardonic. P. G. Wodehouse weighed in with the Market Snodsbury *Argus-Intelligencer,* but then rather let the side down with the humdrum Peebles *Courier* and Basingstoke *Journal.*

Arthur Conan Doyle was among those whose imagination decidedly avoided waggish nomenclature. In his Sherlock Holmes stories he customarily used actual newspapers, and when he did on rare occasions feel moved to invent them, he gave them pedestrian names like the North Surrey *Observer* (in "The Adventure of the Retired Colourman"), the *Daily Gazette* (in "The Adventure of the Red Circle"), and the *Daily Herald* (in *The Valley of Fear*).

Dorothy L. Sayers was pretty much in the same vein with the *Evening Banner,* the *Morning Star,* and the *Evening Wire.* But Agatha Christie came up with a few wry jibes such as the *Daily Megaphone,* the *Evening Shriek,* and the *Daily Flicker.*

Some other notable inventions by mystery writers include Lillian Jackson Braun's macabre *Daily Fluxion* (which in medicine means "an unnatural flow of blood") and the *Pickax Picayune,* Jane Langton's Boston *Improviser,* Hampton Charles's *Daily Negative,* Sarah Caudwell's *Daily Scuttle,* and M. C. Beaton's Lockdubh *Listener.*

Occasionally life imitates art, as in the case of William Makepeace Thackeray's fictional *Pall Mall Gazette,* "written by gentlemen for gentlemen," in his 1849 novel *The History of Pendennis.* In 1865 two London entrepreneurs, Frederick Greenwood and George Smith, decided to establish a newspaper and, gentlemen or not, they could think of no better title for it than Thackeray's.

Louisa May Alcott in *Little Women* conceived of two sensational newspapers, the *Weekly Volcano* and the *Spread Eagle,* the former of which is now the name of a real weekly newspaper in Tacoma, Washington.

Other novelists—perhaps still awaiting real newspapers to adopt their invented names—include Ian McEwan (the *Judge* in *Amsterdam*), E. Annie Proulx (the *Gammy Bird* in *The Shipping News*), J. K. Rowling (the *Daily Prophet* in the Harry Potter books), and Lemony Snicket (the *Daily Punctilio* in several of his acerbic works). *Punctilio,* in case it has momentarily slipped your mind, is from the Latin *punctum* ("point") and means "meticulous attention to details." It should go without saying that it is a fictitious newspaper.

Comic strips and popular adventure stories are a fertile field for news-paper names. The *Daily Planet* and the *Daily Bugle*, which we have en-countered in previous chapters, are two notable examples, from the "Superman" and "Spider-Man" series, respectively. The *Planet*, whose symbol is a large globe, is edited by Perry White and employs Clark Kent (alias Superman) and Lois Lane as reporters, and Jimmy Olsen as a copyboy. In the early Superman comics, Kent worked not for the *Plan-et*, but for the *Daily Star*, named by one of the original Superman cre-ators, Joe Shuster, for the Toronto *Star*, which he delivered as a boy. When Superman began to appear in newspaper comic strips, however, the fictional daily was changed to the *Planet*, in order to avoid conflict with actual newspapers called the *Star*.

DC Comics, publishers of the "Superman" and "Batman" series, has evolved an elaborate network of newspaper connections in Metropolis, Superman's home, and nearby Gotham City, where Batman hangs his cape and pointy-eared mask. Bruce Wayne, alias Batman, owns the *Daily Planet* in Metropolis, and *Planet* editor White once worked for the Gotham *Gazette*. The *Planet* has a plethora of rivals including the *Daily Star* (the former *Planet* name resurrected for a tabloid), the *Daily News*, the Metropolis *Sun*, and the Metropolis *Eagle*. The *Gazette* likewise has plenty of competition in Gotham City with the *Times-Tribune*, the *Examiner*, the *Globe*, and the *Daily*—all fictional, of course, although with names that are used by real newspapers.

Not to be outdone in the media biz, Marvel Comics has created its own news empire in the *Daily Bugle*, which first appeared in *Amazing Spider-Man* #51 (1967), created by Stan Lee and John Romita Sr. The *Bugle* is published by J. Jonah Jameson and edited by Robbie Robert-son, who frequently buys photos from the freelance Peter Parker, a.k.a. Spider-Man. As part of its editorial policy, the *Bugle* frequently runs scurrilous attacks on Spidey, even though his circulation-building ex-ploits are their editorial bread-and-butter.

Other pop-media papers include the *Flash*, where glamorous, so-phisticated Brenda Starr, Reporter, in the comic strip of the same name, has worked since the 1940s. Britt Reid, also known as the Green Hornet on radio and TV, is the editor of the *Daily Sentinel*. (He's also the great-nephew of the Lone Ranger, whose name was John Reid—both created by the same writer, George W. Trendle.) In *Big Town*, a radio series that began in 1937 and continued on television into the 1950s, combative editor Steve Wilson (originally played by Edward G. Robinson), aided by star reporter Lorelei Kilbourne, led the crusading *Illustrated Press,* whose motto was "The freedom of the press is a flaming sword; use it justly; hold it high; guard it well!"

The movies and television have given us dozens of fictional newspapers, among them the *Tally-Ho* on *The Prisoner;* the *Picayune Intelligence* in Frostbite Falls, on the *Rocky and Bullwinkle Show;* the Hooterville *World-Guardian,* the "almost-daily" newspaper on *Petticoat Junction* and *Green Acres,* which failed to publish only once, September 10, 1924, a day on which "nothing happened"; and a newspaper that clearly was invented by someone who has been through the agony of publishing one, the *Daily Miracle,* a tabloid in the movie *The Paper,* whose motto is "Never let the truth get in the way of a good story."

Citizen Kane, Orson Welles and Herman J. Mankiewicz's extravagantly praised film biography of a tycoon loosely based on William Randolph Hearst, features newspapers in New York and Chicago called the *Inquirer.* The *Inquirer*'s New York competitor is the *Daily Chronicle.* Other invented newspapers referred to in the film are the St. Louis *Inquirer* (part of Kane's chain), and, in a montage reporting Kane's death, the Chicago *Globe,* the El Paso *Journal,* the Minneapolis *Record Herald,* and the Detroit *Star.* Fictitious foreign-language newspapers are also pictured in *Citizen Kane,* including Moscow's *Ezhednevnaya Gazeta* ("Daily Gazette"), Paris's *Le Matin* ("the Morning"), and Spain's *La Correspondencia* ("the Mail").

Los Angeles is the setting of many television shows (because that's where they are produced, and it's cheap to shoot on location—duh), and as a result it has spawned more fictitious newspapers than any other city. Among the papers you might read in L.A. if you were a character on a TV show are the *Sun* (on both the *Debbie Reynolds Show* and *My Favorite Martian*); the *Star (Dear Phoebe);* the *Gazette* (on three different shows); the *Post-Gazette* on *Our House;* the *Daily Banner* on *Duet;* and probably the most famous, the Los Angeles *Tribune,* whose city editor was Lou Grant, who, after losing his job with WJM-TV on the *Mary Tyler Moore Show,* got a show named after his own character.

Howard Brenton and David Hare's play *Pravda* invents London's *Daily Victory, Daily Tide, Daily Usurper,* and *Daily Snake,* as well as the Leicester *Bystander.* The quintessential play about the newspaper world, Ben Hecht and Charles MacArthur's *The Front Page,* is set in Chicago and uses a paper called the *Herald-Examiner,* which had been an actual daily in the Windy City at one time (and was also the name of a Los Angeles paper). In the 1931 movie, the newspaper's name is changed to the *Post,* which also actually existed in Chicago. The *Morning Post* is also used in *His Girl Friday,* the 1940 remake of *The Front Page.* By the time a television series was created from the movie in 1959, the newspaper was changed again to the Center City *Examiner.*

The *Flintstones,* the TV parody of modern life set in the Stone Age, had two daily papers, the *Granite* (edited, of course, by Lou Granite) and the *Slab.* Deftly satirical names are found in the soap opera *All My Children* (the *National Intruder*), the TV series *The Naked Truth* (the *National Inquisitor*), and the animated TV comedy *The Family Guy* (the *Quahog Informant*). The Springfield *Shopper* on *The Simpsons* (of which an actual example has existed in Springfield, Illinois, since 1975) was somehow the result of mergers by papers known as the *Times, Post, Globe, Herald, Jewish News,* and *Hot Sex Weekly.* Shelbyville, Springfield's twin city, has a newspaper called the Shelbyville *Daily*—which is published once a week.

The height of whimsy is perhaps found in the *Herald-Star,* the newspaper in mythical Lake Wobegon, Minnesota, on public radio's *Prairie Home Companion.* At first blush, it may sound like a very commonplace name that Garrison Keillor invented for a town that teems with off-the-wall establishments, such as Ralph's Pretty Good Grocery, Bertha's Kitty Boutique, the Side Track Tap, and Our Lady of Perpetual Responsibility Catholic Church. The *Herald-Star*'s name becomes whimsical only when you know that it was chosen by its editor-publisher—Harold Starr.

17

All in Fun

People have always liked to have fun—sometimes veering toward the scatological—with the names of their hometown newspapers. By altering the spelling or by devising a roguish pun, wags invent satirical parodies of newspaper names that theoretically target the perceived failings of the papers in question, and in so doing produce gales of raucous laughter. Or not. Gather around for more examples of this high-spirited persiflage than your funny bone can possibly absorb.

The London *Evening Standard,* for example, is hilariously referred to by some of its readers as the *Sub-Standard.* In Dallas, the *Morning News* is sometimes called the *Morning Snooze.* And of course the Atlanta *Journal-Constitution* is raffishly referred to as the *Urinal-Constipation.* Get the idea? If you like these jests, here are a few more (along with the real names of the papers being parodied, so that you can't possibly be confused). If you don't like such jests, skip down a few paragraphs to the anagrams; maybe you'll find them more amusing.

Try these on for yuks: the Ravenna *Wretched-Courier (Record-Courier),* the *Virginian Pile-It-On (Pilot),* the Akron *Reekin'* or *Leakin' Urinal (Beacon Journal),* the Raleigh *Nuisance-Disturber (News & Recorder),* the Montgomery *Agonizer (Advertiser),* the Fort Worth *Startle-Gram (Star-Telegram),* the *Empty Prize (Enterprise),* the *Tribulation (Tribune),* the *Regret (Gazette),* the San Jose *Murky News (Mercury News),* the *Comical (Chronicle),* the Jackson *Carrion-Dredger (Clarion-Ledger),* or the *Pain Dealer (Plain Dealer).*

And don't forget the Omaha *Weird Harold (World-Herald),* the Halifax *Chronically Horrid (Chronicle-Herald),* the Arizona *Repulsive (Republic),* the Orlando *Slantinel (Sentinel),* the Wauchula (Florida) *Hard-*

ly Adequate (Herald-Advocate), and the Anderson (South Carolina) *Impotent Male (Independent-Mail).* Well, enough of that. Maybe you can try it on your own hometown newspaper with even more hilarious results.

Come to think of it, there are some actual newspapers whose names are funnier. Take the *Spinal Column* in Waterford, Michigan, for example. The founders of the paper asked their financial backers to suggest names, and then drew one from a hat. The investor whose name was chosen was a chiropractor, and you can guess what was on his mind, and thus the weekly paper has been known by that name ever since. Presumably its editorial policy has plenty of backbone.

The Scottish are good at inventing satirical names. Two online papers cry out for mention. One is called the *Wreckered,* which promises satire, sports, lifestyle, and "comedy news," whatever that may be. A branch of the Scottish Socialist Party publishes an online paper that is called—really—the *Ratcrotch.* Please don't ask.

Online, news stories are served up as if every day were April Fool's Day by the *Onion,* the *Loon News,* the *Frumious Bandersnatch,* the *Baloney Press,* the *Spoof,* the *Bean Soup Times,* the *Bongo News,* the *Big Fat News,* the wonderfully named *Daily Telegiraffe,* the *Framley Examiner,* and many others in an increasingly crowded cyberfield.

This type of fun, of course, long predates the Internet. In 1830 in Philadelphia there was a paper called the *Tickler,* edited by one Toby Scratchem. And in Chemung County, New York, in 1831, there was a paper that liked to stir things up that called itself the Fort Henderson *Meddler.*

Mergers of newspapers can produce names that are a mouthful. Sometimes they're also funny. Woody Allen, in his film *Annie Hall,* suggests that the magazines *Dissent* and *Commentary* might merge into a new one known as *Dysentery.* Wordsmith Anu Garg, on his Web site wordsmith.com, cites the actual case of a merger in 1939 between two papers in Chattanooga, Tennessee, the *News* and the *Free Press,* which, for a brief period—until someone tardily noticed the unintentional humor—resulted in a paper known as the *News-Free Press.*

Set your mind to it, and you can come up with nifty titles that might result from the merger of actual newspapers such as the *Light-News, Eagle-Eye, Telegraph-Post, Express-Mail, World-Atlas, World-Almanac, World-Record, Record-Star, Clipper-Blade, Reflector-Mirror, Life-Guard, American-Eagle, Voice-Echo,* or *Standard-Citizen.*

For whatever reason, probably mere chance, mergers seem to have oc-
curred with uncommon frequency between certain named newspapers.
For example, there are at least sixteen newspapers known as either
Herald-News or *News-Herald,* fifteen called *News-Journal,* thirteen
Sun-News or *News-Sun,* and eleven *News-Leader.*

Then, of course, like the famous three-named poets who fill nineteenth-
century anthologies, there are the three-named newspapers, which are
saddled with the fruits of multiple mergers and are almost never called
by their full names. They include the Athens (Georgia) *News-Banner-
Herald;* the Manitowoc (Wisconsin) *Herald Times Reporter;* the Middletown (New York) *Times Herald-Record;* the Newton (North Carolina) *Observer News Enterprise;* and the New York *World-Telegram & the
Sun* (usually known as the *World-Telly*), which in a later merger became
the *World-Journal-Tribune* (called the *Widget*), and then collapsed, one
might suppose, under the weight of its name.

The history of the Pittsburgh *Post-Gazette* is a lesson in merger ma-
nia. The paper was founded in 1786 as the Pittsburgh *Gazette.* In 1828
it was sold and renamed the Pittsburgh *Gazette & Manufacturing &
Mercantile Advertiser.* The following year it was sold again and revert-
ed to plain *Gazette.* In 1866 it was sold yet again to the *Commercial* and
renamed the *Commercial Gazette.* In 1900 it changed hands once more,
became the plain *Gazette* again, then merged with the *Times* and was
called the Pittsburgh *Gazette-Times.* In 1924 the *Gazette-Times* and the
Chronicle-Telegraph both came under the ownership of William Randolph Hearst, who must have felt he had an embarrassment of riches, because in 1927 he agreed to swap the *Gazette-Times* for a paper called the
Sun owned by his associate Paul Block, who also owned the *Post.* Block
renamed the resulting paper the Pittsburgh *Post-Gazette,* and so it has
remained since then, having also absorbed the *Sun-Telegraph* and the
Press along the way. Whew, what a journey!

A columnist for the Houston *Chronicle,* Loren Steffy, has jumped into
the newspaper name game by proposing, jestingly, one assumes, that the
Chronicle change its name to *CommUnoGen.* "I know at first blush it
sounds like an airborne virus," he writes, "but it reflects our singular
commitment to the community as we generate communications among
Americans of all cultures." Houston, Steffy says, has abounded with
made-up company names that mean nothing: Dynegy, Entergy, Cinergy,
Mirant, and the notorious Enron, to cite a few, and he thinks the same
kind of nomenclature should be applied to newspapers.

Eric Shackle, the retired Australian journalist who created a miscellany-filled e-book called *Life Begins at 80 . . . on the Internet;* Anu Garg, a self-described wordsmith and computer scientist from the Pacific Northwest; and William Tunstall-Pedoe, who runs a Web site called Anagram Genius from Cambridge, England, have all made anagrams from the names of newspapers. Many of them are either quite appropriate or highly amusing, depending on your point of view.

Some of the gems they came up with at their various Web sites include:

New York Times—The monkeys write
The Scotsman—Hasn't cost me
The Daily Telegraph—The really hated pig
The Straits Times—It is the smartest
Chicago Sun-Times—Amusing, choicest
Chicago Tribune—Cohabiting cure
Cincinnati Post—Ants picnic on it
The Plain Dealer—A dire lethal pen
Detroit Free Press—Feed its reporters
El Paso Times—Aims to sleep
Fort Lauderdale Sun-Sentinel—Faultless return on deadline
Los Angeles Times—So elegant, smiles
Newark Star-Ledger—We're grand talkers
The Oregonian—One giant hero
Seattle Post-Intelligencer—Genteel tall receptionists
Houston Chronicle—Run hot cliché soon
Vero Beach Press-Journal—Jocular, sharp—even sober!
The Washington Times—White hot assignment
The Washington Post—News photos at night

A final note of caution: Do not attempt this feat at home unless you have access to a computer-generated anagram-maker! Trying it on your own may lead to *delirium tremens* (Intel murders me!), *dementia praecox* (tree coaxed an imp!), or *catatonia* (ain't a taco!).

18

So Sue Me

You cannot have failed to notice in these pages that the same name is often used by many unrelated newspapers in different communities. As an example, the *Times* in New York is a different entity from the *Times* in Los Angeles, and they are both different from the *Times* companies in London, or Altus, Oklahoma, or Gadsden, Alabama, or Bombala, New South Wales, Australia. In fact, there are hundreds of newspapers that call themselves the *Times*.

So—could you start your own newspaper and call it the *Times*—or any other name that might already be in use? Well, sort of, but not exactly. You probably could not set up shop in, let us say, Poughkeepsie, and operate a newspaper there called the Upstate New York *Times*. You would most likely hear from a highly expensive and needlessly pompous Manhattan law firm within a matter of days, if not hours, threatening you with dire consequences unless you ceased and also desisted your publishing activity, lest your Poughkeepsie readers mistakenly think that you are affiliated with a downstate paper with a very similar name. On the other hand, it is likely that you could send a whole squadron of news vendors to hawk a paper using the name *Times* in White Rock, South Dakota (population eighteen), and evoke no protests from anyone, except perhaps an occasional gray wolf or black-footed ferret. Location, location, location.

The guiding principle in determining whether one entity's name may properly be used by anyone else is whether such use is likely to cause confusion in the mind of the public. In general, a newspaper, like any other company or product, may protect its identity, preventing others from using its name and other distinguishing characteristics in a manner that might have an adverse impact on its reputation or its sales. You will recall, of course, that insofar as newspapers are concerned, this principle was established in 1648 by the British House of Lords when it gave John Dillingham the exclusive license to publish the *Moderate Intelligencer,* ordering a rival using the same title to desist.

Today a newspaper customarily protects its identity through the use of trademark law. A trademark may be a name, a slogan, or a logo and is typically registered with the government, but it may also be protected by common law, if it has been in use in a given market area. A newspaper's trademark encompasses what is referred to as its "trade dress"—the type font in which the name is printed on the nameplate, any unique colors or design elements used in its logo, and sometimes even the graphic format of its news pages.

The protection afforded by a trademark is typically limited to the specific geographical area in which the paper is marketed. Often this area is denoted in the title of the paper.

But like everything in life, especially law, it can get messy. Otherwise we wouldn't need lawyers and courts, would we? Publishers can become extremely possessive about anything that they believe might lure a reader or an advertiser away from them. At the top of that list is another publication using the same name. Especially for newspapers that market themselves nationally or internationally, conflicts over the use of a name can arise. Naturally, as you can tell by the delicate sound of lawyers' lips smacking, this conflict leads inevitably to threats of litigation, which may be sufficient to intimidate the faint-hearted or shallow-pocketed upstart. Sometimes actual lawsuits are filed, and that makes for interesting claims.

New York's *Village Voice* has become known for zealously asserting its claim to the near-exclusive right to the word *Voice* as a newspaper title. The paper apparently feels threatened by other publications using this title, fearing that even though other *Voice*s may be in small communities a continent away, befuddled readers will somehow mistake the Hot Springs (Arkansas) *Village Voice* and its coverage of the fishing derby on Balboa Lake, with the hip, in-your-face, politically sassy journal brimming with attitude that emanates from Greenwich Village. It seems of no relevance to New York's *Village Voice,* which was founded in 1955, that it was not the first to use the name, or that dozens of newspapers calling themselves the *Voice,* with various modifiers, date back at least to 1831.

The *Village Voice* sued the Bloomington (Indiana) *Voice* in 1998, and the Indiana paper agreed to change its name to the Bloomington *Independent.* Similarly persuasive threats resulted in changes at the Dayton (Ohio) *Voice* (to the Dayton *City Paper*) and the Tacoma (Washington) *Voice* (to the Tacoma *Reporter*).

Attempts to halt publication of other *Voice*s, however, have met with less success. *Voice*s in Beachwood, California, and Cape Cod, Massachusetts, as well as the one in Arkansas, continued to be heard, despite protestations from the feisty Manhattan publication. In an editorial response to the *Village Voice*'s claim that its use of the name could cause confusion, the Cape Cod *Voice* asserted, "We chose the word 'Voice' because it seemed like that is what we are aspiring to be, Cape Cod's voice. That choice had nothing to do with Greenwich Village, which is a great place to visit, but we choose to live here. It had nothing to do with a self-described urban 'alternative weekly' that is now part of a chain of such papers and no doubt much more successful than this little Voice. We are not in any conceivable way piggybacking on those people or capitalizing on their work."

The Cape Cod paper even drew support from author Norman Mailer, who as one of the founders of New York's *Village Voice* gave it its name. Mailer, one of America's literary giants since his first novel, *The Naked and the Dead,* in 1948, wrote in a letter to the editor of the Cape Cod *Voice:* "The notion that you must change the title of the Cape Cod *Voice* because the corporate legal and editorial types who now own the *Village Voice* feel that your presence might come to a possible future loss of profit for them is enough to make one retch. It's monstrous. It violates everything the *Village Voice* stood for over the decades." The letter ended, "Yours in outrage."

Even the two words *Village Voice* taken together can be found in numerous uses other than the New York paper. In a recent Googling of "Village Voice," the first thirty hits (out of a total 1,900,000) included newspapers in New South Wales, Australia; Hot Springs Village, Arkansas; Salado, Texas; Var, France; and Washington, Connecticut; a rural arts touring program in Winkleigh, England; a bookshop in Paris (which pays homage to the New York newspaper); and an interactive video database of "the efficacy of localized ontology in the dissemination of narrative" in Somalia. Be sure to pick up a couple of those on your next trip to the newsstand.

In the fall of 2005 the *Village Voice* was merged into a company called New Times—which publishes a chain of newspapers variously called the *New Times,* the *Observer,* the *Press,* the *Weekly,* and the *Express,* among others. Any attempt to monopolize that profusion of much-used names should keep a lot of lawyers busy!

The fictional *Daily Planet*—Clark Kent's paper—can also be cranky about others using its name. The lawyers it employs to assert its claims are not fictional, but all too real, as one student newspaper discovered. In 1979 the *Obstacle,* published at Chicago's Richard J. Daley College, decided to change its name—and with a name like that, it's easy to see why. The whimsical new title they adopted was the *Daley Planet*—get it? Well, DC Comics, owners of the Superman franchise, got it—but they didn't like it. According to *Time Magazine,* the *Daily Planet* sued the *Daley Planet,* claiming trademark infringement, injury to business reputation, and engagement in deceptive practices. In reply, the student paper lamented: "Great Caesar's ghost! If we'd known there'd be so much trouble, we'd have changed our name to the *Gotham Globe* or the *Daily Bugle.* Then we'd only have to worry about bats and spiders knocking at our office, and not the Man of Steel."

Corporate forces also descended upon another hapless newspaper, this one in Newburgh, Maine, distributed free out of the trunk of its publisher's car and containing material written by and for children. It was called the *Small Street Journal*—until guess who objected. That's right, mighty Dow Jones, publisher of the *Wall Street Journal,* claimed trademark infringement. Silly as such a lawsuit may sound, there must have been method in Dow Jones's madness; the corporate giant now advertises its own *Small Street Journal,* a classroom edition with articles on money matters for kids.

The venerable word *Journal* itself has been the subject of legal wrangling. Some years ago the *Wall Street Journal* attempted to gain exclusive rights to the name *California Journal* for a regional edition of its paper. Oops! Trouble was, there was already a magazine with that name. After a protracted legal battle, the Wall Streeters came out on the losing side, so they folded their tents and silently stole away.

The Case of the *Pescadero Pebble,* although you won't find it in the Perry Mason series, illustrates another type of identity problem, which has arisen with the Internet. "Cyber-squatters" are entrepreneurs who register domain names that are identical or similar to established businesses and then either use them for their own purposes or offer to sell them to the company in question. In the *Pescadero Pebble* case, a newspaper in San Mateo County, California, known as the *Half Moon Bay Review and Pescadero Pebble* filed a complaint with the World Intellectual Property Organization that another individual had registered the domain names "pescaderopebble.net," "pescaderopebble.org," and "pescaderopebble.info"—all of which were in conflict with the newspaper's own Web site at "pescaderopebble.com." The tribunal agreed. Well, who wouldn't?

To show just how seriously some people take a newspaper's name, three journalists in Inez, Kentucky, were prepared to go to jail rather than give up using the name of the *Mountain Citizen*. As the Associated Press tells the story, the Martin County water board chairman, annoyed by several articles critical of the water system over which he presided, acquired the right to the paper's name when the publisher inadvertently allowed the incorporation to lapse. The owner, the publisher, and the editor continued to issue the paper as the *Mountain Citizen* and were hauled into court. The judge fined them five hundred dollars each for contempt, but allowed them to continue using the name when the water board chairman withdrew his objections. All's well that ends well, even if there's no final word on whether the water well's water's well.

How far will a publisher go to protect a name? The answer, apparently, is as far as necessary—even to the extent of demanding the right to use names it doesn't want to use. The Toronto *Globe & Mail,* fearful of impending competition from a rival, took steps to acquire the trademark rights to seventeen newspaper names just to keep anyone else from using them. It filed applications for the *Times,* the *Independent,* the *World,* the *Telegraph,* the *Nation,* the *Citizen,* the *Colonist,* the *Canadian,* and *Today,* with several variations on them. It might have sought the *Star,* the *Sun,* and the *Post* as well—but, oops again, someone was already using them. Next time, maybe it'll ask for the moon.

Philip Anschutz, the billionaire publisher of the tabloid *Examiner*s in San Francisco, Washington, D.C., and Baltimore, is so in love with the name of his paper that he wants to spread it around the entire United States. Anschutz's company, Clarity Media Group, has filed an application for trademark rights to the *Examiner* to be used for general-circulation newspapers in fifty-nine additional American cities. Be on notice that there may be an *Examiner* in your future—if there is not already a paper with that title—if you happen to live in Albuquerque, Atlanta, Austin, Birmingham, Boston, Buffalo, Charlotte, Chicago, Cincinnati, Cleveland, Columbus, Dallas, Dayton, Denver, Des Moines, Detroit, Fresno, Fort Lauderdale, Fort Worth, Hartford, Honolulu, Houston, Indianapolis, Jacksonville, Kansas City, Las Vegas, Long Island, Los Angeles, Louisville, Memphis, Miami, Milwaukee, Nashville, New Orleans, New York, Oakland, Oklahoma City, Orange County, Orlando, Palm Beach, Philadelphia, Phoenix, Pittsburgh, Portland (Oregon), Providence, Rochester, Sacramento, St. Louis, St. Paul, St. Petersburg, Salt Lake City, San Antonio, San Diego, San Jose, Seattle, Tacoma, Tampa, Tucson, or Tulsa.

And please remember—you read it here first.

Books

Ackroyd, Peter. *London: The Biography.* New York: Anchor Books, 2000.

Baker, Thomas Harrison. *The Memphis Commercial Appeal: The History of a Southern Newspaper.* Baton Rouge: Louisiana State University Press, 1971.

Bleyer, Willard Grosvenor. *Main Currents in the History of American Journalism.* Boston: Houghton Mifflin, 1927.

Boyce, Charles. *Shakespeare A to Z.* New York: Facts on File, 1990.

Boyce, George, James Curran, and Pauline Wingate, eds. *Newspaper History from the Seventeenth Century to the Present Day.* Beverly Hills, Calif.: Sage Publications, 1978.

Breen, Timothy. *The Marketplace of Revolution: How Consumer Politics Shaped American Independence.* Oxford: Oxford University Press, 2004.

The Cambridge Encyclopedia of the English Language. Ed. David Crystal. Cambridge: Cambridge University Press, 1995.

The Cambridge Fact Finder. Ed. David Crystal. Cambridge: Cambridge University Press, 1993.

Clark, Charles E. *The Public Prints: The Newspaper in Anglo-American Culture, 1665–1740.* New York: Oxford University Press, 1994.

The Columbia Encyclopedia. 6th ed. Ed. Paul Lagassé. New York: Columbia University Press, 2000.

The Compact Edition of the Oxford English Dictionary. Oxford: Oxford University Press, 1971.

Frank, Joseph. *The Beginnings of the English Newspaper, 1620–1660.* Cambridge: Harvard University Press, 1961.

Herd, Harold. *The March of Journalism: The Story of the British Press from 1622 to the Present Day.* London: George Allen and Unwin, 1952.

Kluger, Richard. *The Paper: The Life and Death of the New York Herald Tribune.* New York: Alfred A. Knopf, 1986.

Kobre, Sidney. *The Development of the Colonial Newspaper.* 1944. Reprint, Gloucester, Mass.: Peter Smith, 1960.

———. *Foundation of American Journalism.* Tallahassee: Florida State University, 1958.

Lee, James Melvin. *History of American Journalism.* Garden City, N.Y.: Garden City Publishing, 1917, 1923.

The Merriam-Webster New Book of Word Histories. Springfield, Mass.: Merriam-Webster, 1991.

Mott, Frank Luther. *American Journalism: A History of Newspapers in the United States through 250 Years, 1690 to 1940.* New York: Macmillan, 1947.

Neussel, Frank. *The Study of Names: A Guide to the Principles and Topics.* Westport, Conn.: Greenwood Press, 1992.

Opie, Iona, and Peter Opie. *The Oxford Dictionary of Nursery Rhymes.* Oxford: Oxford University Press, 1997.

Oxford Companion to the English Language. Ed. Tom McArthur. New York: Oxford University Press, 1992.

The Portable Handbook of Texas. Ed. Roy R. Barkley and Mark F. Odintz. Austin: Texas State Historical Association, 1993.

Shaaber, M. A. *Some Forerunners of the Newspaper in England, 1476–1622.* London: Frank Cass, 1966.

Smith, Anthony. *The Newspaper: An International History.* London: Thames and Hudson, 1979.

Spears, Richard A. *Slang and Euphemism.* New York: Signet New American Library, 1981.

Starr, Paul. *The Creation of the Media: Political Origins of Modern Communication.* New York: Basic Books, 2004.

Stephens, Mitchell. *A History of News: From the Drum to the Satellite.* New York: Viking, 1988.

Stewart, Powell. *British Newspapers and Periodicals, 1632–1800: A Descriptive Catalogue of a Collection at the University of Texas.* Austin: University of Texas, 1950.

Sutherland, James. *The Restoration Newspaper and Its Development.* Cambridge: Cambridge University Press, 1986.

Taft, William H. *Show-Me Journalists: The First 200 Years.* Marceline, Mo.: Heritage House, 2003.

Tarpley, Fred. *Jefferson: Riverport to the Southwest.* Austin: Eakin Press, 1983.

Tebbel, John. *Compact History of the American Newspaper.* New York: Hawthorn Books, 1969.

Webster's New International Dictionary of the English Language. 2d ed. Springfield, Mass.: G. & C. Merriam, 1949.

Westmancoat, Joan. *Newspapers.* London: British Library, 1985.

Web Sites

Note: In addition to the following, the Web sites of many of the individual newspapers mentioned in the text were invaluable sources of information.

Bartleby. www.bartleby.com.

Beeville, Texas, City of. www.beeville.net/TheHistoricalStoryofBee CountyTexas.

Black Hills Newspapers. www.rootsweb.com/~sdrcsgr/newspapers.htm.

British Library Catalogue. www.bl.uk/catalogues/newspapers/welcome .asp *and* www.bl.uk/collections/britnews.html.

Cambridge History of English and American Literature. www.bartleby .com/cambridge/chapterindex.html.

Cox, Kristy. "Bill Barlow." Campbell County High School, Gillette, Wyo.www.ncteamericancollection.org/litmap/barlow_bill_wy.htm.

Crookshanks, Ben. "The Feast of the Ramson." Road to Adventures. www.roadtoadventures.com/misc-articles/ramps.html.

Early America. www.earlyamerica.com.

The Editors Weblog. www.editorsweblog.org.

Electric Scotland. www.electricscotland.com/canada/caledonia/caledonia_ 7.htm.

Encyclopedia Britannica. www.britannica.com.

Gale Group. www.galegroup.com/pdf/guide/early.pdf.

Garg, Anu. www.wordsmith.org.

Georgian Index. www.georgianindex.net/publications/newspapers/news- dates.html.

Higgins and Related Maryland Families. www.higginsandrelatedmary landfamilies.com/EasternShoreNewspapers.

Hildesheim City Archives. www.stadtarchiv-hildesheim.de.

Historic Magazines, Newspapers, and Ephemera, 1680–1945. www .historicpages.com/texts/incat49.htm.

Hughes, Timothy. Rare and Early Newspapers. www.rarenewspapers .com.

Indopedia. www.indopedia.org/Daily_Planet.html.

Library of Congress Newspaper and Current Periodical Reading Room. www.loc.gov/rr/news/17th/178index.html.

Library of Virginia Online. www.lva.lib.va.us.

Love to Know 1911 Online Encyclopedia. www.1911encyclopedia.org/ Newspapers.

Maryland State Archives. www.msa.md.gov/.

Mattapoisett (Mass.) Historical Society. www.mattapoisetthistorical society.org/whalingships_history.htm.

McVicker, Mary Frech. "Courants, Messengers, and a Plain Dealer: How Your Paper Got Its Name," *American Heritage Magazine.* www.americanheritage.com/articles/magazine/ah/1994/6/1994_ 6_36.shtml.

Meade, Don. "The Life and Times of 'Muldoon, the Solid Man.'" my space.virgin.net/harry.campbell/muldoonspicnic/DonMeade.pdf.

Memorial University Libraries, University of Newfoundland. www.library .mun.ca/qeii/newspapers/.

Murray County, Georgia, Museum. www.murraycountymuseum.com.

Netstate. www.netstate.com/states/intro/ia_intro.htm.

Newseum. www.newseum.org/todaysfrontpages/flash/.

North Carolina Newspaper Project. http://statelibrary.dcr.state.nc.us/ ncslhome.htm.

North Carolina Office of Archives and History. www.ah.dcr.state.nc.us/ sections/hp/colonial/Nchr/Subjects/lefler.htm.

The Origin of Newspapers. mbbnet.umn.edu/hoff/hoff_news.html.

The Paperboy. www.thepaperboy.com.au/welcome.html.

Pedoe, William Tunstall. www.AnagramGenius.com.

The People's Almanac. By David Wallechinski and Irving Wallace, 1975. www.trivia-library.com/b.

Quinion, Michael. www.worldwidewords.org/weirdwords/ww-pic2.htm.

Readex, Division of NewsBank, Early American Newspapers. www
.readex.com/scholarl/eanplist.html.

Redlands (Calif.) Area Historical Society. www.illustratedredlands
.com.

Rostock Historical Newspaper Corpus from 1700 until Today. www.tu-
chemnitz.de/phil/english/chairs/linguist/real/independent/llc/
Conference1998/Papers/Schneider.htm.

Shackle, Eric. *Life Begins at 80* [e-Book]. http://www.bdb.co.za/
shackle/articles/shuttle_pirate.htm.

Tennessee Encyclopedia of History and Culture. http://tennesseeencyclo
pedia.net/.

Times (of London) Online. http://www.timesonline.co.uk/article/
0,,696–36873,00.html.

Tri-Counties [Chemung, New York, and Bradford and Tioga, Pennsyl-
vania] Genealogy and History. By Joyce M. Tice. www.rootsweb
.com/~srgp/articles/hms01dr.htm.

TV Acres. www.tvacres.com/newspapers_glance.htm.

United States Newspapers. http://www.50states.com/news.

The Victorian Dictionary. www.victorianlondon.org/.

Wikipedia, Newspapers. http://en.wikipedia.org/wiki/Category:News
papers.

Williams, Edgar [former Philadelphia *Inquirer* staff writer]. www
.philly.com/mld/inquirer/news/local/6135296.htm.

World Association of Newspapers. www.wan-press.org/article7321.html.

World-Newspapers.com. http://www.world-newspapers.com.

General Index

ABC, 2
"Abou Ben Adhem," 24
Abraham, 155
Adams, John, 86
Adams, Samuel, 70, 95
Addison, Joseph, 24, 26, 73
Age of Reason, 47
Age of Reason, The (Paine), 89
Aiken, Clay, 110
Aitken, Max. *See* Beaverbrook, Lord
Aitzing, Michael von, 10
Alcott, Louisa May, 168
Algonquin Round Table, 134
Allen, Woody, 173
All My Children, 171
American Philosophical Society, 89
Amsterdam, 168
Anderson, James, 68
Anglo-Saxon Chronicle, 40
Annet, Peter, 25
Annie Hall, 173
Anschutz, Philip, 150
Anson, Karen, 121
Apollo, 84
Arcadia University, 3
Archer, Thomas, 17
Areopagitica, 47
Argus, 113
"Arkansas Traveler, The," 165–66
Ark of the Covenant, 130
Around the World in Eighty Days, 88, 149

Artemis, 134
Associated Press, 180
Astaire, Fred, 165
Athena, 112, 115
Atlantic Charter, 132–33
Atlas, 113–14
Audubon, J. W., 136
Audubon, John James, 136
Aurora (goddess), 85
Aurora (magazine), 86
Aurora borealis, 86

Bache, Benjamin Franklin, 85–86, 95
Ball, Bert, 120
Barkley, Doc, 117
Barnum, P. T., 162
Barrow, Minnie, 99
Barrow, Morris C., 99
Batman, 169
Baylor University, 155
BBC, 2
Beaton, M. C., 168
Beaverbrook, Lord, 7, 32, 36, 167
Beaver College, 3
Bee, Barnard E., 106
Beecher, Henry Ward, 70
Bell, Alexander Graham, 151
Bell, Horace, 110
Bennett, James Gordon, 33, 76–77
Berthold, Henry, 153
Bible, 40, 97, 121, 130, 155
Bierce, Ambrose, 24

Index of Newspaper Names